Also by Jasvinder Sanghera

Shame

JASVINDER SANGHERA

Daughters of Shame

First published in Great Britain in 2009 by Hodder & Stoughton
An Hachette Livre UK company

1

A CIP catalogue record for this title is available from the British Library

Hardback ISBN 978 0 340 96206 0
Trade Paperback ISBN 978 0 340 97802 3

Typeset in Sabon MT by Hewer Text UK Ltd, Edinburgh

Printed and bound by Clays Ltd, St Ives plc

Hodder & Stoughton policy is to use papers that are natural, renewable and recyclable products and made from wood grown in sustainableforests. The logging and manufacturing processes are expected to conform to the environmental regulations of the country of origin.

Hodder & Stoughton Ltd
338 Euston Road
London NW1 3BH

www.hodder.co.uk

To all those courageous victims and survivors of forced marriages and honour based crimes, and sadly to those who lost their lives at the hands of such heinous crimes. To those who work tirelessly to effect change – you are not alone.

AUTHOR'S NOTE

To protect the identity of the men and women whose stories are told here, names have been changed, as have other identifying features such as jobs, physical descriptions and places.

Daughters of Shame

PREFACE

I was brought up to keep secrets, ugly secrets about bullying, coercion and fear which were all part of everyday life in our family. I believed it was shameful to discuss things with outsiders and that if I did I would compromise our honour – *izzat* – the most important thing in my mum's life. That's why I didn't tell anybody when she showed me a photograph of the man she said I had to marry. I knew it wasn't right; I knew I was too young to leave school or get married, and it felt all wrong being forced to marry a man I didn't know, but I didn't tell. I kept the secret and it festered inside me, feeding on my feelings of shame, resentment, fear and guilt.

I ran away rather than go through with that marriage and my family disowned me: 'You have shamed us. You are dead in our eyes,' my mum said. I kept that secret too. As I struggled to make my way in life I kept my head down and my eyes averted: I didn't want people knowing how worthless I was.

I was on a listening skills course when, finally, I shared my story with a virtual stranger. She was called Alicia and to my amazement, as the torrent of truth spilled out of me, she didn't recoil, she didn't reject or ridicule me. She sat there and she listened, and when I had finished she said she understood. That was a turning point.

About eighteen months later I met Ayesha and learnt that mine wasn't the only Asian family held together by a suffocating web of secrets. Karma Nirvana – the charity I founded to help women whose lives were blocked by cultural and language barriers – was in its infancy and Ayesha was one of its first clients, so locked in by her misery that I thought initially I would never reach her. It was an instinctive decision to tell her my story and it worked. She listened and then she told me in turn about her life – raped by her brother when she was eight, betrayed by her mother who knew but turned a blind eye, forced into a marriage that she fled from. As she laid down each awful, agonising incident for our inspection she found she could let it go. She saw her past through my horrified eyes and it lost its hold on her. She realised, as I had done, that she was the victim not the perpetrator of a crime.

I was Ayesha's turning point and knowing that has shaped my life. I realised that in listening to her, bearing witness to her suffering, I had made her feel valued as an individual, possibly for the first time. I watched that feeling change her, so that she began to believe in herself, to see she had a future – even one she might enjoy. I knew then that I had found Karma Nirvana's purpose: supporting women like Ayesha – whose suffering so often makes mine a pale shadow – is the cornerstone of everything I do.

But I have also tried to batter down the wall of secrecy. I realised that by staying silent, women like Ayesha and me were making it impossible for anyone to help and I wanted to change that. I started journeying across the country telling my story, and that of other women like me, time and again. It wasn't always easy. With your head above the parapet, you feel very alone. I often felt exposed and scared.

Two years ago the publication of my autobiography, *Shame*, brought publicity to my campaign. Invitations to speak to the very people I wanted to reach – the police, health workers, social workers: all the people on the front-line – poured in so fast that at times now my working life feels like a blur of conference platforms, station platforms, new faces and places. Sometimes I arrive home late, and struggle to find anything left inside myself to give my children. I am often tired, but I am also empowered by the fact that people are listening. They have woken up to the fact that forced marriage, honour-based violence and murders in the name of honour are not confined to far-off, foreign countries: they happen right here, in Britain; perhaps in the house next door.

Shame also gave people the courage to come forward and ask for help. Calls to Karma Nirvana tripled, almost overnight, and they have never fallen back again. Each new day brings with it women – and increasingly men – who say that they read the book and realised for the first time that they are not alone; that there are people out there who will understand what they have been through. I listen to those stories – more than even I imagined – told by women who have been drugged, beaten, imprisoned, raped and terrorised within the walls of the homes they grew up in. I meet women whose families treat them like slaves. I listen and I am humbled by their resilience. I feel privileged to hear these stories and proud to stand beside those who tell them as they set down the burden of the past and start to rebuild their lives. I draw strength and inspiration from their courage.

My decision to write *Shame*, to lift the veil of secrecy that cloaked my family, was not taken lightly – I knew it would extinguish all hope of reconciliation between us – but it has been vindicated by all the people who have said to me: 'I read your story and it gave me permission to tell mine.' You will find some of those people here, in these pages. Some of them are very dear to me: they have become, in a way I could never have anticipated, the sisters I lost, the aunties my children never had.

As I see it now, *Shame* was a catalyst: it paved the way for these, the stories of the *Daughters of Shame* that I've been waiting to tell.

I

Sometimes I lie awake at night thinking about Uzma Rahan. In the photograph I've seen of her she looks so confident with her gold jewellery and her full red lips and her coloured hair. 'Flashy,' my mum would have said, the corners of her mouth turning down in disapproval. I don't agree: to me she looks beautiful and bold. But that's not how I see her as I stare into the darkness, trying to lie still, fighting the temptation to toss and turn. Lying there in the silence of the night, I see what the policemen would have seen when they found her in her bedroom, four weeks after she died.

I try shutting my eyes against the image but it's no good because it's inside me, it's what my imagination conjured from the horrific details I know to be true. There must be scene-of-crime photographs showing what Uzma Rahan's body looked like but Detective Inspector Brent Hyatt didn't put them in his presentation; there are some things that even delegates to a police conference aren't strong enough to see. But he did describe what happened: Uzma was battered to death by a baseball bat wielded by her husband, who had bought it specifically for the purpose. Forensics saw evidence of twenty-three blows.

What could anybody do to deserve that?

Uzma wasn't born here – she came to Manchester from Pakistan for an arranged marriage with her first cousin, Rahan Arshad – but she liked Britain and she quickly adapted: she got part-time jobs as a beautician and a dinner lady, she cut her hair, she started wearing fitted, western clothes. She was an ordinary woman just like any one of us except, perhaps, she was gutsier, greedier for life than most.

But then allegedly she started having an affair. She tried to keep it secret but according to the papers everybody knew about it; it was reported that her lover's wife even sent a text message to Pakistan telling Uzma's family there. Her husband, Rahan Arshad, hadn't liked the make-up and the tight clothes and the admiring glances that she drew from men, but it was the affair that drove him to divorce her and sell the family home and by the time Uzma was thirty she was destitute and living with her three children in a council house.

If only she'd stayed there she might still be alive, that's what I keep thinking.

But she didn't. A year or so later, her husband bought a new house and asked her to move back in with him and attempt a reconciliation, and she agreed even though she foresaw the danger. 'Count the days until he kills me,' she said to her brother, even as she packed her bags. She *knew* he would want to revenge himself on her, but she can't have thought, even for a second, that he would harm their children otherwise she would have stayed in her council house. That's what I think.

Brent showed pictures of the children in his presentation – posed school photographs for which some teacher had hurriedly smoothed their hair down, told them to smile. I was in the front row and I sat there looking at them – such young, trusting, eager-to-please faces – and tears that I didn't even try to stop streamed down my cheeks. Uzma's husband, their father, killed all three.

He killed Uzma in the bedroom and then he went downstairs to the living room and called the children down, one by one. The oldest of them, an eleven-year-old boy, was dressed in his football strip; the next one down, aged eight, was wearing his Spiderman outfit. Their little sister, Henna, was only six. In the paper it said that two of them had wristbands on, tight strips of plastic that had given them access to rides at a funfair in Blackpool where they'd all been on a family outing the day before they died. I bet it was the boys that were wearing them; little Henna wouldn't have been tall enough to go on most of those rides.

Lying in bed in the dark, I hope against all hope that of the three children, she died first.

What must they have heard and seen? What unimaginable terror must they have felt as they crouched upstairs, pressed against the wall, blocking their ears against the sound of blows and yet straining to hear, waiting their turn. Three such young, innocent lives lost, for what?

'I had to stamp out that fucking bitch's bloodline,' I've been told that's what Arshad said.

2

The vision I first had for Karma Nirvana was very straightforward and – now I look back on it – almost innocent. I was inspired by the terrible death of my sister Robina, who burnt herself to death to escape her husband. It seemed to me then that hers was a uniquely awful fate; I didn't know as I do now that desperate women like Robina – and terrified women like Uzma – exist across Britain, often in cities I know like the back of my hand. But I did think there would be other women like my mum. She was my other inspiration: she spent four decades in Derby but never learnt a word of English. Mum died a stranger in the land she lived in but never called home.

In the years after they died, still raw with the loss of them, I was driven by pain and guilt. I was unable to reconcile myself to the fact that I didn't avert Robina's agonising death. I wanted to, I tried to, but Robina wouldn't listen to me because I'd been disowned. When I ran away from home, desperate to avoid the marriage that Mum and Dad were trying to force me into, my mum declared that I was dead to them. Since then I've been an outcast in my own family and, as such, my opinion didn't – doesn't – carry any weight.

As for Mum: she died without ever saying she was proud of me. I chose to embrace the freedom offered by the country that she brought me up in and although I don't regret that, I was struggling with the fact that she left me feeling I had disappointed her. By living the life I wanted, I had let her down.

Out of this morass of emotion came my vision for a charity that would help women like Robina and my mum, women whose lives were being blighted by cultural and language difficulties. Karma Nirvana was in their honour and their memory so I set it up in Derby, their home town and mine. Looking back now I realise I had no idea of the scale of the problem I was tapping into, I wasn't even sure what problems I was going to find. But I didn't have to wait long to find out; it very quickly became clear that, time and again, the women who came to us for help were suffering honour-based violence – appalling cruelty meted out by whole families, not just by their husbands – and forced marriage.

What struck me as I sat with those women and listened to them – hijabs pulled close around their bruises, faces taut with misery, voices strained – is how young they were. They came to us as battered wives but they were barely more than children. Children who must have known of or suspected their fate before it happened, but who had no idea of where to turn for help. That's why, when I began working to get Karma Nirvana's name and its intentions known, schools were one of my early targets and that hasn't changed.

I keep in touch with all the schools in our locality; I ask to speak to the person in charge of child protection and try to make them aware of the issues surrounding teenage girls and forced marriage. It's not always easy. A lot of the schools don't want anything to do with me. They say the things I'm talking about are 'culturally sensitive' and they don't want to upset parents. One headteacher went so far as to say, 'We don't have anything like that here, we're a progressive school.' And I wanted to say, 'Oh yes? Well what about the girl who was strangled by her brother while her mother sat on her legs? Murdered by her own family because they thought she was pregnant by a man she wasn't married to. She went to your school didn't she?' I wanted to say that, but over the years I've learnt it's sometimes sensible to hold your tongue.

It was through one of the local schools that I met Fozia. Heather Jackson, the deputy headmistress of the school she was at, rang me up to talk about three of her year ten girls, all of them aged fifteen.

'Fozia is the one I'm really worried about,' she said. 'I don't know if she'll tell you but she has issues with self-harm. The other two, Rashpal and Kuljit, just seem disaffected. They used to be keen students with flashes of real promise but now they're both bolshy; it's as if their enthusiasm is being squeezed out of them bit by bit. I'd appreciate some insight into what's going on at home, and I'd really like a bit of input from someone who understands their cultural background more than I do, Jasvinder. As I see it, the problem for all three of them is that they need to be teenagers, but they come from families where that doesn't seem to be allowed.'

I agreed to go into the school and talk to them. I went one day in late May; Heather greeted me warmly and ushered me into her office, a small room with a couple of desks in it and a whole wall of books and files. I sat down and then I heard her heels tip-tapping down the corridor as she went to get the girls.

'Rashpal, Kuljit and Fozia,' she said moments later as the trio stood bunched in the doorway, staring at their feet. Fozia was wearing a hijab and the other two had long hair that flopped forward, screening their faces so all I could really see was the tops of their heads. Heather shot me an encouraging glance and then closed the door. Keeping their eyes downcast, they shuffled forward to sit in the chairs I'd placed opposite mine. As they sat down all three slid backwards, moving their seats as far away from me as the confined space allowed. There was an awkward silence, broken by a snort of laughter from the one in the middle, Kuljit. Hands flew up to faces, all three suppressed conspiratorial smiles.

Where to begin with them? I cleared my throat.

'Miss Jackson thought you might like to talk to me?'

Silence.

'Do you know why?'

Muffled giggles.

'Did she tell you anything about me?'

'That you know my dad.' The words were muttered so quietly that I couldn't be sure who said them, but I think it was Rashpal, the tallest of the three who was sitting on the right.

I stopped, nonplussed. 'What makes you say that? What do you think I'm doing here?'

Heads stayed firmly down. Kuljit doodled on the back of her hand with a biro. Fozia chewed the skin at the edge of her thumbnail.

'Come on, you may as well tell me, we can't just sit here. Who do you think I am?'

There was another long silence before Rashpal, speaking

even more quietly than before, said, 'You're a friend of my dad's. We know he sent you.'

'I'm not, I . . .'

'Well you must know someone who knows him, you're in the network.'

'I'm not part of the network, I can promise you that. The charity I run, Karma Nirvana, helps women overcome cultural and language barriers. Most of the women who contact us are south Asian, a lot of them are very young, like you. A lot of them are being abused at home by their families, or their in-laws. Some of them are afraid of being forced into marriages. Some of them are . . .'

'Excuse me, Miss, could I ask you something,' said Fozia, looking at me for the first time. She was much the smallest of the three, hardly bigger than a child, but I was struck by the fact that she looked older than her years, and careworn. She had none of a young girl's bloom. Her face, framed by her hijab, was dominated by the biggest brown eyes you've ever seen. 'Can we go outside for a minute because the thing is,' she bent down and, with a broad grin, produced a packet of ten Marlboros from her sock, 'I need a smoke.'

Rashpal and Kuljit backed her up with a chorus of, 'Oh yes, Miss, please Miss.' I hesitated, gauging the tightrope I had to walk in order to maintain control without increasing the hostility of this close-knit gang of three. How to win their trust? I thought back to my fifteen-year-old self and was suddenly caught – almost smothered – by the memory of longing to live a normal teenage life.

'Do you know what?' I said, and even to me my voice sounded firmer and more confident. 'When I was about your age I came home from school one day and my mum showed me this photograph. She said, "Look here, this is the man you are going to marry. What do you think?" I can remember that day as if it were yesterday. The man had a really stupid haircut, and he was much smaller than me but that wasn't the point. The point was, I was fifteen and I didn't want to marry anybody.'

Fozia had hidden her cigarettes again and all three were looking at me now with genuine interest. I could tell by their body language – leaning back in their seats, still keeping a distance between us – that they weren't yet prepared to trust me but they had definitely dropped their guard a little.

'What did you do?' asked Kuljit.

So I told them. About running away and being disowned and struggling to make a life without any support from my family; about bringing up my children on my own. I told them about Robina burning herself to death because she was so unhappy in her marriage. They were really shocked by that. Even now, months later, I can remember how they edged their chairs forward as they listened. It was as if they were being physically drawn in by my words. And they had questions, so many questions. 'What did you live on?', 'How did you manage without your mum?', 'Do you miss your family still?' They were all talking together and butting in and a couple of times I had to say, 'Please, wait your turn, I can't hear any of you when you all speak at the same time.'

I'm not sure who started it, but gradually a few bits and pieces from their own lives started trickling out. The slap from a brother, 'because he saw me talking to a boy. We were talking about homework!' The confiscation of mobile phones, 'I've told her, I've said, "Mum, *everybody* has one." But she knows it's just the white kids.' And then, suddenly, there was this from Rashpal:

'You know when you were locked in your room, right? Well that's what happens to me. Every night. Someone told my mum I've got a boyfriend. But I don't. I never did. I keep telling her but she won't believe me. Soon as I get back from school she locks me in my room and I have to have my meals in there, I'm not even allowed down to eat with the family.'

And all at once Fozia and Kuljit were chipping in with, 'That's right Miss' and 'My mum did that to me too once but only for a couple of days.' The details were pouring out but they were talking to each other as much as to me; sharing long-protected secrets. It was frustrating. Having won their trust I realised there was nothing I could do with it while I had to contend with them as a trio. By the time Heather Jackson returned a few minutes later, I'd made a decision.

'Yes, I think it has gone well.' I glanced quickly round for affirmation and was pleased to see all three of them nodding. 'But I think it would be even more constructive if I could talk to each of them on their own. What do you think?' The three girls looked at one another but, ignoring Heather's questioning gaze, none of them spoke.

'I don't see why not,' Heather said, checking her watch. 'Right, Rashpal, Kuljit. Will you go back to your classroom, please. Fozia, are you happy to stay here and talk to Jasvinder on your own?'

Taking her non-committal shrug to be assent, Heather ushered Rashpal and Kuljit out of the room, and I turned back to Fozia who, having lost the support of her friends, seemed newly shy. I reached across to still her hands which were pulling at the sleeves of her sweatshirt, rolling them down below her wrists. That's a habit I've often noticed in self-harmers. Maybe they think they're making sure that nobody can see the ladder of cuts up their arms, the row of crudely carved rungs, some old and faint and silvery and then the new ones red and raw. But to me the fiddling and sleeve pulling is such a giveaway; I see it as another cry for help.

I left my hand where it was, pinning her small, hot fists in her lap and said, 'So, tell me a bit about yourself. Tell me about your family.'

'My family? That's some story,' she said, looking up at me and rolling her eyes, making it a melodrama, as if I was sitting there waiting to be entertained. I've learnt since that Fozia always makes a joke of things when she's embarrassed and knowing her as I do now – how reluctant she often is to talk at all about the things she's been through – I look back at that afternoon and I'm amazed she found the courage to share so much.

'I'd like to hear about your family,' I said, dead serious.

She looked me straight in the eye and I could feel her mood change. 'You won't tell my dad I told you?'

'I won't tell him, I promise.'

'You don't know him, right? You *did* say you don't know him?'

'I don't know him or – as far as I'm aware – anyone who knows him. This is just between you and me, Fozia.'

'That's okay then. It's just that me and the others, we thought our dads sent you to find out what we're thinking; if we're up to anything.'

'This is nothing to do with your dad. Heather Jackson asked me to come because she's worried about you – you and the others. She says you are bright intelligent girls who are not getting any work done. She thought there must be a reason for it. She thought you might like to talk to someone.'

'What's the point of getting my work done, when I'm just going to fuck off and marry some Paki?' Fozia spat the words out.

I looked at her questioningly, hoping she'd carry on.

She avoided my gaze, turning to look through the window, feigning interest in the empty playground. 'I think my mum and dad are planning to get me married off to someone in Pakistan. That's what they done with my older sisters, three of them and I think that's what they're going to do with me. I'm fifteen now and I'm the next in line.'

She looked up and examined my face as if checking to see if I found this credible. What she saw must have convinced her that I did, because she went on, 'I've only told this to one person before you, you know.'

'Who was that?'

'My best friend. I told her because one day a whole lot of us were sitting on the games field and one of my friends shouts out, "Who thinks they are going to get married first?" So my other friend looks at me and straight away she says, "Fozia, I think Fozia will get married first." I didn't say anything because I thought that was right and I wished it wasn't, but all the others were going, "Is that right, Fozia, do you think so?"' She pushed her fingers – stubby, ink-stained, child's fingers – into her eyes to stop the tears. The skin around her nails was chewed raw. 'I still can't forget that conversation, it made me feel so different. It made me feel really alone.'

'And what did your best friend do?' I prompted.

'I asked for her advice. Afterwards, I asked her what she'd do, and she said, "if I was you I'd do it, I think you should go through with it." The difference is that she is the only daughter in her family, her mum is like her best friend, whereas I've got eight sisters, I'm the second to last, and I could never sit down with my mum and tell her how I feel.' Tears were running down Fozia's cheeks now, and she swallowed hard to get rid of the sob that was threatening to choke her. 'My mum is scary, she has mood swings and she's very controlling. If I tell her I got in trouble at school and say it wasn't my fault, she doesn't believe me. She always says it was my fault.'

Fozia stopped talking and gave a heavy sigh and at that moment she looked so young, so child-like, that I felt a stab of fury at the thought of her being pushed into a loveless marriage, her childhood cut short for the sake of her family's status. Her pause was filled with the clamour of the bell, followed instantly by the sound of doors opening, voices loud with the pleasure of release, the clatter of dozens of pairs of eager feet.

'Dinner time,' Fozia said, as if these noises needed explanation.

I nodded. 'Do you like school? Do you want to go to college?'

She cocked her head to one side, considering the question. 'I've been really bad in school. I've got excluded loads of times. I've got lots of detentions. But . . .' she stopped and grinned at me. 'School is the best, it's heaven. When I step into the school grounds in the morning I think "YES". It's just me and I can be whatever I want. I love it. School is my time for enjoying myself . . . Do you remember the six week holiday? Did you have that? To me that's a killer because home is so tight. I'm not allowed to go out. I'm not allowed to wear western clothes. Six boring weeks with no music, no *EastEnders*, no English programmes. All we can watch is Bollywood movies.'

After this burst of enthusiasm, she fell silent.

'What do you think your mum wants for you?' I asked her.

There was another sudden mood switch, another heavy sigh.

'She has low expectations for all of us girls. My brother, she strokes him and says, "You are my son and you are going to go to work and make me proud of you," but she doesn't want that for us. If she sees me sitting in the living room with a book out she says, "You're not going to sit in an office or do A levels so what you got a book out for?" I even get told off for reading the Harry Potter book. I do my homework when my dad is there because he's really supportive, he wants me to have an education. He always says, "Look the teacher in the eye; make sure she knows you're paying attention". He wants me to do well—'

She stopped, brought up short by her own confusion. Her voice had softened at the mention of her father and I could sense her wrestling with the fact that this man whom she obviously loved dearly, whom she trusted and respected, now seemed to be betraying her.

'He's always wanted me to do well, that's what I don't understand. That's why I said to him, about the marriage, "Why are you doing this? This is not like you." And he said, "Well, look, I'll have a conversation with your mum and see what she says." So, he had that conversation and afterwards it was like talking to a different person, even his tone of voice was different. It was all flat and expressionless. He just said, "You've got to get married." That's all he'd say—'

The look she gave me was almost challenging.

'He's my dad and he's really understanding, but I've never had the courage to look him in the eye. Can you believe that? It's like this fear I've been brought up with, it's a kind of respect but it's more fear really.'

I nodded and as I did so Fozia's face was blotted out by an

image of my own dad. I saw him standing by the back door of our house in Dale Road; in my mind's eye he was leaning against the door frame enjoying the evening sun before he set off for the night shift at the foundry. I saw him smoking a cigarette, his hand cupped round it in that distinctive way he had. It was such a vivid image that I could almost smell the smoke, sharp and tangy against the sweeter smell of the hair oil that he always wore. I felt the hairs on my arms stand up, and I cleared my throat loudly, almost afraid that I might speak to him. I forced myself to focus on Fozia.

'When were your sisters married?' I asked her.

She thought for a minute. 'I think I was nine. We went in the summer holidays and when we came back I'd missed two weeks of year four. My family's *Baba* in Pakistan said to my dad that he wanted three girls of marriageable age and that's why we went, but we didn't know that until later. At the time we thought we were just going on a holiday. Even when my dad took my sisters off to buy new dresses they didn't catch on. It wasn't until we'd been there about two weeks that the marriage preparations started: my aunties were cooking all this Asian food and big crates of Coke and juice were coming into the house and that's when my dad told my sisters they were getting married.'

'How old were they?' I asked her.

'Khalida must have been twenty-two, so Raveeda was eighteen and Heba was sixteen. Raveeda really didn't want to go through with it.' Fozia was leaning in towards me now, caught up in her story, her eyes wide as saucers. 'She was screaming and crying out, "No Dad, I don't want to get married," and my other sisters were crying. Then suddenly my dad pinned Raveeda up against the wall and held a knife to her throat – I don't even know where he got that knife from, he must have had it hidden in his clothing – but he was shouting and yelling, and saying he would kill Raveeda if she didn't go through with it. She was so terrified . . .' Fozia paused and looked right past me as if she could see, over my left shoulder, her sister's tear-stained face, the panic in her eyes, the way she flattened herself against the wall, trying to shrink from the glinting blade and the icy rage in her father's eyes. I felt my own skin prickle. 'It was scary to witness that,' Fozia said so softly it was as if, for that moment, she was talking to herself. 'My mum could be like that and it would be quite normal for her, it wouldn't have affected me in any way, but my dad is a softer person, he's very gentle. For him to do that was very surprising.'

'Had they met the men that they were going to marry?' I felt a twinge of shame at the note of urgency in my question. In all the years I've been listening to these stories, supporting the women who tell them to me, I've never managed to detach myself; my mind always flits back to the photograph on my mum's mantelpiece, the stranger who was earmarked for me. It can make me feel guilty, survivor's guilt I suppose: my sisters all went through with the marriages my parents made for them, but I escaped. Why should I have been the one to cheat my destiny?

'They'd seen them, that was all. At least I know Khalida had. Her in-laws came to the house and when this lad came in my mum whispered, "What do you think of him then?" Khalida should have guessed then that she was getting married because that was the opposite of how Mum was normally. Normally she was more like, "Get away from him, he's single," even if she saw you talking to a cousin.

'My third sister, Heba, she never saw the man she had to

marry though – or only in a picture. Hers was working away and when the time came for the *ruksat* she had to do her part over the phone.'

'How long did your sisters have to stay in Pakistan?'

'It must have been about six months. We came back home after the engagement party and it was only my dad who was there with them for the *ruksat*. That was filmed and we used to watch the video at our house. It made me so sad, I'd be crying inside when we watched it. My sister, Khalida, you see her holding onto my dad, crying her eyes out. There's no sound on the film, but it's so easy to read her lips. You can see her saying, "Please don't leave us here." My dad's saying, "Don't worry, it will be all right." He and my mum didn't care about them being unhappy. When Khalida got raped by her husband she told my dad, and he said, "That's not rape, it's a husband's right." That was his answer; I was really shocked to hear it.' Fozia's voice was fading to a whisper and I had to strain to hear her final sentence. 'It scared me, Jasvinder. I don't want to go through that.'

The clangour of the bell startled both of us. The noise from the playground – which had seemed a distant hum while Fozia was spilling out the sad details of her sisters' unhappiness – grew louder as the kids began pouring back into the building. The room seemed to vibrate slightly as dozens of pairs of feet thudded down the corridor.

'You understand what I'm on about don't you?' Her voice was still so low that she could have been speaking to herself. Perhaps she was. But she turned her attention back to me as she said, 'My dad might kill me, Jasvinder. Believe me, he said he would.'

'I do believe you.'

'I came downstairs one night at about eleven o'clock; I didn't know anybody else was still awake until I saw a light on in the living room. The door was half shut but I stopped just beside it and I could hear them talking. It was Mum, Dad and my oldest sister. I heard my mum say, "We'll take her off to Pakistan and get her married." Then my sister said, "But what will you do if she runs away again?"

'Again?'

Fozia sighed as my interruption broke her thread. She looked drained and exhausted.

'Don't worry,' I said quickly. I didn't want to make this any more of an ordeal for her. 'Go on. You can tell me about that later.'

'That's when I heard him say it. My dad said, "If that girl runs away again I'll kill her, don't doubt my word. I'd rather a daughter dead and myself in prison than stand here and let the shadow of dishonour settle on my family." His voice was so hard and cold when he said it Jasvinder, it really frightened me. It wasn't like him. Me and my dad have always had a special relationship. I was brought up to be scared of him but he was always special to me—' Her voice tailed away again and we sat silent for a minute. Fozia was chewing at her fingernails.

'I just know it's nearly time for me. They want me married now,' she said eventually.

'Okay.' Fozia's pallor told me it was time to stop talking. I was tired too. I felt battered by the cruel realities of this child's life. 'Now you have told us we can look after you. Here is my number, you can call me whenever you need to. I'd like to speak to Miss Jackson before I go. Do you know where I'd find her?' Fozia stood up and at full height she looked half the size of my Maria, who was only eleven then. She seemed so young and so vulnerable that I stood up too and hugged her. As she melted into me – so desperate for love and reassurance – I wished I could take her home.

Minutes after Fozia had left the room, Heather was back with a mug of tea in each hand. 'I should think you need this. How did you get on?'

'She says she's already run away from home once . . . did you know that?' I asked. And of course Heather did. It had happened a few months previously; Fozia had left home and gone to stay with Raveeda who, like Heba, has now left her husband and is struggling to bring up young kids on her own. Heather found out about it because, while she was there, Fozia took an overdose. Paracetamol they think it was. She didn't take enough to knock herself out, in fact she was still well enough to come to school the following day. It was only because her best friend noticed that she was really pale and miserable that anyone found out. When Fozia admitted to it, the friend told the school nurse, who packed Fozia off to hospital.

'She was off for about a week. I saw her when she came back and I asked her why she'd done it. She said it was for the freedom it gave her. She said nobody knew she'd done it, and that was a wonderful contrast to the way her parents usually watch her twenty-four seven. It was the one thing in her life she felt she could control.

'The parents visited her once in the three days she spent in hospital. Apparently the only thing they said was that she'd better not dare do that again. Can you understand that attitude, Jasvinder?' Heather rested her cheek against the warmth of her coffee cup. 'I know I can't.'

The hospital discharged her to her family and Fozia was back in the situation she had fled from. A couple of months later she ran away again and this time found accommodation in a bed and breakfast. 'The trouble there was that her self-harming became too serious.' Heather sighed. 'She cut herself quite badly and left blood all over the bathroom, and the bed and breakfast wouldn't keep her after that.'

I sighed too. 'I'm sure they wouldn't. Poor child. It must have felt as if, once again, her cry for help had been ignored.'

Some time later – in one of the many, many conversations I've had with Fozia – I asked her if she had ever considered going to the police when she was living at home and frightened for her life.

'The police?' There was an incongruously adult note to her contempt. It's surprised me several times when we've been talking about the things she's been through.

'Shall I tell you about the police? They came round to my sister's place with my dad when I was there. My dad had been round before hammering on the door and kicking at it but I wouldn't talk to him, so he reported me missing and came back with the police.' Her cheeks were flushed with anger and she was rushing the words out, almost tripping over them in her haste.

'There were two police officers, an Asian guy and a white guy who was with him, but he didn't speak to me. The Asian guy said he wanted to talk to me alone and I thought that was good. But when I said to him, "They're trying to force me into marriage and I don't want to go home, please don't make me go home," he turned round and said, "You and I both know this is what happens in Asian families. I think you should go home and go through with it." He was the first adult I dared speak to about it and that's what he said.'

3

Nowadays more than fifty-five per cent of the agency calls we get at Karma Nirvana are from police officers, either making referrals or wanting advice or information. Increasingly we are asked to go and address police forces, to explain the issues surrounding forced marriage and honour-based violence; as I write this there is a list of twenty-two forces waiting to hear my presentation. Because the police are such important allies, I never refuse.

I always start off by talking a bit about my own experience, but as the years have gone by I've added the stories of other women who have suffered and – in the most shocking cases – died in the name of honour. Heshu Yones was one of the first I knew about and to my mind is still one of the most terrible. Heshu was sixteen and had everything to live for. I've seen photographs of her at her comprehensive school, laughing with her friends. I've seen photographs of her lolling on her bed at home, smiling into the camera, surrounded by the paraphernalia of teenage life. She was beautiful, vibrant, intelligent – and now she's dead. Her father killed her. He stabbed her seventeen times before slitting her throat and leaving her to bleed to death in the bathroom of their council flat in Acton. The knife he used was twisted, bent, and the tip of it was broken off with the ferocity of his attack.

The scene-of-crime photographs are almost unbearable. Heshu's mutilated body, slumped on the bath, looks like a human sacrifice, which in a way I suppose it was. Heshu was sacrificed in the name of honour; killed by her Kurdish Muslim father because – as he saw it – she had shamed him by having the temerity to choose a Christian boyfriend.

Heshu knew what the consequences might be; letters read out in court showed that she had already suffered at her father's hands. One, written in defiance, said, 'Hey, for an older man you have a good strong punch and kick. I hope you enjoyed testing your strength on me, it was fun being on the receiving end.' She was frightened for her life long before he came to drag her from her bedroom, knife in hand. She told her teachers at school that she thought she was in danger; three times she sought help from them and three times she somehow got ignored. And then it was too late.

Detective Inspector Brent Hyatt told me about Heshu at the police conference where we first met. He is part of the Metropolitan Police Serious Crime Directorate and a member of its Honour Killings Working Group; this was the first case of this kind he had to handle. 'I was innocent then Jasvinder,' he told me. 'I thought Heshu's dad might need protection when people found out what he'd done. I thought his son would try to revenge his sister's death and I thought he'd be attacked by the other blokes in prison but I was wrong on both counts. His son congratulated him on redeeming the family's honour and the other Kurds in Belmarsh gave him a hero's welcome.'

Brent also told me that Heshu's father was sentenced to life with a minimum tariff of just eight years before he was considered for release. Apparently the judge said it was 'a tragic story arising out of irreconcilable cultural differences between traditional Kurdish values and the values of Western society'. As if that was an excuse! To me that's tantamount to saying that the impulse to kill your daughter in the name of honour is understandable; somehow less appalling than any other kind of murder.

Trying to explain the concept of honour is one of the hardest things in my presentation. Asian people don't question it: they're swaddled in it from the moment they're born, it's as though they absorb it along with their mother's milk. Honour – *izzat* – is the cornerstone of the Asian community and since the beginning of time it's been the job of girls and women to keep it polished. And that's really hard because so many things can tarnish it.

Wearing lipstick, owning a mobile phone, cutting your hair; any of those things could be said to bring dishonour on a family because those are all signs that a girl is getting westernised, which is what Asian families fight so hard against. They'd lock up their daughters for months on end rather than let that happen. When I was a girl my mum was always warning me against white people with their dirty white ways. She slapped me once because I said I'd like to buy a pair of jeans.

When I finish my presentation, I allow a good half hour for questions and I always need it. A lot of people use me as a confessional. What I've said makes them look back on cases they've handled in the past and wish they'd acted differently. I remember the chief superintendent of a police force in northern

England telling me the story of a young Asian couple he'd dealt with years before. Their families reported them missing and a massive search was launched, he said, with dogs, helicopters, the whole thing. 'Eventually we tracked them down in London and because they were so young we took them home, even though it wasn't what they wanted.' His voice fell away and he said, almost to himself, 'They begged us not to send them home, she was crying, he was insisting it wasn't safe and yet we ignored them . . . why?' His eyes met mine and they were stained with guilt. 'Until today I never realised what that might have meant to them. I know the boy was sent to India but as for the girl . . . With what I've learnt today, I hate to think what happened to her.'

After years of cold calling, hammering on closed doors, sending emails that I could never be sure had been opened, it is gratifying to know that Karma Nirvana's voice is being heard by the police. Steve Allen, head of the Metropolitan Police Violent Crime Directorate, even came to the office recently to see the project at first hand. It was good to see him here, because he and I had a feisty relationship at the start. I met him when I wrote to the Metropolitan Police Commissioner Sir Ian Blair to complain about how little was being done to combat honour-based violence in this country. When the letter arrived on Steve Allen's desk he sent for me – and on the day we met, kept me waiting for ten minutes outside his office, just long enough for me to think that he might never come out! We laugh about it now. I've heard him say to people: 'So many letters of complaint land on my desk, but Jasvinder was different – she wouldn't let go.'

It took me quite some time to persuade him to visit us but eventually he agreed to combine it with talking at a conference on honour-based violence that I organised in Leeds. He looked almost nervous when he arrived in the office; I think he was unsure what to expect. We're based in a business centre on an ordinary Derby street and there is nothing about the room we work in that immediately suggests the urgency and intensity of the work we carry out each day. I remember him looking round: cream walls, our five desks, the conference table, the tray with kettle, coffee, biscuits, the pin board covered with leaflets and newspaper cuttings. Everything he saw was ordinary and unremarkable.

But then he clocked the blue box in its place on top of the filing cabinet by the door. He flashed me a look, eyebrows faintly raised. I shrugged as if to say, 'Yes, that's how it is.' He's a policeman; there was no need to explain that it's a panic alarm, that if the button on the top of it is pressed a clutch of his colleagues will be at our door in seconds. It was installed the day after the family of a young woman I'd helped threatened to chop me into little pieces if I didn't reveal her whereabouts. It was meant as an emergency measure, not something permanent, but each time it's about to be removed something else unsettling happens and it stays. The staff and I tracked Steve Allen's gaze as he looked back at it and, just for a second, time froze as we all stood and stared at the innocuous looking thing: our safety net.

'Let's have a coffee; Anna would you—?' I said, keen to move the moment on. I felt a little uncertain myself but just as I was wondering how to get the day started one of the phones did the job for me. That call – Shazia took it as I remember – was followed by another and another and another until the day began to blur. Between calls each one of us tried to brief Steve Allen, to put him in the picture about who was on the phone and why, but sometimes there was barely time. 'That woman,' I remember saying as I put down the receiver, 'is eight and a half months pregnant. She already has two children under three. She lives with her in-laws and her husband controls her life completely: she's not allowed out alone, she's not allowed to use the telephone, she's not even allowed to choose what television programmes she watches. She rang once before to discuss the fact she wants to leave him and now she's going to. She's asking for refuge provision.' I broke off to call across to my secretary Anna, 'We need a place for a pregnant woman with two children from tonight if possible – can you start ringing round?' Then I turned back to Steve Allen. 'You know what has finally persuaded her to leave? After the other two babies were born she was expected to resume cooking and cleaning for her husband's family – seven of them – the day after she got back from hospital. When she complained she was tired her mother-in-law kicked her and within a week her milk had dried up. She says she can't live through that again.'

Some of the calls we had that day came from women we know well and have been supporting for some time. There was Aaliyah, mother of five daughters, the eldest of whom told her three years ago that her daddy had been sexually abusing her since she was twelve. Aaliyah's initial reaction was to shake and slap her daughter, to tell her off for lying, but the girl stood up for herself and refused to retract her claim until eventually Aaliyah believed her and went to the police. That's when the extended family became involved. 'Don't prosecute him.' 'Don't shame us.' 'Don't you see this will dishonour us – and anyway, what harm has been done?' On and on they went until Aaliyah dropped the charges, a change of heart which left the police feeling understandably frustrated.

Luckily, a few months later, she changed her mind again. To this day I'm not sure why, but I should think the conversation in which her seven-year-old said in all innocence, 'Mummy, did you know Daddy's got a snake that grows when you touch it?' played a large part. And I hope the support we gave her helped too. That father is in prison now: he got two years and he'll be on the sex offenders register for another ten. His family don't see that as a problem. They said to Aaliyah when he was sentenced, 'Don't worry, when he comes out you can all go back and live in Pakistan, you'll have no trouble with child protection issues there.'

In almost all the cases we deal with the police have played a part – or will do. Abhir rang in that day as well. She's a forced-marriage victim. When her father discovered she had a white boyfriend he whisked her off to Pakistan and found her an Asian husband quicker than you could say consent. In fear of her life, Abhir played along with it; she got married and then did everything necessary to call her husband over. But once he arrived here and started beating and abusing her she couldn't stand it any longer. Late one night, when everyone in her household was asleep, she stood shivering in the darkness by the telephone and – feeling blindly for the numbers, whispering into the mouthpiece – she begged her old boyfriend to come and rescue her.

Looking back she thinks her mother might have overheard her, or possibly it was one of her sisters but she found that thought too hard to bear. Anyway, someone did. When the agreed time came Abhir's boyfriend's car can't have been at the curb more than sixty seconds. He drew up, she ran out carrying a few possessions in a plastic bag, she leapt in and they pulled away – with a car full of her uncles and brothers right behind them.

Because they were on a high bridge when the uncle who was driving tried to run them off the road, he was charged with attempted murder. 'Obviously that's good, Steve,' I said when I'd finished telling him the story. 'But the trouble is that once Abhir had given the police her statement, they simply said goodbye to her, they offered her no support at all. And to my mind that's not good enough.'

I think that hit home. I know, anyway, that Steve Allen was affected by what he learnt in our offices. At the conference the next day when his turn came he took the stage and said, 'There's my presentation, read it if you want to, but having observed at first hand the work being done by Karma Nirvana these issues have moved from my head to my heart and it's from my heart that I'll be speaking.' And it was.

We need that kind of empathy trickling down from the top. Time and again I have frontline officers – the men on the beat – saying the same thing to me, 'You know what it's like? A girl goes missing, or turns up covered in bruises and you have your suspicions, but it's always being drummed into us: be careful of cultural sensitivities, steer clear of what you don't understand. The last thing we need is another accusation of racism.'

4

Early that summer Gordon Riches, who had been my tutor when I was an undergraduate at Derby University, came to Karma Nirvana to try and persuade me to do a PhD on honour-based violence. He said he had read about the work we were doing in the local paper and he thought the issues it raised needed exploring. He waved aside my protests that I wasn't an academic, that I was intimidated by the language of academia, by its need for theory and analysis, even by the people it attracted. 'Believe in yourself,' he said. 'This is your area of expertise. How *do* the women who have endured this sort of abuse survive? How did you do it? What were your strategies and coping techniques? When your family disowned you why didn't you just roll over and die? Come on Jas, if you could find the answer to those questions, there are hundreds of women out there who could benefit. You wouldn't just be gathering knowledge for the sake of it, you know that. We need this information.'

Gordon understands me too well: I've often described some of the more damaged women we meet as 'dead people walking', and I've spent hours coaxing them to engage with life again, often without success. I don't know what separates them from those who recover and go on to live fulfilling lives, but I've often asked myself that question and now I was being encouraged to find out.

I told Gordon I would consider his proposal, but even as I said it I was laughing in disbelief that – having left school without an exam pass to my name – I should now be considering a doctorate. In the past education has always been a means to an end for me: when my relationship with my second husband, Maria and Joshua's father, became intolerable I knew I needed some qualifications in order to support my children on my own. I did my A levels and then a degree so that I could earn a proper living. The idea that I could study something just because I found it interesting was right outside my frame of reference, but it certainly appealed.

Gordon suggested I put together a proposal, which he said would involve spending a few hours in the university library discovering what research had already been done, then deciding what I might add to it. Often I found it easiest to sneak a bit of time to do that after I'd dropped the kids at school and before I went into Karma Nirvana: at that early hour I usually had the library to myself. I used to spend half an hour scouring the shelves for anything relevant and then leave with my shoulder bag bulging with books. I still tried to be at Karma Nirvana before the phones started ringing off the hook and if the traffic wasn't too heavy I usually managed it.

Most days I arrived to find Shazia sitting behind her desk, taking messages off the answering machine. When I arrived, she would pause the tape to fill me in. 'There's a day's work here already. Three, no – four requests for you to give a presentation;

I'll get Anna to call them back. Two people wanting refuge places: I'll sort them. Madeleine from social services; she wants to talk about a fifteen-year-old girl who is five months pregnant and whose parents won't let her have any medical care. Do you want to do that? Wait: I'll put her number on a Post-it. Here you are.'

As I reached for the scrap of paper I smiled at the memory of Shazia as she was when I first knew her: a pair of hunched shoulders and a cream-coloured cap pulled right down so that the peak covered everything except her chin. That's all we could ever see of her: her chin and her plaits – you could see those because she was usually fiddling with them.

I met Shazia when she was living in a refuge in Stoke-on-Trent.

I was managing the refuges then and she was a resident who had made a complaint. I went round at the end of the day to hear it. I was on my way home and I remember checking my watch as I unlocked the door and thinking: 'This shouldn't take long. With a bit of luck I'll have the kids' supper on by six o'clock'.

I found Shazia sitting at the kitchen table; at least I presumed it was her – she was safely hidden behind her cap.

'Shazia?' She nodded her head almost imperceptibly. 'I'm going to make a cup of tea. Would you like one?'

I can't remember now how long it was before she lifted up her eyes and looked at me. Until she did I just kept talking, telling her my story, hoping she was listening and that my experience would strike a chord with her. I can't remember what first made her laugh, or the first thing she said that made my eyes sting with tears of sympathy. But I do remember that when I stood up to draw the blue checked curtains the window was all steamed up from the heat of cooking and the moon was high in the sky. Shazia made me Asian food that night. I can still see her standing by the oven, stirring the dahl, lifting the spoon to her lips to taste it before turning to me, 'I hope it's all right, do you want to try?' And then, with this great big smile on her face, 'I've been so lonely, you don't know how good it feels to have someone to eat with after all this time.'

It was almost two a.m. before I left the refuge.

Shazia says now that she trusted me immediately. She'd been living in refuge accommodation for six years at that point, and all that time her story had been trapped inside her. It was as if she had been waiting to tell me. She sat with her hands in front of her on the pine table, her fingers tightly laced together, and the words tumbled out of her so fast and fluently that I knew the thoughts she was expressing had been going round and round inside her head, teasing and tormenting, until she felt she would go mad trying to make sense of them.

And what sense could she make of a life that began to take cruel turns long before she was forced into marriage? There was abuse in her childhood so private and appalling that I might be the only person she ever tells about it. That was the first betrayal she experienced. Then there was loss: her best friend was fourteen when she was murdered by her own father.

Shazia told me about the last time they were together. It was a teachers' training day and with all those free, indolent hours in hand she and Samina decided to wander up to the park and see what was happening. No one else was there so they sat, side by side on the swings, scuffing their shoes in the dust and enjoying the feeble warmth of the spring sun on their shoulders. They were so engrossed in their conversation – they were imagining themselves stretched out on a beach in some far-off, foreign land – that they didn't hear Samina's father coming up behind them.

The first Shazia knew of it was Samina's startled cry of pain, the way the swing seat jerked and got caught in the bend of her friend's left knee as she was dragged off it, backwards. 'He was pulling her by the hair, shouting about her truanting and I was shouting too, trying to tell him that it was an inset day, we weren't supposed to be in school, it was like a holiday. But he wouldn't listen, perhaps he couldn't hear. He was so angry, so busy forcing her along in front of him.'

What happened next was reported in all the papers. Shazia looked it up a few months back. This is from the *Mail on Sunday:*

> Mohammed Riaz, 41, killed 14 year old Samina with an unlicensed Colt 45 revolver, then shot his wife and another daughter before killing himself. Detectives, who believe that there were often rows about schoolwork, are working on a theory that the unemployed father was so ambitious for his children that the argument turned to a blood bath.

Shazia went round to Samina's house a few days after her friend died, she checked that no one was watching before ducking – quick and furtive – under the fluorescent police tape. It felt morbid and she says she was ashamed of that, but she had to convince herself of what had happened. She found it hard to believe that something so terrible could be true – until she got inside. Inside, she said, it was so cold and quiet and still, Samina and her family so completely gone, that the house felt like a morgue. While she was there she opened Samina's drawers and quickly took out one of her cardigans. 'I suppose it was stealing, but I needed something to remember her by and I told myself that no one else would know.'

The following year Shazia's parents took her out of school and kept her at home in readiness for the marriage they were planning for her. The family GP, an Asian, wrote sick note after sick note explaining her absence, although he never once examined her. 'I knew he was doing that, but still I hoped that someone – a teacher or a social worker – would come to my house to see how I was. At first I couldn't believe that everyone had forgotten about me, but after a few months I had to accept the fact they had – either that or they just didn't care. I felt completely helpless and abandoned,' Shazia said.

She was seventeen when she was taken to Pakistan by her parents and forced into marriage with a man she did not meet until the wedding. She begged them not to leave her there, but they did: 'You need time to make this relationship work', they said, confiscating her passport and with it any hope of escape. Shazia refused to give in and relinquish control of her life. She struck a deal with her husband: if you don't force me to consummate this marriage I will do as you wish and fill in the forms to sponsor you into England. 'He didn't mind,' she said. 'He made it clear from the start that all he wanted was a passport.'

Back in Birmingham, she stuck to her side of the bargain, but she also wrote to the British Embassy explaining her plight. In all she wrote seven times in the hope that her husband would not be given a visa but, even though she gave a friend's address so her parents couldn't intercept an answering letter, no response was made. In desperation, three weeks after her husband arrived in England and – with his visa safely in his hand – started trying to kiss and cuddle her, she decided to leave. She called the police and asked to be given safe escort from her home and although she had smuggled some of her things into plastic bags in readiness, when the moment came – with her mother wailing and shrieking at the door and her father standing yelling by the police car – she left the bags behind. 'I took almost nothing with me, but I did have Samina's cardigan, I was wearing that.'

She spent her first few days in bed and breakfast accommodation just ten minutes from the family home; she didn't have the money to go any further and besides, there was nowhere else she knew. Having seen her safely there, the police considered their job done; they offered no further support. 'I used to sit in my room and talk to my family as if they were there on the bed beside me. It made me feel less lonely. I know it sounds crazy but although they had hurt me so much I still missed not being with them. I wasn't used to being alone, it made me feel as if the whole of me was empty.'

She moved on when her father tracked her down. 'I think he did it through my National Insurance number, I know he's got a friend at the job centre.' After that she kept moving until I found her in Stoke-on-Trent, caught in a limbo between the horrors of her old life and a new life she longed for but couldn't envisage. For six years her days had passed in a fog of hopelessness, wandering aimlessly through streets in which everyone else seemed to be walking with a purpose, staring blankly at daytime television, sitting lonely on her bed.

'The thing is Jasvinder, I want to make something of myself. It's all I think about. I've given up everything and I don't want that to have been for nothing. I'd like to help people – like you do.'

'You will,' I said. And it wasn't just words, it wasn't empty reassurance. I knew from the start that Shazia could put her experience to good use. She gave a sort of snorting, disbelieving laugh. 'How can you say that? Look at me. I live in a refuge. I've got no qualifications . . .'

I said, 'Shazia, if you believe in yourself you will do it. Trust me, not only will you do it, you will do it with me.'

That was three years ago; twelve months later Shazia started working with me at Karma Nirvana. She's brilliant at it. I watch her supporting other women and she shines with radiance and compassion. Those qualities were always there but she just needed someone to bring them out – someone to love her. And I do love her. For all she's been through, she never allowed her spirit to be crushed and I admire that.

I'll never forget the first time she shared the platform with me at a conference. She was trembling like a leaf – she still had that cream cap on, I don't know how many months it took me to persuade her to leave it off – but she looked directly at the audience and introduced herself. 'My name is Shazia, I'm a victim of forced marriage and I'm a survivor today. When I was seventeen my parents took me to Pakistan. They said it was for a holiday but after two weeks they told me I was getting married—' She broke off then. I remember the look of panic in her eyes as she turned to me and mouthed, 'Will you take over now?' and the flush of pleasure on her cheeks as she sank back onto her chair and the audience rose to their feet to applaud her. That was only eighteen months ago and now we all joke that we can't shut her up!

Shazia is like a daughter to me, she's like one of my own and she and my eldest daughter Lisa are inseparable. The truth is I'd adopt her if I could but she's still got her own family. Not that she's seen them for the last nine years. She walked out of the house that day and her mum has never allowed her back. Out of all of them, the one she really misses is her little brother. He must be thirteen now and he's grown to adolescence believing that Shazia was killed in a car crash all those years ago. How could his mum make him live with that?

The first time Shazia showed her face on television (it was a big deal for her: she'd been talking to the media for several months but always with her face in silhouette) her mum was on the phone next day: 'How dare you? Have you no shame? Don't you see what this does to your family?' It was the first time they had spoken in years but Shazia stood her ground. I was standing there beside her as she pushed her shoulders back and lifted her chin and said down the phone, 'So what are you saying Mum? That it's not true? That you didn't do those things to me? Can you really deny it?' She stood up to her without flinching and to me that was the final proof that Shazia would survive.

A weighty legal document arrived in the office, sent by some solicitors in Liverpool. They had asked me to be a cultural expert in the custody case of two children who had been removed from their parents. The document explained why, but it was well over one hundred pages long and ever since Anna put it on my desk I had been battling to find the time to read it. One evening at five o'clock when we turn the phones off, I got it out and promised myself I would read at least a third of it before I went home. I had barely reached page ten before I knew I'd read it right through. I was so wrapped up in it that I completely forgot the passing of time.

The woman whose children had been taken away was called Fatima. The only girl among three brothers, she was born and brought up in Liverpool where, with the rest of her family, she lived in a community – all Asian, mostly Muslim – kept close by the fact they all lived in the same street and, where possible, picked spouses from the same family. It was a scenario very typical in the cases that I see.

Some years previously Fatima had married a man from Pakistan (an arranged marriage for certain, if not forced) and brought him over; his name was Rafiq and he was some years older than her. The trouble for this couple started when Fatima's youngest brother's wife ran off, taking with her their new baby boy. The document named the errant wife as Jamilah, but said very little else about her. I presume she ran away for the same reason that so many of the women we see flee from their families: she had been bullied and abused to the point when she couldn't endure any more.

Whatever the reason, Jamilah's husband and his brothers were furious, enraged by her independence and her disrespect. When she sent word that she was in a refuge and had no intention of coming back, they determined to find her. For six months they looked, scouring Liverpool and then fanning out to search the surrounding cities. I'm sure they had many willing helpers, sharp eyes and ears from the Asian network, but they had no luck. Eventually they stopped looking – but they didn't give up.

Even as I write this I find it hard to believe what happened next. As a mother, it seems to me inconceivable that Fatima did what she did, but there it all is, written down in black and white. She has never denied it.

One late spring evening at about six o'clock, Fatima dialled

999. Her kitchen was on fire, she said, and her children had been abducted. The emergency services rallied immediately, arriving at Fatima's three-bedroom semi minutes later to find her outside in the garden, wringing her hands and gabbling about a woman called Jamilah, her sister-in-law who, she said, had both started the fire and snatched the children. 'She fell out with my family and this is her revenge,' Fatima wept.

Even as the firemen fought the blaze which, by the time they arrived, had consumed the kitchen and was lapping at the stairs, the police found this story far-fetched. But it was the way Fatima knew which direction to take to find the children: 'I think she set off this way . . .' 'My guess is she will have taken the number eleven bus . . .' that really gave the game away. Her son and daughter, aged five and four, were found crouched beside one of the A roads leading out of Liverpool. They were huddled together, their faces smeared with snot and tears.

That image haunts me. It was dusk by the time I left the office, and as I drove home I kept looking at the houses that I passed. Some of them had their curtains drawn against the evening's chill, but there were others where the golden glow of electric light spilled out onto the pavement and seemed to me to symbolise all the warmth, comfort and safety that a home is supposed to be about. Why would any woman jeopardise that? What twisted emotion could drive a mother to endanger her own children?

In my mind's eye I could see those children – barely more than toddlers – doing what their mummy asked them, waiting where she left them, trusting her to come back soon, just like she said. I flinched at the thought of the traffic thundering past them, at the dust and dirt thrown up at their level, smudging their faces and caking their hair. My arms ached to hold my own children tight. In doing what she had done Fatima had gone against the most primitive maternal instinct: to always, under any circumstances, protect your child.

To be honest, when I first finished that report, as I stacked the pages neatly on my desk, I couldn't see what there was to talk about. My first instinct was to ring the solicitors and say, 'Don't let her near those children. She's a mad woman. Any other woman would make a better mother.' But as my road home wound out of Derby and on to the village where I live my view softened a little. Fatima wasn't mad – at least, no one seemed to think so. Her story about Jamilah was disproved by CCTV footage taken in the refuge at the time of the blaze. Also, two bus drivers on the number eleven route remembered her. 'She definitely had two kiddies with her, she was holding their hands,' said the one who watched her alight at a stop near the A road. 'No, she was alone, I'd swear to that,' said the one who picked her up again twenty minutes later. Fatima had been proved to be a liar, but being a liar doesn't make you insane. And there was nothing in the report to suggest that, in the past, she had been anything other than a loving, conscientious mother.

I parked outside my house, which backs onto fields, miles from the Asian area of Derby where I'd spent so many, many years feeling I was watched and judged. Moving here was the best thing I ever did, but I still find it hard to believe that – all on my own – I bought this house and made it a home for my family. Maria, now in her second term at secondary school, shouted hello from the living room where she was watching television with her younger brother, Joshua. 'I've finished all my homework, Mum, and Lisa's home. She picked us up and now she's in the kitchen.' I could smell something delicious and I smiled to myself. From the time Lisa was tiny I always wanted her to go to university and when she decided to read law I was just so proud. I'd always sworn I wouldn't be the typical Asian mother, grooming my daughters in domestic skills to make them more marriageable, but at that moment – tired and hungry – I was really pleased that Lisa had chosen to learn how to cook.

5

'Jasvinder?' The voice on my mobile phone was barely more than a whisper. 'Jasvinder? Is that you?'

It was a Saturday and I was in the park with Maria and Joshua. They were on their bikes and they pedalled on as I stopped to try and make out what this anonymous voice was saying. 'Are you able to speak up a little?' I asked, raising my own voice against the noise from the kids on the swings just beside me.

'I found your number in *Marie Claire* magazine. I—' The line suddenly went dead but then, just a couple of seconds later, she was back. 'Sorry, I had to ring off because I thought I heard my mum coming up the stairs; she might still come so I have to be quick. I'm locked in my house. I'm in Bournemouth. They want me to marry my cousin. I don't even know him, but they won't listen to me. I'm a prisoner; I've been locked in for two years. I've got to get out. I can't stand it any longer.' She stopped and gulped a breath. 'I need help.'

I was absolutely focused. I had no idea who I was talking to, but as soon as she said she was locked in I knew I had to help. An image of Heshu Yones's ravaged body flashed across my mind. This stranger sounded frantic; if she was at the mercy of her family, danger could be imminent. I spoke quickly: 'Are you ever left alone? Do you think you could get out? If you can, there are all sorts of people who can help you.'

My mind was racing, running through refuges that might have a space for her. I stood stock still, scared the line might start breaking up if I kept moving but at the same time aware that, ahead of me, Maria and Joshua were still pedalling on. I was willing them to stop and when Maria looked back over her shoulder, checking I was still in sight, I gave a wave signalling that I wanted her and Joshua to turn back.

'I don't know.' The girl's voice was quiet but urgent; she sounded educated, almost posh. 'There are padlocks on all the doors and my stepdad's even gone and put barbed wire round the garden wall. I don't know how I could get out. And if I did, where would I go?'

I wanted time to think but I knew that wasn't possible. In my experience, when a girl has made up her mind to run she usually finds a way to do it. I couldn't procrastinate. This young woman was hundreds of miles away but she was desperate and I had to reassure her. 'There is help for you,' I said. 'There are safe houses, refuges, people to support you. I would support you. Believe me, you will be okay.'

'But how . . . Wait, that's Mum. She's coming. I have to go.' Her phone went dead.

For a few moments I stood there, hoping she'd ring back, that it had been another false alarm, but she didn't. My pulse slowed but I felt anxious and fretful and I couldn't put her from my mind. As best I could, I got on with my morning.

I was cooking when my mobile rang again. At first I couldn't make out anything except the jagged sound of panting but as I turned down the radio I could hear a steady beat beneath the breathing: the rhythmic drumming of feet. And then that voice again, well-spoken even *in extremis*: 'It's me, Kiren. I've – done it – Jasvinder – I've – run away – I'm – out.'

'Kiren? The girl from Bournemouth? You're out. I didn't expect . . . How did you manage it?'

'Keys – my stepdad's pocket – parents in town. Please – for fuck's sake – tell – me what –should I – do.'

'Where are you?'

'Alleyway – hang on. I'm – going to – stop.' For a full minute the line was filled with laboured breathing. 'That's better. Got my breath. I thought my fucking heart was going to burst. I didn't dare stop until I'd got past all the neighbours. I don't think anybody knows me here.'

'Kiren . . . That is what you said your name was?' I had the phone clamped beneath my ear as I washed my hands. 'Kiren, you have to call the police. Dial 999—.'

'No, no way. I don't want the police involved. I haven't done anything wrong.'

'That's the point, Kiren. You haven't done anything wrong and the police should protect you. Trust me, dial 999.'

Next time she rang – not more than an hour later – she was almost hysterical. 'They want to take me home. They won't fucking believe me about the marriage. They don't believe me about my stepdad beating me. They keep saying that it's just a family tiff and lots of young girls have them and the best fucking thing is to go home and sort it out. I can't do that!' Her voice cracked and I heard her gulping in air, struggling to regain control.

'Don't let them take me home, Jasvinder. You said they'd help me. My stepdad will kill me if he sees me, I know he will. He said if I tried to run away he'd kill me and dump my body somewhere no one would ever find it. They won't fucking believe me. You've got to help me, Jasvinder. Please.'

'All right. Okay. Try to keep calm.' I took a deep breath myself. 'Right: I know what to do. I'm going to ring a friend of mine. He's a Metropolitan police officer. He's in London. I'm going to ring him now and see if he can help. Stay where you are. Don't let them take you home. Do you want me to speak to someone there? No? Okay. Just hold on.'

I rang Brent Hyatt and he answered. How many police officers do you know who would pick up their phone on a Saturday afternoon while they were off duty? As quickly as I could I outlined the situation and asked if he could help. Without a second's pause he said he would.

Kiren owes a lot to Brent and she would be the first to admit it. Thanks to him an incident room was set up and a proper statement taken. Then, when that was done, he insisted an officer drive Kiren up to London, to Victoria station, where he said he would take charge of her. He said he'd find her somewhere to sleep for that night and then, between us, he and I would sort out something more permanent. That evening he booked her into a small hotel, an inexpensive travellers' place but it was clean and – most important – it was safe. He saw her checked in and then he went off and bought her a few essentials: toothpaste, toiletries, a chicken kebab. I can just imagine him whisking round some store: toothbrush, face cream, anti-perspirant. He's a practical man is Brent.

I can imagine her too at that moment. Sitting alone in an unfamiliar room, trying not to breathe too deeply in case she inhaled the cold, faintly sickly smell of strangers. She'd have been straining her ears to catch the sounds – a door slamming perhaps, a snatch of conversation drifting down the passage – small bits of proof that she was not alone in the silence that surrounded her. I bet she put the TV on. I would have done. Anything to create an illusion of company in the terrifyingly lonely world she'd just created for herself.

The next morning Brent took her to the bus station, gave her £60 to tide her over and put her on a coach to Wolverhampton where I had found her a refuge place. He stayed to wave her off and then, as soon as she was out of sight, he rang me.

'It was awful Jas,' he said. 'She didn't say a word and she was pale as a ghost. When she'd found her seat on the bus, she sat there with her forehead pressed against the glass just staring into space with tears pouring down her cheeks. I felt like I was sending her to the end of the earth on her own. She's going to need a lot of support.'

It was ten days after that I first met her. I arranged to meet her at the bus station in Wolverhampton. It was a stormy day with a heavy, lowering sky. People on the street had their heads down and their shoulders hunched as if the clouds were pressing down on them. I remember looking up the street and finding myself staring at a very tall, slim woman who was tottering along the kerb towards me. I have to say tottering, there's no other word for it. I kept expecting her to lose her balance and fall right off her boots, which were baby pink PVC with the highest heels you've ever seen.

I caught her eye and she smiled and then she waved at me.

My first thought was, 'No. There is no way that can be

Kiren.' Only a couple of days before Kiren had rung up and asked me how to buy jeans. 'What sort of shop?' 'What size?' 'What style?' Two weeks ago she'd never even worn a pair of jeans, she certainly wouldn't be into freaky footwear.

'Jasvinder?'

'Yes.' Now she was close up I could see that the make-up she was wearing was about an inch thick.

'I thought it must be you.' She leant up against the lamp-post. 'Sorry I'm late. Nobody told me what hard work it is walking in high heels. Fuck me it's difficult. But I love it. I've never worn a pair of boots before because I've never been allowed.'

We went to the nearest coffee shop – it was hardly fifty yards away but even for that short distance she was wobbling and grabbing at my arm. We were laughing so much by the time we sat down it felt like we had known each other for years. But when the waitress had taken our order – two coffees, two teacakes – Kiren suddenly turned serious.

'I'm really grateful to you, Jas,' she said. 'I wouldn't have got through the last few days without you. It's been such a relief to have someone to ring.'

'How is it in the refuge?' I asked her.

'It's okay. It's not an Asian refuge, is that why you chose it? I'm glad, I didn't want to go to an Asian place. The ladies there are lovely, they've looked after me and I've made quite a few friends. I even cooked some of them Asian food – like they were my own family.' Her voice was deliberately bright but her eyes told a different story. She looked tired and scared.

'What's your own family like?' I knew practically nothing about her background. Since she ran from her parents' house, all our conversations had been about the practicalities of getting her set up in a new life. Now the details of what she'd fled from came spilling out.

'There's my older brother, he's at Birmingham University; I've got a little sister and then there's my mum and my stepdad. My real dad died of cancer when I was about six and my stepdad turned up soon after. He came over from Pakistan to marry my mum and now he lives on my dad's money. He's never done more than cleaning jobs himself. I just came home from school one day and he was there, upstairs. I was like, "What are you doing here?"'

Things went wrong from the start. The first time he told her to do something Kiren – who was grieving for her dad and confused by the presence of this stranger who had walked into her home and, worse still, into her mum's bed – refused. 'Why should I? You can't make me. You're not my dad,' she said. So he hit her. And once he had proved that might is right he carried on. First there were Asian clothes to wear; if not at school then as soon as she came home. Then trips to the mosque started. Soon Kiren's mum was wearing a hijab. 'He was always telling us we had to be like this or that. I went to a Christian school – there were only about three Asians there – but he'd say, "don't listen to your teachers; they don't understand us, we Muslim people are different." But I didn't want to be different like that. I didn't want to be one of those Asian women who just sit at home and cook and clean.'

I couldn't imagine Kiren as one of those women. Sitting opposite her in the café that morning – in her ridiculous boots and her jeans, with her long black hair streaming down her back and too much make-up on her beautiful pale skin – I found it hard to believe she was even Asian. 'My family's from Afghanistan. They live in the northern province of Pakistan.

We speak the same language as the Taliban – not that that's something to be proud of,' she said.

It was her stepdad who arranged her marriage, to one of her first cousins. Kiren had grown up assuming that one day – far in the future – the subject of her marriage would come up. But she didn't expect it to happen when she was fifteen, and why would she? She was one of three Asians in a school full of white girls, all of them just starting to giggle and flirt and fancy boys. As far as her friends and classmates were concerned, marriage was a lifetime away. So when Kiren's mum woke her up one Saturday morning and told her she was going to get engaged Kiren said flatly, 'I don't want to.'

She might as well have saved her breath. Her mum wasn't interested in discussing it; she had Kiren out of bed, into her best gold sari and downstairs just as the house was filling up with relatives. 'It was exciting in a way, with all the family there and lots of people bringing gifts and all the tables covered with Asian dishes.' Kiren dropped her eyes as she said this, as if embarrassed by this small connivance in her fate. But the excitement faded when it came to the exchange of rings. Face to face with a boy she'd never met before ('the person was eighteen,' she said, as if trying to detach herself from him as far as possible by her choice of words) she felt awkward and embarrassed. 'I watched the video of it later and I look really upset. By that stage I was wondering, "what the hell is going on here?"'

Of course once the deal was done Kiren's life at home became that much harder. She felt she was walking on eggshells. Her stepfather was determined to domesticate her so, while all her school friends went home to do their coursework or watch television or text each other, Kiren had to do all the housework and then cook the family's evening meal. If she refused he would beat her and then lock her in her room. Once he punched her so hard that she couldn't open her mouth properly for two weeks.

'There was no point telling my mum, she was just as bad in a way. She always had a violent temper. When me and my brother were little she used to take our clothes off and whip us with her belt, not for anything bad, just for little things like having fun or messing about. I think she was taking her anger out on us. It sounds really weird saying it, but we lived in a reality where having parents who hit us was the norm.'

Being good Asian children they never hit back, not even on the day that her mum hurled herself at Kiren with such force that they both landed on the floor and Kiren found herself struggling to breathe as she tried to prise her mum's furious fingers off her throat. 'She tried to strangle me a few times before that, I learnt to wear a scarf to cover up the marks.' Kiren shrugged as if to brush away the hideous image of her mum – the person she believed she should love, respect and honour – forsaking all tenderness and dignity and lunging at her like a mad woman.

Under such circumstances, it's not surprising that Kiren ran away.

'It was a spur of the moment thing really. I had this one Asian friend and she and I had sometimes talked about running away but we never made a plan or anything. One day we were in the playground and I was feeling really pissed off with my stepdad and I just said, "I'm not having this anymore, let's go today." At first my friend didn't want to but then she said she would. I don't think I'd have done it on my own. I was really scared the police would stop us, I think she was too, we were in our uniforms you see. We didn't have anything else and then

– you won't believe this Jas – it started snowing. I thought I was going to freeze to death, my feet were blocks of ice.'

When they arrived in London and paid up-front to spend one night in a hotel – 'I didn't know such places existed, Jas. It was dingy and the furniture had cigarette burns and it stank' – they had to face the fact that the money they had left would just about buy them a couple of packets of crisps. 'But I thought we'd be all right because you see I've got this uncle and only a few weeks before he rung me and said he'd got a flat in London and I was welcome to go there any time if I needed somewhere to stay.'

What foresight her parents must have had. Imagine their pleasure when their troublesome daughter walked right into their trap. When Kiren rang her uncle he was warm and welcoming: of course they could come and stay he said, why, he'd even pick them up. He took Kiren and her friend back to his flat, sat them down – and then fetched Kiren's parents. 'Honestly, Jas. I thought I was going to faint.'

And well she might have done. 'We went home and it was bad, I was really frightened and scared. The first thing was, Mum held a knife to my throat and she was like, "I'll cut your tongue off." Then I went upstairs and they followed me and my stepdad was beating me up and my mum was shouting at me, she said, "If you don't listen to us and do what we say, your stepdad is going to rape you."'

When Kiren said this I felt my stomach shrivel with disgust and horror and it must have shown on my face, because she answered my unspoken question. 'Yes, it's true. It must be two years now but the words go round and round in my head. I still find it hard to believe my own mother said that but she did. And believe me, she'd have stood there and watched him do it. As it was she let him fling me into the bath before they went downstairs and left me.'

That was the end of what little freedom Kiren had known. She was escorted to and from school by her stepfather, who started insisting that she wear a hijab. After school, once she had completed her own chores and the cleaning jobs she was expected to help her parents with, she was confined to her room. She wasn't allowed out, friends weren't allowed in. She used to sit there and listen as her parents and her little sister talked, ate, watched television – carried on their normal humdrum lives as if they didn't have a care in the world, let alone a prisoner in an upstairs bedroom.

'I tried to get out, Jas. After a few weeks of thinking about it I decided if I could get to the doctor he might help. I dreamt up some excuse for going, backache or something. Mum insisted on coming with me – I was prepared for that, I knew she would, so I didn't make a fuss or anything. But when my name got called and we went into the room, before she could even sit down I said, "Actually Mum, I'd like to see the doctor by myself."

'Can you imagine how scary it was for me saying that, Jas?' Kiren leant right across the table as she said this, her eyes wide, her hair falling forward like a curtain. 'I knew Mum would beat the hell out of me later on, but I also knew that if I said it in front of the doctor she couldn't argue, she'd have to leave the room.'

I could imagine that, and I could also imagine the tangle of fear and frustration Kiren must have felt when the doctor – a white, middle-aged man – said, 'That's a very serious allegation. Are you sure you're not exaggerating? I see no sign that your parents are beating you. Where are your bruises?' 'As if they would have let me out of the house on a day I had visible bruises,' said Kiren with contempt.

Heaving the sort of sigh that left her in no doubt as to what he thought about timewasters, the doctor agreed to alert the social workers who would shortly pay a visit. 'I thought they would come and see me at school but they didn't, they went to my house *while* I was at school and what did they see? A nice house and my mum all smiling and full of lies and that was that. They never came back. But when I got home I got the beating of my life.'

Once Kiren had finished her GCSEs, her stepdad called a halt to her education: 'Why would you need A levels? All a wife needs to know is how to cook and clean.' Her world shrank to her bedroom where she passed the time sewing and daydreaming about a world in which she had a good job, her own home, a lovely man in her life. Sometimes, lured by the apple-pie perfect American families she saw on television, she dreamt of being adopted. And for the last year she was incarcerated, she kept the copy of *Marie Claire* which had my number in it under her bed. 'When I felt down I used to get it out and read your article; it gave me hope.'

'Can I get you anything else?' said the waitress pointedly as she reached between us, with hardly an 'excuse me', to take our empty cups. I checked my watch. It was 5 p.m. and time I headed back.

'Tell me Kiren, when you made your statement to the police did you tell them everything, like you've just told me?'

'Yes, I did it when I first left home, before I went to London.'

'And are you going to prosecute your parents?' I tried to sound neutral, to keep any note of hope out of my voice, but the truth is that I really wanted her to say yes. When the House of Commons voted not to make forced marriage a criminal act what they did – and I'm not saying they realised this –was to confirm what most girls like Kiren think already: that their parents' actions are quite within their rights, that it is they – those who run away to escape forced marriage – who are the perpetrators not the victims of a crime.

Kiren chewed her lip and, pulling the ketchup bottle towards her, began picking at its label. She didn't meet my eye as she answered, 'Yes, I *think* I will.'

6

'Jasvinder? It's Heather. I need to talk to you about Fozia.'

I'd just dropped Joshua at school and was nosing my car back into the traffic. 'I'll call you when I get to Karma Nirvana. Give me about ten minutes.'

As I drove towards the office I was trying to remember when I last spoke to Fozia. Ten days ago, or was it more than that? Last month? She'd sounded quite cheerful anyway, but then that was Fozia. She must have rung me four or five times since we first met six months ago, but she never said much after we'd done 'Hello, how are you'. It was as if she just wanted reassurance that I was there if she needed me. And now it seemed she did. There was such urgency in Heather's voice that I didn't wait until I reached my desk; I rang as soon as I'd parked the car. 'What's happened?'

I should have expected it I suppose, if not from Fozia then from one of the other young Muslim girls we had on our radar at the time. It was coming up to Hajj, and many devout Muslim families travelling to Mecca to perform their devotions might think it convenient to give the trip an extra purpose. 'Fozia has seen plane tickets to Pakistan; she's seen her parents making preparations. She's worried that they're going to take her with them and force her to get married.'

In my mind I started whipping through the protocol of getting a minor removed from her home, but Heather had the edge on me. 'We've obviously got to act quickly but I think I've bought us a couple of days. I've written her parents a letter saying that it's exam time and any parent not ensuring that their child is in school is liable to be prosecuted. With luck, that will stop them taking her anywhere at least until the end of the week.'

'Right,' I said. 'I'll contact her social worker – you did say she has one, didn't you?'

'Yes, she first made contact when Fozia ran away.'

When I rang the number Heather gave me she said at once that she remembered Fozia and put me on hold while she went to get her file. As concisely as I could I gave her an update on the situation and once I had finished talking she said, 'Obviously I must see Fozia again and assess her case. Let me just look at my diary.' There was a pause, a rustling of paper. 'Yes, I should be able to do it early next week.'

'Next week!' I paused and took a deep breath; sounding shrill wasn't going to help. 'I don't think we can afford to wait until next week. The beginning of Hajj is six days away, Fozia has seen the plane tickets but her parents still haven't mentioned the trip to her. Hajj is such a big deal – I don't need to tell you that – you've got to admit that it's strange not to talk about it. It's one of the reasons Fozia is convinced that the real reason for the trip is to force her into marriage . . .'

'I don't agree, I know this family and I don't think they are capable of that sort of behaviour.'

'But you can't be sure. I really think this is an urgent child protection issue; I think we should listen to what Fozia herself says. Why would she invent these fears?'

It took me a good half hour to convince her but eventually she agreed to move on the case immediately. She put in a call to the local police, asking that Fozia be collected from school and given safe escort to collect her possessions from her parents' home.

'And where will you send her?' I asked when rang the Social Worker to confirm this was happening. 'You know she is very keen to stay in Derby, she has always said. . .'

'I'm afraid that's out of the question for safety reasons; Fozia's safety has to be our first concern.'

I could see her point of view, I felt the same initially. When I ran, I ran as far away from my home town as possible and most of the runaways I've met since have done the same, but Fozia was adamant: it was her family she wanted to leave, not her home town. When I saw how unshakeable she was in this, I had to support her. I know from experience that if the girls aren't happy where they go, the pressure for them to return home is that much harder to resist. And I also felt that she was very young to be so isolated; if we kept her here in Derby she would only be a bus ride from familiar faces, if she was sent further afield I was afraid she might be overwhelmed by loneliness.

'I think in this instance between us we can manage her safety. I think we should respect her wishes and I'd like to be able to keep an eye on her,' I said. 'If we uproot her from her physical as well as her emotional landscape I don't know that she'll cope. I know I couldn't have done when I was her age, could you?'

But what I said made no difference. By the end of that day Fozia was on a train on her way to a refuge in Chesterfield – and this is what shocked me – she was all alone. The two white police officers who escorted her home to pick up her belongings should have stayed with her until she reached the refuge but they didn't; they took her to Derby station and left her there. Perhaps they didn't realise how young she is: she does look older than her years.

It seemed so wrong to me that fifteen-year-old Fozia, who had woken up that morning cocooned by the sounds and smells of the house she had lived in all her life, should find herself that evening making her way, without company or comfort, to a city she had barely heard of and would certainly not have been able to locate on a map. To my mind that's when she started going downhill.

She told me what had happened when she rang the next day, and her voice was still thick with tears. 'It's not like me to cry, Jas. I'm not a crying person but I can't seem to stop, I was crying all night. When I went home to get my stuff my mum was there and she was shouting things like: "You'll never be happy" and "You'll never be successful," and my sister was there too and she was shouting, "Do you hear what she is saying, are you listening?" That's when the fact of leaving them really hit me hard.'

Her account of her journey up to Chesterfield tore at my heartstrings. Dumped at the station with her ticket, she waited until she was on the train before plucking up the courage to ask the man in the seat next to her if she could borrow his mobile.

'There were people I really wanted to say goodbye to, people who are important to me, Jas and I didn't want them left wondering what had happened to me.'

She needn't have worried about that: the news of her departure was travelling like wildfire.

'First I rang my best friend. I wanted to tell her how much I was going to miss her, but she wouldn't talk to me; as soon as she heard my voice she cut me off. I rang again thinking I'd just lost the signal but the phone rang and rang and she didn't pick up. I've known her since primary school: how could she do that?'

The reaction she got from her sister Raveeda upset her even more. Raveeda's son Daniyal is the apple of Fozia's eye, she's forever talking about him and she's got this dog-eared picture that she always carries. 'I rang Raveeda to say "tell him goodbye from me," "tell him I'll come and see him when I'm settled." He's only a baby, he only started walking last week, so I know he wouldn't understand the words, but Raveeda knows how much he means to me. I was hoping she'd talk to him about me, maybe show him photos, you know. . .' There was a pause, an audible sob. 'I hoped she'd keep me alive in his mind. But she's not going to do that Jas, do you know what she said to me? She said, "Don't bother visiting. Daniyal won't want to see you. I'm going to make sure that he grows up to hate you."

'She's going to make him hate me, Jas and he won't know different. All last night, I kept hearing her saying it, over and over, it was like a tape recorder had got jammed inside my mind.'

The line went very quiet for a while after she said that. All I could hear was Fozia swallowing her tears and I sat there, clutching the receiver, wishing I was close enough to hold her.

Eventually I said, 'Is there anybody there at the refuge you can talk to?'

'Well, they're all much older than me; I'd say they are in their forties and fifties. And I'm the only Asian.'

Out of the corner of my eye I could see Anna, one of Karma Nirvana's volunteers, mouthing at me, 'Detective Sergeant O'Leary is here to see you.'

I knew I had to wrap up the conversation quickly. O'Leary had travelled a long way to see me and I had promised him a clear hour of my time before I had to leave the office at midday. 'Okay, Fozia,' I said, trying not to sound hurried. 'I have to go now, but I want you to remember something. We're all here: me, Anna, Shazia. Ring whenever you need to, there will always be someone free to talk to you.'

Detective Sergeant Stephen O'Leary was from the British Transport Police. He was working on the investigation into the death of Navjeet Sidhu, an Asian woman who earlier in the year had flung herself under the Heathrow Express at Southall. She had her kids with her, a little boy of not quite two who she was carrying in her arms and a five-year-old daughter who, the CCTV cameras show, she was holding by the hand. She and the girl died instantly but the little boy – he was called Aman Raj – survived for about two hours.

I remembered the case well. It was all over the papers at the time and as I read the reports my heart went out to Navjeet, a stranger whose story reminded me of so many of the women who contact Karma Nirvana, women whose parents bring them up in the West and, as they reach adulthood, insist that they conform to the cultural values of the East.

The facts of Navjeet's case seemed clear. She was born and

brought up in Southall and then, at the age of twenty, taken to India where she underwent an arranged marriage. She had spent six years working as a receptionist at Sunrise Radio, but in 2004 she gave it up in order to care for her children; thereafter the family survived (one paper said struggled to survive) on her husband's postal worker's salary. The couple had undergone a brief separation during which time Navjeet went to America but on her return they decided to give their marriage a second go. On the day of her death, she hung around on the station platform for two hours before she made her fatal jump, telling a station worker who questioned her that she had brought her children to see the fast trains. Some reports claimed that hours before she jumped she had phoned her husband to say, 'I'm going far, far away and I'm taking the children with me.'

Inevitably friends leapt in to offer their views: one reportedly said that Navjeet had the perfect mix of British and Asian values and was 'so happy go-lucky' that she would never have contemplated suicide; another claimed to have heard her say recently that she was desperately unhappy and needed help. There was speculation that she was ground down by the traditional Sikh values of her Indian-born husband and his family and that they bullied her because her mother was divorced. Some reports said that she was taking medication for a depression that started when her first born child was a girl.

O'Leary's report was so confidential that he refused to trust it to the post; in fact he wouldn't let it out of his sight, I had to read it through while he sat opposite me, resting his coffee cup on my desk. Much of what it said had already been in the newspapers but there were certain insights about her home life which made me realise how unhappy she must have been. When her husband went back to the Punjab, Navjeet, left in England, was isolated and lonely, battling to bring up their two children all alone. Eventually her mother-in-law persuaded her to go to India and apologise to her husband. This she did: on her knees and in front of his whole village she begged for his forgiveness. Still, he refused to return until Navjeet had promised he would not have to help with any of the household chores. That came out at the inquest and so did the fact that when Manjit arrived at Southall station, just minutes after Navjeet had jumped, he walked straight past the bodies of his wife and daughter and went to his son.

I found it hard to read that report. Try as I might I couldn't stop my mind flicking back to Robina, my precious sister who, like Navjeet, found herself trapped in a tormented marriage and chose as an escape route a horrible death. Robina set fire to herself and died of burns to ninety-five per cent of her body. She was even younger than Navjeet when she did it, only twenty-four. I've always said that in Asian families suicide can be a cleaner form of murder and when I think about Robina's agonising end – which was watched by her husband, he was there when she lit the match – the only comfort I can draw is that her death certificate doesn't say she killed herself. It says that the cause of death was 'severe burns caused when she poured paraffin over herself and set light to herself in the bathroom of her home . . .' And then it says 'there being insufficient evidence to show why she did: open verdict.'

Navjeet didn't have that to dignify her death. The verdict for her was suicide and unlawful killing of her two children. In the eyes of the world they were the real tragedy of this case. It was them that O'Leary wanted to talk to me about, he wanted to know why I thought she had taken them with her, what was in her mind. The answer seemed clear to me: she didn't want them to be brought up in the life that she had found so suffocating, she saw killing them as preferable to passing on a legacy of misery. I told him that, and also that in my opinion Navjeet's arranged marriage had involved an element of force.

The misery didn't end with the death of Navjeet and her children. Six months later Navjeet's mother, Satwant Kaur Sodhi – who had been 'inconsolable' since her daughter and grandchildren died – went, as she often did, to Southall station to stand where her daughter last stood. It was from there that she too hurled herself into the path of a high speed train. Neighbours said that in recent months Satwant had often talked about how lonely she was; one anonymous friend alleged that she had been plagued with remorse over having arranged Navjeet's marriage. A suicide note written in Punjabi seemed to confirm her sense of guilt and loss.

Even then it didn't end. Her suffering and Navjeet's seem to draw other similarly unhappy women to the area. I recently read a report put out by the route manager of a national rail company which claimed that one third of rail suicides in the previous twelve months had occurred on track going into London Paddington, track that went through predominantly Asian areas like Slough and Southall. In one week there were four suspected suicides in four days on the line between Slough and Paddington. The manager said that a 'disproportionately high number' of the total fatalities in the area were women of Asian origin. That didn't surprise me: it's been on record for some time that the suicide rate among young Asian women is three times the average for women of other ethnicities. It seems to me sad that it's not until the suicides impact on a national railway company that this is news.

7

One cold, grey morning about a fortnight after Fozia had gone to Chesterfield I walked round the back of the car to open the boot while Maria and Joshua were scrambling to get ready for school. I was carrying a big saucepan that I was going to lend to Shazia, who was coming with me in the car to Liverpool that day to interview Fatima and her husband Rafiq. I thought she could take it when I dropped her home afterwards.

I was calling to Joshua to make sure he had shut the front door properly as I pulled the boot open and it wasn't until I slammed it shut again that I saw the words scrawled in the dust: large, shaky capitals spidering across the back window:

NO SHAME

My heart skipped a beat. My first instinct was to look around me and my head flicked quickly left–right–left. Was there anybody there? Anyone I didn't know? Anyone watching me? But there was nobody to be seen outside our little row of houses;

no parked cars that I didn't recognise, no one on the other side of the road, nothing at all out of the ordinary. Except those words, screaming off the back of my car.

NO SHAME

Who wrote them? That was the question burning my brain as – without even thinking about it – I pulled the sleeve of my suit jacket taut and scrubbed my forearm across those two angry, accusing words. I couldn't stand looking at them. I wanted them gone. It was as if in some unformed, primitive part of my brain I believed that by rubbing them out I could rub out the threat they represented.

Suddenly my legs felt weak and insubstantial, as if they had been drained of muscle, flesh and blood. 'Evidence. You've just destroyed it.' The thought skittered through my mind as I turned to lean – almost to hold myself up – against the back of the car. But it was blown aside immediately by more pressing concerns. When was it done? When were those words written? Was it done right here, last night, while we were sleeping? Does this person know where I live? Please, not that, please. Let it have been done somewhere public and impersonal, not right outside my house, not here.

I mentally rewound the previous forty-eight hours of my life, playing back my memories with a manic jerkiness. Yesterday: come back by train from London, collect car from the station car park: STOP. No, it was too dark to see and besides I approached the car from the front. The day before: leave the office through the back door, into the car park: STOP. No, it was nearly half past five and the bulb in the car park's lamppost has been out for weeks. I buried my face in my hands, trying to remember. Oh God, when did I last notice the back of the car?

'Mum. Mu-um! What are you doing? We're going to be late.'

It was Maria, calling from the front of the car.

'Coming.' I inhaled deeply twice, trying to still my heart, calm my breathing. The kids mustn't see me scared. I climbed into the driving seat and as I steered onto the road and headed for Derby I tried to force myself to concentrate on what Joshua was saying about football practice that afternoon, but it was so hard. My mind was flicking through my case load: I had found refuge spaces for two girls on Wednesday, but neither of them was from anywhere near Derby, not that that matters when you've got the Asian network, but still it seems unlikely their families could have found me so fast. At the beginning of the week I had advised that pregnant teenager about mother and baby hostels, would her father be the type? I'd spoken to Fozia who knows how many times since she left home, could it be her family?

As if on auto-pilot, I pulled into the kerb outside Joshua's school and sat there as the children gathered their things. 'Mum,' Joshua sounded aggrieved. 'You haven't answered me. Who's picking me up today? I've asked you twice already, are you okay?'

'Of course I am. Sorry, I was thinking about something else.' I turned to face him, hoping that I looked and sounded calm. 'Lisa's picking you up today, but I'll see you at home later. Maria, are you okay to walk the rest from here? Bye then.' I waved, forced a smile.

The drive across Derby to pick up Shazia seemed to take an eternity and without the kids there to be brave for I found it hard to keep control. I could bite hard on my lips to keep myself from howling out loud but I couldn't stop the tears that were pouring down my cheeks.

'Do you think I'm over-reacting Shazia?' I said as soon as I'd told her. 'Tell me that I'm being silly, that it's just some kids . . . a prank.'

Her soft face creased with concern and she was twisting her hands in distress as she said, 'I'd love to say that Jas, but I can't. It's not what I think. I think you should call the police. Just hear what they have to say. Go on. Maybe they can reassure you.'

They did their best. I drove to the station and gave my statement, but even before I'd finished giving all the details I knew what they were going to say, 'I'm sorry Jasvinder. You were absolutely right to come and tell us, but there's not much we can do. We've got it all noted down. We'll keep in touch and you must be extra vigilant. Remember all those things we told you, about varying your route and where you park your car? Be sure to do them, don't forget or get careless.'

I couldn't stop thinking about it, all the way to Liverpool. Shazia was very supportive; she listened, she did her best to reassure me. 'You don't know it was done outside your house, Jas. Think about it, it's much more likely to have been someone in town.' With endless patience she tamped down each new anxiety. 'No, I don't think you were irresponsible to let Maria walk to school: she's fine. If there was any problem you would have heard by now.' By the time we reached the office of the Children and Family Court Advisory Support Service (CAFCASS) where I was due to see Fatima I felt almost calm.

Gillian Symons, Fatima's social worker, was tall and brisk; the hand she thrust out for me to shake was cold as stone. I introduced Shazia as my note-taker and explained that, unlike me, she speaks fluent Urdu. I didn't share the fact that I was keenly aware that what I said about Fatima and Rafiq could affect their family for years to come and I thought it would be useful to have another perspective on their problems.

The room CAFCASS had provided for us was an enormous, anonymous space in which right away I didn't feel comfortable. There was a partition concertinaed against the wall so I pulled that across, blocking out the corner of the room that was cluttered with a well-worn selection of toys, and the space we were left in immediately felt cosier. I had expected the usual hard-backed plastic seating but instead there were a few armchairs, large and comfortable. Shazia and I manhandled them into a circle.

'Is there anything else I can get you?' Gillian Symons was already half-turned, on her way out of the room to get Fatima when I saw a flip-chart pushed back against the wall. The top sheet of paper suggested that the last person to use it had been giving some sort of talk on motivation. Words like ACTION, ATTAINMENT and PROGRESS were scrawled in bright green capital letters and linked by a complex system of arrows.

'Yes,' I said, picking up the chart and bringing it over to stand beside our trio of chairs. 'Could I have some clean paper?'

'What are you going to do with that?' asked the CAFCASS rep, curious.

'I don't know,' I said and at that point I didn't. 'I just have a feeling that it might come in useful.'

I'm not sure what I had expected Fatima to look like, but her appearance surprised me. Perhaps she had dressed to impress in her shimmering Asian suit, which was a deep blue laced with gold. On her right wrist she had a jangle of bracelets and she was wearing an unusual pair of high-heeled flip-flops. Her plain black headscarf framed her face which was pale and pinched and almost childlike – without any make-up on she barely looked nineteen, although she must have been older. She was very nervous. She sat perched on the edge of her chair with her shoulders hunched up near her ears and her hands forever fiddling, twiddling the corners of her scarf. As her bangles slipped back down her arm I noticed how thin her wrists were; her knees and ankles, pressed together, were bony and prominent beneath her Asian suit.

I introduced myself and gave her a few quick details about Karma Nirvana and how I had come to start it and then, when I saw she was really listening, I said, 'I'm not a police officer, I'm not a social worker or a psychologist. I'm here to listen to your story and see if we can get another perspective on it. Do you understand that?'

'Yes,' she said. 'They told me you were the cultural expert.'

Then, when Shazia had introduced herself, I suggested we get started. I asked Fatima to tell me what had happened. She nodded and, without any pause for thought, began to talk. Right from the start she was emphatic about how much she and her husband loved their children, so much so in fact that soon I felt obliged to say, 'Hang on a minute. I'm a mother; can you explain to me – as a mother – how you could abandon your two small children on a busy road where they could have been killed or abducted and, not only that, you set your house – their home – on fire. Imagine some other woman did that – not you – and you got to hear about it. What would you think about that woman? Would you think she was a suitable person to look after her children?' I spoke as gently as I could but I wanted to surprise her, to jolt her into seeing things from a viewpoint other than her own.

It worked. Her face crumpled and she began to cry loudly and without inhibition, letting the tears run down her cheeks and into her lap. 'I didn't want to hurt them, I love them,' she sobbed, but still she tried to justify her actions. 'I was at fault, yes. But I felt it was important to find Jamilah, I was worried for her baby. How could she cope with him all alone, without the support and guidance of her husband?'

She was working herself up, and I could see this wasn't going to get us anywhere. I held up a hand as if to stop the flow of words. 'Wait. Let's forget about all that for a minute, Fatima. I'd like to know about you. Tell me a bit about your life. Let's start with your childhood.'

'My childhood?' She could not have sounded more surprised if I'd asked her to recite her shopping list. 'Why do you want to know about my childhood? No one has ever asked me about that before.'

'Well, I'm asking now. I'm interested.'

She looked at me pleadingly, willing to cooperate with my strange request but at a loss as to how to begin, so I prompted her, 'Tell me about your mum, what's she like?'

Fatima's eyes filled with tears again when I said that, but she held herself together and proceeded to tell me her story. It transpired that her mum had died when she was little, leaving her the only girl in an all-male household. She had missed her terribly – still did – but for the sake of her father whom she adored she did her best to fill the hole her mum had left in all their lives. From the age of about ten she rushed home from school each day to cook and clean and keep the house in order.

'And what about your brothers, did they look after you?' I asked her.

Her eyes widened and the way she stretched out her 'y-e-e-e-s' made me think she was wondering exactly how much information to trust me with. 'They always looked after me, they were always very protective, even when I was young—' Her voice petered out.

'Was that a good thing?' I asked, trying to keep my voice neutral.

'Mmm.' Fatima's head weaved from side to side as she debated what to tell me. Suddenly she gave a decisive little nod: she'd made her mind up. 'One day at school, when I was five or six years old, we had a sports day, just for the youngest children. The races were not serious, everything was done for fun. In one we jumped in sacks, in another we had to run holding eggs in spoons and we also did what the teacher called a three-legged race when we had to run in pairs with our legs tied together. We were allowed to choose our partners but I wasn't quick enough to make my choice. It was the teacher who put me with David, I didn't choose him. The teacher took us by the hands and said, "that leaves you two to go together." What could I do? I couldn't say I wouldn't do it.' Her voice became shrill as she sought to justify herself.

'But why shouldn't you have run with David? Why did it matter?' I asked, genuinely baffled.

She looked surprised, as though the answer was obvious and I was being obtuse. 'My brothers didn't like it. I don't know how they knew, but someone must have told them and when I got home they hit and slapped me. They said I was shameful to allow my leg to be tied to a white boy's, they said I should not have held his hand. They said I had disgraced the family.'

'So, that's when it started,' I said, addressing the remark softly to Shazia, but Fatima picked up on it, seemed to take encouragement. 'As I grew a little older I realised that there were all sorts of things my brothers did not want me to do. Not only was I not allowed to touch boys, I couldn't talk to them. I couldn't wear certain clothes, any western clothes really. I couldn't go to the shop by myself. I couldn't choose the man who I would marry. And all this was due to honour – *izzat*. *Izzat* was the most important thing in our house.'

Perhaps it was the word 'important' that sparked the memory, I don't know, but suddenly I had a flashback to an exercise we did on the first counselling course that I attended. I stood up and moved the flip-chart so that it was facing Fatima. Then I drew three circles on it, each one inside the other, and in the centre one I wrote in big letters: ME.

'That means you. We're going to try to find out a bit about how you see yourself,' I said to Fatima. 'Now, I want you to list the things in life that are most important to you and I'm going to write them in that centre circle. I should think most of them will be people.'

She thought for several moments before saying, 'The children, my family, my husband . . . and *izzat, izzat* should really be there because that's very important to me too.'

'Is that it?'

She nodded.

'Now, in this next circle I am going to put the things in life that you enjoy doing, things that are just for you.'

This time there was a very long pause. She sounded uncertain when at last she ventured, 'Being part of the community?' And then, more confidently, 'Cooking, looking after the children.'

I wrote those down, then said, 'But those are the things you have to do. I meant things that you like to do, going for a walk maybe, or watching television.'

She opened her mouth as if to say something, but then she just shook her head.

'What about shopping. For instance, did you enjoy shopping for your pretty suit?'

'I'm not allowed to go shopping without my husband. I'm not allowed to go anywhere without my husband except taking the children to school and back.'

The three of us sat in silence for a couple of minutes, all staring at the flip-chart, at the few words that summed up Fatima's life. I needed her to understand the implication behind those words and after a while she did.

Almost to herself she said, 'I lead my life for other people, that's it, isn't it. There is nothing there at all for me.' She began to cry again, not the noisy wailing of before, but a silent stream of tears down her cheeks. She cried for some time and then she said, 'I never realised that before. I never thought about it, but that is always how my life has been. These last months I have spent so much time talking, talking, answering the questions of policemen and of social workers but you are the first person who has had any interest in understanding me.'

Again we were quiet. I felt we might be on the edge of a breakthrough, but I was also aware that Fatima needed a bit of time to reflect. I wanted her to see herself – as I did – as a victim of the system that surrounded her every moment of every day. That fact didn't excuse her criminal actions, but it made them easier to understand.

'Jasvinder?' She moved forward in her chair, leaning closer towards me. 'There is something I want to tell you.'

Again we waited, and this time it felt like an age before

her words came out in a rush, dumped like a heavy burden she had been carrying and was longing to set down. 'I did what I did because my brothers told me to. I was scared to refuse them. They told me they would hurt me and take my children away if I did not obey them. They sat me down and gave me instructions: where to take the children, how to start the fire. You think I would dare to go on a bus by myself without permission? You think I was not scared for my children beside that road? You think I did not pray for their safety every minute they were out of my sight? Later my brothers were angry with me for dialling 999 too soon, but I was so scared.'

'You have several brothers, Fatima. Which one told you to act as you did?'

'I can't tell you that Jasvinder.'

'When you made your statement to the police, you did not implicate anyone in your family. You said you acted by yourself.'

'They would have killed me and my children if I had done anything else.'

'Are you willing to go back to the police now, to disclose this?'

Fatima's eyes widened in panic and she shook her head vehemently. 'No, no. I could not do that. Please, don't try to make me. Believe me, things will go very badly for me if you do.'

'But it might mean that you or your husband could have your children back?'

Her head went on shaking, a sad little metronome, and I felt myself torn between frustration and pity. Fatima clearly loved her children, there was no doubt in my mind about that but she was too frightened of her family to protect them. She had proved that when she followed her brothers' criminal instructions, she was proving it now she refused to use the truth to defend herself. How could I honestly say she would act any differently in the future? Who could predict the risks to which she might expose herself and her children? What other demands – in the name of honour – might her brothers make?

Fatima looked up at me, again she leant in close. It was as if she felt she had fulfilled her role in some unspoken bargain and she was now waiting for me to fulfil mine. 'Please help me get my kids back, Jasvinder. Please help me, I love them. They're my kids, they ought to be with me.'

'I know you love them, but I can't promise anything,' I said.

The CAFCASS officer came to escort Fatima from the room and then she came back with Rafiq. I was very curious about him because he had barely featured in anything I had read or heard about this case. Fatima scarcely mentioned him beyond insisting that he had nothing to do with her actions, or the planning of them. I had no idea what to expect.

He turned out to be a tall, thin man, correctly and soberly dressed in an Asian suit and skull cap. His manner was nervous, almost apologetic, and he kept ducking his head in a series of strange little bows. As far as possible he avoided all eye contact. Because the only language he speaks or fully understands is Pushto, CAFCASS had provided an interpreter for him. As they walked into the room together Shazia fetched another chair and we expanded our little circle to let them in.

Once he was sitting down I found him surprisingly forthcoming. He too was full of tears and lamentations and his distress seemed genuine. 'My children, my poor children, I must have them back. What has my wife done? I cannot believe she did this.'

'Were you not aware of her plans?' I asked and the interpreter relayed the question.

'No, I knew nothing. I went to work. My work is in the factory of one of Fatima's brothers. I went to work, I came back and there at my house are the police.'

'Did Fatima tell you what she has just told me, that in everything she did she was following instructions from her brothers? The fire, abandoning the children, the story that she told the police—'

He stopped his tearful sniffing and immediately sat up, ramrod straight.

'I knew it, I knew they had done it. Fatima would not do these terrible things herself.'

'Of course this throws a different light on Fatima's case, but Rafiq, there is a problem. Fatima is not willing to repeat this in court. She refuses to implicate her brothers for fear of what they might do in revenge.'

His face grew hard, determined. 'She must say it, for the sake of our children she must. I will make her and if she refuses I will divorce her.' His insistence blunted my sympathy. Before my eyes the bereft father became a bullying husband, another domineering male in Fatima's life.

'Do you not worry about reprisals from her brothers? Are you confident they would not hurt your children?'

Concern flashed across his face. His demeanour changed again and he was once more pleading. 'Please, please help me to get my children back. Can you not understand that my children are Muslims, they need to be with Muslims. Do you know the foster parents they are with are white people, white people have dirty ways, many white people smoke—'

The interpreter relayed all this in a deadpan tone, his face and voice expressionless, but Rafiq's emphasis was clear to me and Shazia even though we speak no Pushto. No foreign language could disguise the contempt with which Rafiq spat the word 'white'. He was into his stride now, berating the foster parents because they took his four-year-old daughter riding, muttering again about the tendency of white people to smoke.

'Please ask him to stop, this negative attitude isn't helping anyone,' I said to the interpreter, turning away from Rafiq to show my disapproval, lest the interpreter's monotone should leave him in doubt. 'Tell him that his children are being well looked after, that all reports show his children's foster carers are doing a good job.'

Rafiq pitched forward slightly in his seat; for a moment I expected him to argue with me, but then he slumped back. At that moment I felt exhausted by both Rafiq and Fatima. They were trapped, both of them, by the cruel and rigid thinking of the society they had grown up in, the only society they knew. They had colluded in the destruction Fatima's family had wrought and although I ached for the injustice of it I couldn't at that point see how I could help. I sighed heavily and turned back to Rafiq.

'How important is *izzat* to you?' I asked him.

'Not very, not at all. The welfare of my family is my main concern,' he said, so quickly that I was fairly sure he was saying what he thought I wanted to hear rather than what he genuinely felt.

'And if your children came back to you, how would you protect them from the influence of your wife's family which, in the past, has not been good?'

'Not good, no.' He agreed, again I thought too rapidly. 'I would move away from Liverpool, I would not see them.'

'But how would you manage? Do you know anyone else in England you could turn to? It is very hard to manage without any sort of family and besides, don't they employ you?'

No matter how hard Rafiq tried to persuade me that he could survive without his in-laws, I remained unconvinced. It didn't sit with me that a man who, in the past, had had so little influence on his own life could suddenly take charge. I felt the weight of my responsibility to his children very keenly. Shazia and I drove home in thoughtful silence.

As I climbed into bed that night the words NO SHAME suddenly flashed across my mind and for a second fear's icy fingers tightened round my stomach. But then, consciously and deliberately, I relaxed, made myself breathe deeply and slowly: in and out.

'I'm too tired,' I told myself. 'I can't think about that now.'

8

Anna handles my appointments now that things have got so busy. Each month I get about forty invitations to speak to police forces and social services, health visitors, schools, primary care trusts, even the Women's Institute. I hate to turn any of them down but realistically, with all the travelling it involves, I can't manage more than twelve each month.

The talk I give has always provoked shock and disgust among my audiences – I'm invariably struck by the horrified disbelief that spreads like a rash across every single face. But now, increasingly, I find that what I say sparks recognition. The beat bobbies, the social workers, the health visitors, I can see them all thinking, 'I've got a case like that'. And many of them want to discuss those cases and ask for my help. Some weeks I feel that I am getting as many referrals through the talks I give as I do from the helpline at Karma Nirvana.

It was two days after I had addressed a police force in Leicester that I was contacted by one female officer: 'Do you remember?' she said, when Anna put the call through to me. 'We chatted briefly at the end. You had to leave to catch your train but you gave me your card.' She said her name was Sergeant Jenkins and it did spark a memory: a small, fair-haired woman with a sporty figure and ruddy cheeks.

'Mmm, yes.' It was a Thursday, and the first day I had been in the office that week. I had a small mountain of paperwork to get through, and half my mind was still on the email I was reading.

'It's about a young Asian woman we're in touch with. We've known of her for two or three months now. She's twenty-eight but she is still living at home with her family and she seems to think she is at risk from them. At least sometimes she says she is and then she says she isn't. One day she says her life is in danger and the next she implores us not to have any sort of contact with her, saying that if we get involved it will only make things worse.' Sergeant Jenkins paused and gave a heavy sigh. I pictured her desk: in my mind's eye it was tidy and functional, all her paperwork properly stacked, the coffee cup beside her hand. I imagined it like her voice, neat and precise.

'Yes, go on,' I said. She had my full attention now.

'To tell you the truth, Jasvinder, I discussed it with my colleagues and we agreed that she seemed a little unhinged. We thought she might just be an attention seeker. But then what you were saying the other day about the misplaced loyalties of the women that you work with; you know, how – despite everything – they love their families and don't want to get them into trouble. Well, afterwards I couldn't stop thinking about this woman . . .'

'If you say she keeps changing her mind she could well be torn between her fear of her family and her love for them. Tell me a bit more about her. What's her name?'

An hour later, I was still listening. The young woman was called Shabana, and the outline of her story was familiar; in many ways it was like mine. When her mother announced that she had found the man she wanted Shabana to marry, she was surprised to find her daughter reluctant and uncooperative. After an hour or so of being bullied and brow-beaten, Shabana admitted that she was already in love.

'Who with? Tell me,' her father yelled when he came home from work that evening to find Shabana tear-stained on the sofa, her mother and her sister sitting each side of her, guarding her like a prisoner in the dock. 'Tell me his name, you hussy,' he shouted, grabbing her jaw, twisting her face to within an inch of his.

She must be a gutsy girl, I thought, as Sergeant Jenkins – in a tone of utter disbelief – read out what Shabana claimed to have been subjected to that evening. Her father punched her face and tried to strangle her; her sister scratched her, kicked her, pulled her hair. That she held out at all seems remarkable but eventually, inevitably, she caved in: 'His name is John Henderson', she whispered, wrapping her arms around her knees, gathering herself in, trying to make herself as small as possible as she crouched on the floor.

'*HENDERSON*? A *white* man?' her father roared as, with his hands embedded in her hair, he yanked her to her feet. 'You are a disgrace, you disgust me, you are no better than a prostitute.' With the flat of his hand he landed a blow on her right cheek which sent her tumbling to the floor again.

'Get out!' As she dragged herself onto all fours he aimed a kick at her left buttock. 'Get out! I cannot bear to look at you! Get out of my sight!'

'She said she was in such pain that she had to crawl up the

stairs to her bedroom,' Sergeant Jenkins said. 'She said that later that night her sister came up and told her that their dad was going to get someone to cut John's legs off. The sister said they'd already found out where he lived.'

In the heat of their rage Shabana's family forgot to confiscate her mobile phone and that evening she managed to ring John and warn him and she also rang two other friends, seeking sympathy and advice. It was one of these, a girl called Sheena, who alerted the police.

'So we went round to the address Sheena gave us, myself and a colleague, and we insisted on seeing Shabana alone.' There was a note of pride in Sergeant Jenkins' voice as she said this. 'But although she gave us her boyfriend's name and address, "just in case", she claimed that she herself was fine, she said she was perfectly happy, she was on good terms with her family, there was nothing to worry about.'

'So what did you do?'

'What could we do?' said Sergeant Jenkins, and in her controlled way she sounded quite exasperated. 'We left. And then the next day she sends an email containing everything I've just told you, admitting that the only time she's allowed out of her bedroom is to go to work, and adding that her father has shown her a gun and told her that he's not afraid to use it. 'I'd rather see you dead than have my family shamed,' is what she says he said.

'Let's face it Jasvinder, if she's telling the truth, we've got grounds for prosecution. But it turns out that's not what she wants. It turns out that she doesn't want any police involvement. "I'm handling this myself," is what she said.'

'Well, you have to respect that,' I said immediately. 'Believe me, girls like Shabana are very good at assessing their own risk and they are usually also skilled at managing it. Trust what she says. But clearly she needs help. Can you get her permission for me to ring her? Thanks. Let me know what she says.'

9

'I had a call from a guy yesterday,' Anna said. 'Apparently he read the piece about Karma Nirvana that appeared in the evening paper a few weeks back, but it's taken him all this time to pluck up the courage to contact us. He's been a forced marriage victim: it's a few years back now, but he still sounds really cut up about it. He seemed desperate for someone to talk to.'

'Did you get his number?' I asked her.

'Of course I did, and I said I was sure you would call him as soon as you could.'

I decided a face-to-face meeting would be best; at that point I didn't have any experience of supporting male victims and I was worried about striking the wrong note. I wanted to be able to see his reactions. We met at a little place just down Normanton Road. I bought him a cup of tea and a piece of cake and he sat there, shoulders hunched, hollow-eyed, warming his hands on his cup. What I remember most about that afternoon is how lost he looked. He was thirty-one then, but I took him for much younger: in his trainers and his hooded top he seemed more boy than man and behind his street swagger he was shy and tongue-tied. Conversation was sticky initially so I told him a bit about my background to try and put him at his ease. He said afterwards that I made him feel cared about for the first time in years.

Imran is a Muslim; he comes from a family where arranged marriages are the norm and, to be fair, his older sisters and his brother are proof that they can work. Imran admits that. 'My brother didn't want to go through with it, because he'd already set his heart on a girl he met in India but our mum said to him, "No, you've already been promised elsewhere." It was a girl from my dad's family. They got a chance to meet and talk to each other and they got on okay; she's a teacher and well-educated. It's seven years now, and they've got two beautiful kids and they're enjoying life. He's grown into loving her.'

Imran was promised to his uncle's daughter when he was ten years old, although he didn't realise at the time. All he remembers is a family holiday to Pakistan and in the middle of it someone threw a party at which he and the little girl he was told to sit beside were the centre of attention. He remembers screwing up his eyes against the flash of cameras. At ten you don't question your good fortune, do you? Imran just enjoyed it: his smart new clothes, the tables piled high with food and the money people gave him. But he looked uncomfortable as he described it to me; like all survivors I've met he seemed ashamed at the slightest compliance in his fate.

'I never thought about it afterwards, but when I was fifteen my sister showed me one of the photos taken that day. She said, "That's you and the girl you're going to marry" and although she sounded like she was teasing, I knew she was serious. It seemed wrong to me. The girl in the picture was so young, maybe five years old. I said, "No way, that is not going to happen." And she said, "You've got no choice. You have to go through with it. You can't say no, it's a question of honour."'

'You've got no choice.' Imagine saying that to a kid at the very moment in his life when the world is starting to open up and he's getting his first small taste of independence. My mind flashed back to my nephew Sunny when he was that age: he was always off with his mates, his mind full of bands and girls and the brilliant ways in which he was going to make his money. Why would fifteen-year-old Imran have been any different? His sister's words must have felt like a prison sentence. It came as no surprise to me to hear that he rebelled against it.

'I went off the rails. I started drinking heavy, smoking heavy. I was in with the wrong crowd. I got expelled from two schools. I was getting into fights, smashing windows. It was kids' stuff, not serious but still, the police came to our door about four times.'

When his mum suggested a holiday in Pakistan he never suspected anything was amiss; he leapt at the idea. He flew out with his sister who was going to bring her husband back to England, and they stayed with her in-laws in Sialkot for a week before going on to visit their grandmother in Karachi. 'I was excited about going there, I knew Karachi was a big city with loads of shops – I wanted to see it,' said Imran, shaking his head at his naivety.

There wasn't to be much sightseeing. A few days after he arrived in Karachi his brother-in-law woke him up one morning at 5 a.m. 'He was pulling at my arm and saying, "Come on, quickly now, it's time to pray" and I was like, "But I've never prayed, I don't know how to," and he was saying not to worry, that he'd teach me. He had a mug of tea in his hand and a tablet and he said, "Take this tablet, it will help to wake you up more quickly."'

Imran, seventeen years old, in a strange country, befuddled with sleep and – above all – used to trusting people, swallowed it. Before his brother-in-law had hustled him out of the house, through the garden and into an alleyway his head was swimming. He could feel himself swaying and he steadied himself briefly against the side of a parked car. 'Suddenly these hands grabbed me from behind and dragged me into that car. I was trying to fight against it but my arms and legs felt so heavy. It took all the concentration I had just to say, "What's happening?" I was slumped in the front seat and there was this sack full of something really hard and heavy where my feet were. That's all I remember before I fell asleep.'

He was woken by ice-cold water being splashed on his face. Jerked into consciousness, Imran realised that two men had his arms pinioned painfully behind him and a group of others, including his brother-in-law, stood in a semi-circle, staring. 'It was hard to see because we were in this bare brick room with hardly any light. Although I couldn't see much I knew it was a mosque. One of the men, dressed in cream salwar kameez and with a long, tangled beard, stood out from the others; he was an imam. It should have felt like a safe place but with the way they were all staring at me it just felt threatening.'

His brother-in-law stepped forward holding a set of shackles. 'He looked embarrassed and he sounded upset when he said, "I'm really sorry Imran. It's your mum's request, she's asked me to do this because you're so naughty. She wants you rehabilitated."'

I had to stop Imran there, because I couldn't believe what I was hearing. Shackles! I thought you only found those in museums these days. The words burst out of me: 'What did they look like?'

Imran swallowed hard. I think if we'd been somewhere less public than a café in Normanton Road he would have started crying. As I sat there waiting for his answer I noticed the dark circles under his eyes, the tension in his shoulders.

'They were made of iron. There was a chain with a padlock on it to go round each ankle and a solid bar between them to stop me walking properly. Attached to the bar was another chain which had a big iron ball at the end of it.' He paused for a minute.

'My brother-in-law knelt down to put them on me. It wasn't his fault, he was just doing what he had been told. I was crying and begging him not to do it, and he was emotional himself. He was trying to tell me to walk round but he could hardly get the words out. I tried to walk but it was so heavy and the chains rubbed against my ankles. It was really painful, by the end of that first day my skin was red and raw.'

When his brother-in-law left – with more apologies and the promise to come the following week with clean clothes and money for food – Imran said he felt completely desolate, losing his only link to the life he knew. He made to follow his brother-in-law, forgetting all his adolescent dignity and crying out just like a little boy, pleading with him to stay. But by the time he had hobbled painfully to the door, dragging the iron ball behind him, the car carrying his brother-in-law was in the distance, enveloped by a cloud of dust.

'I looked out and there was nothing. Honestly, Jasvinder, I could have been in a desert, there was no proper road or anything. I leaned out further and looked all around and I could see maybe five scruffy handmade houses, all spread out from one another. Otherwise it was just scrubby fields with a few goats and a dirt track. I knew then that I'd been dumped in the back of beyond; I thought, I could die here and nobody in the real world, my world, would know.

'At first I just stood there with the tears pouring down my cheeks but after a while I pulled myself together and looked out again and then I saw there was one sign of civilisation. It was a little shop, just a shack really, with a stack of soft drink crates outside it. I found out later that I could go there; it was the furthest I was allowed to go. It would take you thirty seconds to reach it from where I was standing but with the shackles on it took me nearly five minutes.'

But that day Imran remained indoors. He wasn't alone with the imam; when he finally turned back into the mosque he noticed a long low table at which about a dozen boys were seated. They were younger than him, ragged and barefoot, crouched on the concrete floor as they bent over copies of the Koran, moving their lips as they read slowly and silently, peering through the gloom. These were Imran's fellow prisoners. They didn't wear shackles and they went home to their parents at night, but by day they were as trapped as Imran was: tied to their studies by fear of the imam who – at the slightest sign of inattention – brought his stick down, thwack, on this or that bony spine. 'Or, when he was really angry, he picked them off the floor by their ears; they were screaming and crying,' said Imran.

The imam pushed him down onto the floor, into his place in the line of students, and set a copy of the Koran on the table before him. 'The shackles really dug into me and I was moving them, trying to make them comfortable, when I felt this kid sitting next to me staring. He was looking at the shackles and his eyes were stretched really wide and he whispered, 'What did you do?' as though it must have been something terrible. I told him I'd done nothing, that I didn't know why I was there and he said he felt sorry for me. He was only a little kid, eight or nine years old, but after that we became quite friendly.'

The first night was the worst for Imran. The boys went home and the imam showed him into a tiny room with a narrow bed and a barred window. He brought him food: potato curry and chapattis and a glass of water. He made to leave and Imran called after him, 'You can't expect me to eat or sleep with these shackles on, they hurt me. Look at my skin, it's bleeding.' But the imam shrugged and said, 'I am just doing my job. This is what your mother wants. I am not to take the shackles off until you have read the whole Koran and are ready in yourself to be a better person. Don't worry, you are safe here.'

'I didn't feel safe, Jasvinder,' Imran said, and he wasn't close to tears any more, he was angry. 'I felt abandoned – I didn't even know what part of the country I was in. I was terrified. I couldn't believe that this was really what Mum meant for me. All night long I was thinking she couldn't have done this if she loved me. I was crying till my eyes were sore and my pillow was wet with it. I never slept while I was there, I couldn't. I lay awake thinking that I was never going to see my brothers and sisters or my friends again. Sometimes I'd talk to myself so I didn't feel so lonely.'

To this day I haven't met Imran's mum, I never will meet her. But I've heard him speak highly of her. I've heard the note of pride in his voice when he describes her: 'My mum wore the trousers in our family, Dad had a drinking problem. Every night when I went to bed, every morning when I woke up, the sound in our house was her sewing machine. People dropped off these big bags with the pieces of fabric in them and she worked, day in day out, putting them together. She bought a big house for us – she bought lots of houses – all from that sewing machine.'

Imran's mum was clearly a woman doing the best for her family and I have to believe that in sending Imran to that mosque in Pakistan she thought she was doing the best for her wayward son. But if she could have seen him that afternoon as I did, if she could have seen the hurt and betrayal in his eyes, heard the anger in his voice – raw emotions that he was still feeling, fourteen years later – I wonder whether she would have felt regret.

Imran marked off his days of incarceration on the wall of the cell-like room he slept in. As the hours crept by, tortuously slow, the tedium soothed his panic and blunted the fear and humiliation that were chasing each other through his mind. He was able to think. 'I looked at the chains round my ankles and saw that the padlocks holding them together weren't monster munch; I could break them quite easily if I just had a tool.'

He needed an accomplice and his little wide-eyed friend would have to do the job. Imran didn't rush him. 'Remember back in England I'd been very naughty and to be naughty you have to be clever.' For several days he wooed the boy with money to buy food from the shop then, once he felt confident that he would cooperate, he confided his plan and asked him to find a tool. Next day the child – proud to help, pleased with this promising link to the United Kingdom – came to the mosque with a metal bar concealed beneath his shirt.

'All that day I hid it in my trousers. I waited until two in the morning to see if it would work; I was so scared that I said a prayer before I tried it.'

It did work. He pushed down hard with the metal bar and the padlock sprang open without breaking; better still, it snapped shut again without showing signs of damage. In the silence of the night Imran whooped for joy; he'd been imprisoned for fifteen days and now he knew he could break free.

'Next day I waited until we had our food at twelve o'clock, because I didn't know when I would eat again, then I asked the imam if I could go to the shop. He sent some of the kids with me, to watch me, so there I was, terrified, but trying to hide my fear and talk and joke with them.'

As getaways go, it was laughably slow. I had to smile at the image of a hobbled man 'running away' with a group of kids dancing along in front of him, tugging at his sleeve to get his attention. Imran looked hurt at first, then he smiled too.

'That was just the beginning,' he said. As he shuffled past the invisible mark which was his boundary things changed. When his diminutive 'guards' realised that he wasn't going to stop, their laughter changed to shouting, their voices high and indignant. As Imran broke into a stuttering run their shrill cacophony merged with lower pitched laughter and yells of encouragement. Surprised, Imran turned to see a couple of farmers, scythes dangling by their sides, egging him on. 'I knew then I had to get the shackles off in case they stopped laughing and started to chase me. As I bent down to bang my padlocks open I saw the kids running back to tell the imam.'

Free from the chains, Imran, squinting in the glare of the midday sun, fleetingly surveyed the dusty plain. The heat was intense, settled like a blanket over miles of empty scrub which offered no landmark to give him his bearings. With his sweat-drenched shirt plastered to his body and his heart pounding in his chest, he set off in the direction his brother-in-law's car had gone, running as fast as his bare feet would allow across dirt and stubble and stones until at last, with his chest heaving and his feet cut to pieces, he reached the road.

'It felt like I was running for hours, Jasvinder. Maybe it was two hours, two and a half, I don't know, but when I got to the road there was a water pump and for the first time since I came to Pakistan I thought someone was on my side. I put my whole self under that water until at last I felt cool.'

He flagged down the first bus that came by, scrambling over the back bumper and up on to the roof, clinging on precariously with several other boys. At the first town they reached there was a big bus station with services to cities with names that he recognised: Karachi, Gugerat, Sialkot. 'I decided on Sialkot – where my sisters live – because I'd met some mates there, people who wanted to know me because I'd come from the UK. I thought they might help me. I had hardly any money left so I told the conductor I'd swap my gold watch for a ticket, and he was really pleased.'

In Sialkot he limped on his bare, bleeding feet to a call centre where a boy he'd met worked. 'He's a proper, down-to-earth guy and he said I could stay. His dad said he would contact the British Embassy for me but I was begging him like, please, please, give me a breather, leave it a week before you tell anyone where I am.'

The memory of that week brought a smile to Imran's face for the first time that afternoon. He sat back in his seat and took his time describing how he 'lived in the lap of luxury, eating fruit and watching DVDs'. He didn't try to hide the note of triumph in his voice when he told me that he waited four days before ringing his mum. I could feel the delight he'd had in taking back some power.

'She was very emotional. "Where have you been? We thought you'd been kidnapped," stuff like that. I was really angry with her. I told her I was going to burn down my brother-in-law's house. I told her I wasn't coming home. I made really bad threats.'

And his anger endured. Back in England, he moved away from his family, up to Blackpool where he did a bit of this and that: window cleaning, working as a packer. But the family pressure followed him, needling and niggling at him to get married to the girl to whom he'd been betrothed. 'Dad said, "Do it for your mum". My brothers said, "You can't let Mum down." My sisters said, "Come on, you're hitting the age." I was like "It's never going to happen." But then I got a call from a close family member who said, "Your mum's in hospital, she's really ill."'

How many Asian sons and daughters have had that call, I wonder? And how many mums and aunties, grandmas and grandpas have made miraculous recoveries once the errant child has buckled down and done what the family want. Imran's mum was no different. She wasn't embarrassed by the fact that Imran arrived in the hospital ward to find her 'death bed' curiously unattended. She muttered vaguely about her blood pressure and then got down to business: 'If anything happens to me today it will be your fault, Imran,' she moaned and then, ignoring his protests, went on, sprinkling in a few tears to add to the effect.

'Should I not live after today the only thing I wish for is to know that you are married. Please Imran, will you do that for me? Will you make your mother happy?'

I know Imran well now, I know how big his heart is, but even if it wasn't – what son could resist that sort of entreaty? Of course he agreed, and of course his mum was well enough to leave hospital and wave him off to Pakistan on the flight his brothers booked for him, just five days on.

No time was wasted. When Imran got there the wedding took place almost immediately. The bride was ready – as Imran pointed out, she had been waiting for him all her life. He had it in mind to sabotage the ceremony, to shout 'no' rather than 'yes' when asked to give his consent, but when the moment came, with his extended family looming over him, he didn't dare. 'I would have got killed in the name of honour, I know it, Jasvinder,' he said.

His bride was a pretty girl and intelligent. Imran looked shamefaced, he kept his eyes on the table as he admitted, 'She was upset when I told her that I'd been forced to marry, that it wasn't what I wanted. She didn't understand, she wasn't west-ernised, she didn't know. That first night we sat there and talked all night and she kept crying and saying, "Well, I'm married to you now. What am I going to do?"

'I told her not to worry. I said I'd bring her to the UK. I had to do that, it wasn't her fault we were married and anyway, I didn't have a choice.'

In the face of her disappointment and humiliation, Imran's bride was brave. She promised she would *make* him love her, she said she knew when she came to the UK that things would be all right. But she was wrong. Imran went with his mum to collect her from the airport. 'And I felt shattered; I thought everything that I'm doing, I'm doing it for my family. I'm not doing anything I want.'

They went to live with his mum – there was nowhere else

for them to go – but Imran couldn't stand it. I don't blame him. I hated living with my second husband's parents: the sense of claustrophobia, of your in-laws watching you, the feeling that everybody had their breath held, listening, when you went to bed. You couldn't make a relationship in those circumstances even if you wanted to. After three weeks Imran moved out.

But of course that wasn't the end of it, the pull of home is always so strong and Imran was back and forth, back and forth, trying to make the situation feel better.

He said to his wife, 'In two years time I'll sign your residency papers, but I can't stay here with you now. Don't worry about it, you can stay in England, I'm not going to send you back.'

He said to his mum: 'I did it for you and here she is, but I can't live with her. It's not my fault, we don't relate.'

His mum wasn't interested in how they were relating. She wanted a decision made and she put it to him clearly: either you stay with your wife and we buy you a big house or you don't and we disown you. Choose the second and you can get out and don't come back.

It took him two hours to make a decision from which he's never wavered. As he said to his mum, 'It's not about having a big house. How can I have a nice life with my wife if I don't love her? I'll only leave her for someone else.'

His wife was hysterical as he packed his clothes and with them all the expectations and aspirations she had grown up with. He left home that day and, although she stayed on in his mum's house, he's only seen her once in the seven years since.

'It was the day I divorced her. I'd gone back home to say that's what I wanted to do and all the family was speaking against me. They were trying to brainwash me, saying, "Go on, live with your wife, she's here, sort it out." I couldn't stand it, they were pressing in around me and saying to me, "Do this, do that," until I lost my temper and I went up to my wife and shouted in her face, right close up so there was spittle going on her, "I divorce you. I divorce you. I divorce you." And that was it. My wife started crying and she ran upstairs: that's how Sharia law works; she knew we were divorced.'

Imran's face was contorted by emotion as he said this: guilt, shame, anger, grief – all felt for his ex-wife as much as for himself. As the memories overwhelmed him he buried his face in his hands and we both sat there, silent, contemplating those two innocent lives that had been ruined in the name of honour. When I saw his shoulders start to shudder I went round to his side of the table. I said, 'It wasn't your fault, Imran, you know that.'

His shoulders stiffened as I put my arm round him and then, after a couple of seconds, he relaxed. (He was all skin and bone; it was like hugging a coat hanger.) After a bit he sat up; he was rubbing his eyes with the heels of his hands and he made a crooked attempt at a smile. 'Hugging is what your mum's supposed to do isn't it – but mine never did. She never talked much neither. I've never had anyone I can talk to like I've been talking to you.'

In the years before we met, Imran had been living in an emotional wasteland as he struggled to hold his life together. He was drifting: from Birmingham to Blackpool, Rugby to Derby; occasionally he had his own room ('they were always freezing because I couldn't afford rent and electric') but for the most part he was sofa-surfing or even, sometimes, sleeping on deckchairs on the beach. The work he did was cash in hand and at £4.50 an hour there was never enough of it; sometimes he didn't eat. 'With all the anger inside me I was very aggressive and bad tempered. I was drinking and smoking a lot – anything to ease the pressure in my head.'

That's the reason so many of the young women I see give for self-harming and I've learnt from them that the pressure comes not from anything external but from the vacuum where their sense of self ought to be. Relieving it is not a case of taking anything away, it's about putting something back. Listening to them is the start of that because it acknowledges – often for the first time in years – that they are individuals with a right to feelings and opinions, their own view of life.

As we were strolling back towards Karma Nirvana's offices – I wanted Imran to know where to find us – he turned to me and said, 'For the first time in seven years I feel alive again.' I remember smiling vaguely in reply but even as he spoke an idea was formulating in my mind. Not ten days earlier I had read a government report which claimed that fifteen per cent of the victims of forced marriage and honour-based violence are men. It had set me wondering whether there was a great big hole in the service that Karma Nirvana was providing and, if so, how we could fill it. And here – as if in answer to an unsaid prayer – was Imran, a man whose own experience made him the perfect person to join us as the voice of male victims.

I put my hand on his arm, stopped him in his tracks. 'Imran,' I said. 'How would you feel about doing a bit of voluntary work?'

10

Christmas came and went and as the New Year rolled in Fozia, Kiren and Shabana were almost always in my thoughts first thing each morning. Fozia wasn't doing well. She was struggling to keep the self-harming under control. Late one night in the room of her refuge in Chesterfield she took fistfuls of Paracetamol. 'I didn't plan it Jas, but I was sitting there on my bed and I just felt so much anger.'

She remembers it all very clearly: she went to sleep, woke up a few hours later feeling hot and confused and decided to go downstairs and have a cigarette. Luckily, there was another inmate in the sitting room, doing her ironing, and when Fozia rushed to the toilet to throw up she went to help her, and saw all the undigested tablets floating in the bowl. Fozia was taken to the hospital where she had her stomach pumped. She was kept in for a few days, under observation, but when the medics deemed her well enough to leave, the refuge in Chesterfield wouldn't have her back again.

She was moved to Nottingham and then, because she believed she was being watched there, to Mansfield. 'I've got my own self-contained flat here, Jas,' she told me. 'A real clean freak. I clean all day long, over and cleaning all the time.' She said it lightly – typica I knew her well enough by then to pick up the emb in her voice and she obviously knew it wasn't right.

She was becoming more and more isolated. She told me that she spent a lot of time reading but all too often she had to close the book and leave it because she found the happiness – or unhappiness – of the characters too much to bear. Emotionally she was on the edge. And she wasn't eating, she was quite open about that. 'I'm from a big family and we all used to sit down and eat together. We'd sit on the floor because my dad hated dining tables. "We're not white people – our ways are different," he used to say. He liked to sit cross-legged with his great big belly resting in his lap. I used to enjoy that, Jas, being together as a family, and now I just can't find it in myself to eat a meal alone. Eating is one thing I hate.'

The little contact she had with her family had set her back. One sister, Raveeda, told Fozia that her brother had passed her photo on to his mates so they could look for her. 'I don't like going out now, Jas. I'm scared I'll find them waiting for me round every corner. I only feel safe when I'm indoors.' And the only conversation she had with her mum had left her devastated. When she was telling me about it I had to really focus to understand what she was saying through her sobs. 'She said she wasn't my mother any more. She said she wished she'd killed me while I was in her stomach. She said she always hated me.'

I tried to console her, tried to reassure her that her mum was only getting back at her, but I know it was poor comfort. What sixteen-year-old girl could cope with her mum saying that?

I was advocating for her really hard at that time, trying to persuade social services to let her come back to Derby. 'I think you should try to see it from her point of view,' I said. 'She feels she's being punished, banished from her home town; she keeps saying to me, "Why can I not come back? I haven't done anything wrong." I fully appreciate that you are focusing on keeping her safe but I feel confident that if she were to come back here we could help her to manage her risk. And I'd like to think that, as well as keeping her safe, we can empower her, encourage her to take control of her own life. Don't you think that allowing her to choose where she is going to live would be a good start?' But they didn't seem to hear me. Sometimes I felt I was banging my head against a brick wall.

Shazia went out to Mansfield to see her and I think that did Fozia good because it made her begin to believe what I'm always saying, that friends can become your family. By that stage she was telling me that I was like a mum to her, but Fozia needed a friend too, and that's what Shazia offered.

'I was really scared before she came because I was thinking, what if she thinks I'm shameful when she sees me smoking,' Fozia said when she rang to tell me all about the meeting. 'But—' the word blew out on a gust of laughter 'the first thing I know Shazia herself pulls out a cigarette.'

Shazia's openness impressed Fozia too, the way she was prepared to trust her even though they had only just met. 'She opened up to me and told me about herself and she must have realised how dangerous that was. I could have been one of her family members for all she knows and yet she still told me, I don't think she kept much back. That was a big thing for me.'

We were a lifeline for Fozia at that time and I think it would be true to say the same of Kiren, who was reacting to her independence very differently. Finding herself suddenly free had released a lot of emotions in Kiren, mostly wild and angry ones. It was as if she was over-compensating for all the years her parents had kept her downtrodden and suppressed. Her potential in-laws had been ringing her, furious at the way she'd shamed them. 'I told them there was no way I was going to marry their son, I said I was going to marry someone I was in love with. And when they started threatening me, I just said come and find me then.' Telling me this, Kiren laughed at the memory of her own defiance.

Because she intended to prosecute her parents, the police had placed Kiren on the Witness Protection Programme and before I knew it they had given her a new name and moved her from Cheshire up to Inverness. In time they would give her a completely new identity; meanwhile, as part of the programme, she was supposed to sever all contact with her old life, including me.

'I can't do it, Jas. You're the only person I've got to talk to and anyway I hate it here, I'm miles from fucking anywhere. I'm the only Asian for miles around; I feel like an alien whenever I go out.'

I was trying to distract her, to make her see things in a more positive light when I asked her to tell me what she could see out of the window.

'Nothing!' Her frustration exploded down the telephone. 'There's nothing outside the window except fucking eagles. Nothing to look at, no one to talk to. It's more like a prison here than it was at home. It's not working, Jas. I don't want to be on witness protection, I don't want to prosecute my parents. I just want to forget about the past and get on with my own life.'

I could see why she felt like that, just as I can see why the police feel so frustrated when these girls come forward to complain about the horrors that their parents inflict upon them and then refuse to prosecute. I'd just been seeing it at first hand with Shabana and poor Sergeant Jenkins who was left feeling that her hands had been tied behind her back. I know how hard it is for the police to understand that girls like Shabana and Kiren still love their families despite what they've done to them. It's so difficult to explain that – in defiance of all logic – they long for reconciliation with their families and believe that any police involvement will kill that hope stone dead. I know it seems irrational, still, I argued Kiren's case for her and the police agreed to bring her down to Loughborough and subsequently – in the face of Kiren's refusal to prosecute her parents – they dropped her case. Kiren seemed happier no doubt about that, but, as far as I'm concerned, she soon ran into a different set of problems.

The trouble with girls who have been over-protected by their parents – and that's most Asian girls – is that they have no idea how to handle freedom when they get it, particularly if, like Kiren, they have been locked up for years. Kiren was like a child let loose in a sweet shop. She grabbed at freedom with both hands. She had her hair bobbed, she had nail extensions, she went clubbing with other girls she met.

'I found that quite scary at first. I didn't know how to dance properly. I've never had an alcoholic drink before. My God Jas, I can't believe what I've been missing! And I've never had men's attention like that before, either. It's sort of weird – you know that way they stare at you and it's embarrassing, but at the same time it makes you feel nice?'

Her shyness was easier to lose than her naivety. Early one morning she rang and her usual bravado had been replaced by tears of humiliation. The previous night, she said, she had been talking to some men in a nightclub who seemed 'really nice, really friendly' so when they offered her a lift home she accepted without thinking twice.

'You got into a car with strangers at two o'clock in the morning? Kiren – what were you thinking of?'

'I thought they would take me straight back to the refuge, Jas. Don't worry, I'd have got them to drop me nearby, I wouldn't have shown them exactly where it was . . .'

'It's not that, Kiren. It's you I'm worried about, not the refuge. You knew nothing about these men. How many of them were there anyway?'

'Three, but I told you, Jas, in the club they seemed really nice. They bought me drinks and they were very polite. It wasn't until we got in the car that it all went wrong.'

Suddenly she was sobbing again, it was a moment or two before she could speak. 'I didn't realise it at first but they didn't go anywhere near the refuge, they started heading towards one of the big roads out of town. I told them they were going the wrong way but –'

This time I had to prompt her to stop the silent tears. 'What happened, Kiren? Go on, you know you can tell me.'

'The man sitting next to me suddenly grabbed my . . . you know, there. And he was kissing me, forcing his mouth on mine and using his weight to pin me against the seat. It just happened, out of the blue, and oh Jas, it was so horrible.'

'What did you do?'

'I froze. My mind was telling me I ought to struggle, to make him get off but I couldn't make my body move. It was such a surprise, Jas. I think I was in shock.'

I could hardly bear to ask the next question, I so dreaded

the answer, but I forced the words out of my mouth: 'What happened then?'

'Well, he took his hands off me and the man who was driving stopped the car and they all three were talking to each other but they spoke so fast I couldn't understand what they were saying. Then the man leant across me to open the car door and pushed me out. I fell onto the pavement and I really hurt my elbow –'

'Thank God, that's all.' I felt weak with relief. My heart settled back to its normal rhythm as I said, 'Kiren, stop crying. If a sore elbow is your only legacy from that car journey, you don't know how lucky you are; you really put yourself in danger. Now, we have some serious talking to do before you go clubbing again; are you listening?' Talking as best I could off the top of my head, I condensed all the maternal advice I had given Lisa during years of mothering into a fifteen-minute talk on boundaries. I only hope that some of it sunk in.

Kiren's narrow escape taught *me* a lesson too: thinking about it later I realised how easy – and how wrong – it had been to assume that teaching these young women to look after themselves is simply a matter of making sure they know how to cook and claim their benefits and pay the bills.

When they leave home their innocence and ignorance about the outside world leave them so vulnerable. Giving guidance and advice – being a 'big sister' – to girls like Kiren could, I realised that morning, be one of the functions of a Friendship Network which I had been mulling over in my mind for several months.

In those days it was just beginning to grow out of an idea into something real; I envisaged a support system for young women of the sort who approach Karma Nirvana every day, women who have recently left their homes and been rejected by their families. I was determined it should be a national network and the Forced Marriage Unit – which the Home Office and the Foreign and Commonwealth Office had set up as a 'one-stop-shop' for the rescue and protection of British girls forced into marriage both here and abroad – had agreed to give us funding to train the first nineteen friends/mentors. From my own personal experience I knew it would be a useful service: years ago the struggle to rebuild my life only became bearable when I found some friends – people like Trish – whose care and kindness helped stitch up the gaping hole left in my life when my family rejected me.

'Shabana could use the Network too,' I thought to myself as I sat at my desk, skimming through an email she had sent me, updating me on her circumstances. She bombarded me with emails in those days, me and the police. Each one was long and complicated; they seemed to detail her every thought. I saw them as a drawn-out cry for help, a way of expressing and managing her fear.

When Sergeant Jenkins first told me about Shabana, I referred her case to Brent Hyatt and in recent weeks – on his advice – she'd had her fingerprints and DNA samples taken by her local police force and she had also made a video statement explaining her circumstances. She agreed to do it on one condition: that it would only be used 'if things go wrong'.

I knew that an escape plan had also been made, but – to the police's frustration – Shabana was still refusing to act on it. She was waiting to make sure that once she left her identity would be protected; in particular she wanted her National Insurance number to be changed because she felt sure her parents would try using it to trace her.

I was beginning to be scared that she would procrastinate too long. For safety's sake, she had ended her relationship with John Henderson, but she had also turned down two more of the suitors her mother chose for her, on both occasions provoking vicious family rows. During one of these her sister threatened to call in a posse of black men to rape her. Her father cut out a newspaper article describing an honour killing and left it on her bed. Imagine living with those threats, getting up each day to face such hostility; I wasn't surprised when, in her emails, she started talking about suicide.

I suddenly felt choked by worry for her. I sent a text, asking when I could ring; I needed to reassure myself that she was still there, still safe. I've never rung Shabana except at pre-arranged times, that's how it has always been and I wouldn't go against her wishes. But it hasn't always been easy. More than once she hasn't answered her phone when she said she would and I have been left wondering – panicking as the hours went by – about what might have happened, whether or not she was all right. 'Where *were* you?' I heard myself saying a couple of times, like an anxious mother whose daughter has stayed out too late. She was always quite blithe about it, just like a daughter might be: 'Sorry, I got held up,' or 'Something cropped up.'

When that happened I had to curb the irritation that was lapping round the edges of my relief. I had to remind myself that this was not my daughter but a 28-year-old woman who, at that stage, I hadn't even met.

11

Early in 2007, I received an invitation to the House of Lords from the Liberal peer, Lord Lester. He invited me to attend the second reading of the Forced Marriage (Civil Protection) Act; a bill that he had introduced in order to try and prevent people from being forced into marriage. Of course I accepted; this subject is so close to my heart. I'm not saying that you have to legislate to change a mindset, but the fact is that rape within marriage was considered unremarkable until it was made illegal. In the same way, the victims we see at Karma Nirvana all believe forced marriage is an inescapable and – to the world at large – acceptable fact of life. I hoped Lord Lester's bill would go a long way towards putting that right.

I had never been to the House of Lords before and I was awestruck looking down at the rows and rows of red leather benches and the Queen's magnificent throne. I had invited a survivor to come with me, a young woman recently rescued by the Forced Marriage Unit from a marriage to a much older relative in Pakistan. She was trying to rebuild her life in London – miles from what had been her home in Newcastle – and I hoped that being at the debate might help her recovery by inspiring her to dream and making her believe that anything is possible. We were both a bit overwhelmed. We sat bolt upright in our chairs and when we had something to say to one another we whispered because anything louder seemed disrespectful. We were both riveted from the start.

In his opening words, Lord Lester summed up forced marriage in exactly the way I would. He said it was a form of domestic violence and sexual enslavement and he pointed out that there is a direct link between forced marriages and honour killings. Throughout the debate I was pleased to hear people saying things that I've been advocating for years, things like the need for an infrastructure to support the bill, including mandatory training for all those people like police and social workers who come into contact with victims. Think what a difference that would have made to Kiren when she first ran away. Baroness Butler-Sloss gave worrying figures from the NSPCC showing that in one year ten per cent of calls to the Asian child protection helpline were about forced marriage. Lord Ahmed pointed out that:

> . . . no religion – Christianity, Judaism, Hinduism, Sikhism or Islam – condones this practice. In fact, they condemn it.

He also gave a really clear answer to the question that I'm always asked about why such a large proportion of the Asian community never seems to assimilate into British culture. He said it was because so many of the arranged marriages, let alone the forced ones, take place with people from abroad:

> . . . a marriage takes place and for the next two years the boy or man who has come from abroad will do everything. After

two years there will be a baby from the marriage. But then suddenly there is a break-up once the man has secured his citizenship or right to stay in this country. What happens then? He goes for a divorce and he brings over another bride from India, Pakistan or Bangladesh. This means that the community continues to go backwards rather than move forwards.

It was a long debate but I travelled home that night glowing with a new sense of optimism about what might be achieved. It was the first time that I had heard the issues that I am battling with every day discussed at such a high level and it gave me hope that this might be the beginning of significant change. Lord Lester's bill was subsequently taken up by the government and adapted. The resulting Forced Marriage (Civil Protection) Act received Royal Assent: it gives courts the power to pass protection orders or injunctions preventing or pre-empting forced marriages from taking place. I welcomed it as a first step, but to my mind the issue of criminalisation still needs to be addressed.

Later that same month publication of my autobiography, *Shame*, led to a rash of speaking engagements. Ever since I started Karma Nirvana I have prayed for platforms from which to spread its message, but there were times at the beginning of that year when the roundabout seemed to be spinning too fast, even for me. At the end of every talk I gave – even after the time allotted for questions – there was always a queue of people waiting, wanting to speak to me one-on-one.

One particular occasion has stayed in my memory. I was in Southall, addressing about two hundred people, most of them old Asian women who put me in mind of my mum. My first thought when I saw them was: 'No one here is going to understand me if I speak in English' so I gave the talk in Punjabi. When I told them that to avoid the marriage my mum and dad wanted to force me into I ran away with a boyfriend from another caste – me, a *jat*, with a *chamar* – there was a collective gasp of horror from the audience. Women turned to one another to share their disapproval. It was as if I'd reached right into them and slapped a face.

The formal bit of that evening was over by 7.30 p.m. and because we had to get back to Derby that night Shazia, who was with me, said we had to leave at 8 p.m. But there was no way that was going to happen. By the time we finally left it must have been 10.30 p.m. and I swear I'd heard the stories of half the women in there. Shazia sorted them all out into a queue and they stood patiently, a long line of them in their own uniform of shapeless woollen cardigans buttoned over Asian suits. Each time I looked up and saw the next one, clutching her shopping bag, shuffling towards me on her tired old feet, my heart turned over. For the first time in years I felt a real pang of longing for my mum.

There was so much sadness in the room that night. I heard stories of long empty lives lived with husbands – strangers when as teenagers they were forced to marry – with whom there had never been any common ground. I heard stories of abandonment, disownment, loss and of the longing to go 'home'. One woman leant in so close that the soft whiskers on her chin brushed my cheek and she whispered in my ear that her husband's family had 'dealt with' an errant niece. Another, with tears trickling down her wrinkled apple cheeks, murmured her regret at forcing all four daughters into marriage. The atmosphere was heavy with the burden of their long-held, uncomplaining sorrow, but also – I believe – there was a soft sigh of release.

Sometimes at the beginning of that year I felt as though in telling my story I had unblocked a waterway that had been clogged with misery, freeing a torrent that cascaded round me wherever I turned. *Shame* seemed to have unleashed a compulsion to talk, to tell, to share – so many lifetimes worth of suffering. Each morning my inbox was full of emails bringing stories; hurrying through them, always pressed for time, my mind was left rattling with the sad fragments of other people's lives.

12

It took me about four months to persuade the council, but Fozia was eventually moved back to Derby, first into the YMCA and then into a supported house run by the English Churches Housing Group. Within the first two weeks of being back she took to coming into Karma Nirvana on a fairly regular basis, working as a volunteer, helping to man the phones. She was even starting to do a bit of support work. At first she said she couldn't do it, she didn't have the confidence, but at one point, when it was manic in the office, it just happened. She answered the phone because everyone else was busy and there was a young woman needing help. She listened for a good ten minutes and then she said, 'But you're just like me, innit?' After that she seemed to find her stride. The young woman rang back later and asked for Fozia by name.

I guess we can all remember that day: Fozia was so pleased it actually looked as though she'd grown taller while she sat there, and she had this great big grin on her face. She did a little more and a little more support work after that, and she was good at it: warm, compassionate and surprisingly sensible when it came to lives other than her own. And Shazia was right there beside her, teaching her, encouraging her, passing on to Fozia what she had learnt from me. It used to make my eyes well up when I saw that.

One morning when Fozia and I were first in the office she said, 'Jas, I've got to tell you something. Michelle rang me last night.'

'Michelle? Is she one of your friends?' I assumed Fozia was going to give me some teenage gossip; I thought she was just chatting as if I were her mum.

'You know, Michelle: Michelle-your-niece,' said Fozia, and the penny suddenly dropped for me.

'Yes, of course. I know who you mean, but I've never actually met her. You know how it is Fozia: it's a long time since I've had contact with my family. Anyway . . .' I flipped open my diary, cast an eye down the day's appointments. 'What about her?'

'I think she wants to kill you.'

I looked up from my desk, across the room to where Fozia was standing propped against the filing cabinet, thrusting her hands up inside her sleeves. 'You are joking?' I said, but I could tell from the way her face was crumpling that she wasn't. I tried to ignore that. I came out from behind my desk and went to stand right in front of her. It was all I could do to stop myself from shaking her as I said it again in a voice that sounded too loud: 'You are joking?'

She gave a juddering breath and a tear trickled down her cheek as she shook her head. 'I'm not joking and she wasn't either, she sounded really serious.'

At that moment reason deserted me. I crossed the office in three big strides and shot the bolt across the door. Then I pulled it back again. Shazia would be arriving any minute. Calm, sensible Shazia: 'Please,' I thought. 'Get here quickly.' My mouth felt dry and my heart was pounding. I'd been half expecting threats like this; I knew the publication of *Shame* would ruffle feathers. But still, I wasn't prepared for the feelings of terror that were threatening to overwhelm me. This wasn't an idle threat from an anonymous stranger, this was someone who knew where to find me, knew where my children and I live. I glanced round quickly checking the windows to make sure they were all shut properly. Half of me wanted to close the blinds, but then I thought, 'No, I need to be able to see if anyone is coming.' I stood there, in the middle of the office, trying to think straight.

'Jas?' Fozia's voice was apologetic and so quiet she was only just audible. 'Jas, shall I tell you the whole conversation?' I turned back towards her; she was chewing the skin on her fingers and she looked so young and so frightened that I knew I had to pull myself together. Inside my head I counted slowly to ten.

'Yes, please do. Tell me everything she said. First: why did she ring you? How did she get your number?'

'We were at school together. We weren't friends but she could easily have got my number. I was scared when she rang, Jas. The first thing she said was, 'I'm going to get that bitch'. She was so angry and aggressive. She said she was going to kill you and Lisa too because you wrote that stuff about her grandma.'

Her grandma, my mum: I felt a stab of regret, a momentary mourning for all my shattered family ties. How could it have reached a state when the only thing I heard from my closest relatives was threats, issued through a third party? My heart had slowed back down and I was beginning to feel less frightened, almost angry. 'Are you actually telling me she made threats to kill me and my daughter?'

Fozia nodded, swallowed: 'I'm telling you because I care about you.'

'And would you be prepared to tell the police?'

Again she nodded. 'I recorded it, Jas, on my mobile phone. I didn't get all of it, because I didn't know at the beginning that she'd be saying bad stuff, but once I realised—'

Fozia repeated the story to the police who asked me what I'd like them to do about it. I said I wanted them to talk to Michelle. I wanted her to know she couldn't get away with making threats like that. So they did: two plain-clothes, senior officers went round to her house. They'd planned to have a word with her in the privacy of her own front room but apparently all the family gathered round wanting to have their say too, and there was such a cacophony that in the end the officers had to take Michelle down to the station. They said she didn't deny anything; they said she was very tearful and contrite and I wasn't surprised. She's only a kid and I'm sure her family put her up to it. That's what makes me sad.

13

When I first started speaking on public platforms, the days I was due somewhere I would always leave the house late and with my bedroom looking as if a tornado had swept through it. I can see it now: the wardrobe door open, stuff hanging out of drawers, a pile of discarded garments on the bed, shoes kicked across the floor and me, whirling like a dervish, trying the black top, then the blue, deciding the jacket might be better, and perhaps a skirt instead of trousers, cursing when I found a ladder in my tights. The kids would be eating their Weetabix, and I'd be modelling more outfits than Kate Moss in Fashion Week and demanding to know, 'Does this look all right?' 'Is this better?' 'Or this?' I never felt I got it right, until Maria began to take an interest and then everything changed.

Nowadays she picks my outfits, chooses my accessories and, if I have more than one engagement and I'm going to be away for several days, she packs my case. That's happening more often now that I am travelling not just in this country but to international conferences. The first one I went to was in Dubai and the subject was forced marriage and child abduction. I remember the day I travelled out there, standing in the departure lounge at Heathrow and wondering how – in twelve years that seemed to have rattled past with all the speed of an express train – Karma Nirvana had brought me from the sagging sofa in my front room to this airport: a gateway to the world.

That feeling of dislocation grew stronger eight hours later when I sat in an air-conditioned taxi which whisked me through the gleaming streets of Dubai to my hotel; as I lost my stomach travelling in the lift up twenty-two floors to my room; as I stood on the threshold and stared in amazement at the vast silk-covered bed.

When I was growing up, my parents' idea of a trip was a day out in Markeaton Park, a picnic for all of us kids and the extended family. The park was only half an hour's drive from the terraced house we lived in and yet I remember only two, possibly three of those picnics in the sixteen years I spent at home. In the tight confines of our little life they were a treat, something to be planned for and savoured, an adventure in the quiet monotony of our year.

I kicked off my shoes and stood barefoot on the cool marble of the bathroom floor. The mirror was big and circular and surrounded by light-bulbs like a Hollywood starlet's. I stared into it, trying to recognise myself in these lavish, unfamiliar surroundings. If I had married the man Mum chose for me, Markeaton Park might still be the far point on my horizon; I might now be sitting at home peeling onions and planning my next visit there, a treat for the summer holidays, an afternoon of leisure spent sprawled on worn grass. But I didn't make that marriage and here I am, twenty-five years later, thousands of miles from Derby, the director of a charity, travelling on business, staying in a five-star hotel.

'What am I doing here?' I spoke the words out loud, suddenly uncomfortable with the silence. Karma Nirvana – with its hectic, over-crowded office, and the endless unknown voices on the phone whispering their fears, their pleas for rescue – seemed so far away. How had my vision for a local project to help women like Robina and my mum brought me across the world to the smart sterility of this hotel?

My room suddenly seemed claustrophobic. I grabbed a sun-hat and headed for the roof terrace, I had to get outside. I had come to Dubai to discuss best practice, to share my knowledge of forced marriage with delegates from Islamabad and Mumbai and who knows where else. But why? What had this to do with Shabana, or Kiren or Fozia – all those women who needed me at home?

As if in answer to a spoken question, a woman appeared walking down the passage towards the lift. She was following an affluent looking man and two teenage boys, all three of them dressed in western-style designer clothes. They were laughing and joking with one another. She, the wife and mother, was silent, ignored as she walked ten paces behind them in her full-length burkha, head angled so that – although I couldn't see her eyes – they could only be looking at the floor. From her slumped shoulders to the drag of her feet everything about her spoke of dejection. Her wings had been clipped and here she was, trapped in a gilded cage. In comparison perhaps, Kiren and Fozia were lucky: at least they got away.

The conference was successful. We were there to discuss best practice and the other delegates seemed interested in what I had to say. That trip confirmed to me the fact that although in scale Karma Nirvana might still be a small local project, its reach and influence had spread way beyond Derby. As the year wore on more and more of my time was spent travelling.

I was in Wales when I first met Yasmin. I noticed her in the crowd I was talking to; my attention was caught because she was so absolutely still. Most people fidget while they're listening, they clear their throats, cross their legs, reach in their handbags for something to wipe their nose. But not Yasmin, she was like a statue. Each time I looked her way her gaze was fixed on me, and the expression on her face was so arresting. It was as if she'd been parched with thirst and somewhere, just out of reach, she'd seen something she might drink.

Afterwards I made a point of talking to her. Time was tight for both of us; I had a train to catch and Yasmin, I discovered, works in a women's refuge and had to get back, but we spoke for a few minutes. She told me the outline of her story which essentially was this: she had run away from home six years previously and she was still in hiding from her family. She believed they were looking for her, and in order to evade them she had moved nine times. 'I didn't know there were other people like me out there, Jasvinder,' she said. 'I've never come across anyone who could understand what I've been through. I'd really like to talk to you for longer . . . do you think I could?'

I met her two weeks later in a pub. I got there first. It was an old-fashioned place with leaded windows, varnished floorboards and leather-backed chairs and benches which were stained and worn with age. It wasn't busy: there were four or five men in workmen's overalls standing by the bar, a young bloke with his girlfriend at the fruit machine, a couple of lads playing darts and an elderly man and his wife, sitting side by side in silence, holding hands. I found a table in a corner and I was sitting there with my half pint of Guinness when she walked in. I'll never forget that moment, every head turned.

Yasmin has that effect on people. She's very tall and she carries herself well, her bearing is almost regal. She has very long dark hair and – like Kiren – the pale skin that is common to Pathans. I think it's that, plus her height and her long, slim face that reminds me sometimes of Robina.

I said, 'Tell me about yourself,' and it was as if I had turned on a tap. Three hours later the words were still pouring out of her, prompted by nothing but the smallest interjection. For six years she had bottled up her fear, confusion, pain, anger, sorrow and, I would say, her spirit which is big, vivacious and bold. For six years she had been waiting to tell her story and in me she had a captivated audience.

She started right at the beginning, in a small seaside resort where her father, a first generation immigrant, ran a small business empire selling halal food. He was a very senior figure in the local community and established the town's first mosque. 'Because he played such a dominant role among the local Muslims it wasn't just the Pakistani community we were involved with, it was the Arabs, the Turks, the Bangladeshis: he was humiliated in front of all those people when I ran away.'

Yasmin grew up in awe of her father. 'If he was to walk into a room and I was sitting down, I would stand up. It wouldn't matter if there were fifty seats for him to sit in, I would still stand.' At home they only spoke Pushto and life was very strictly regulated; in fact, she said, she grew up feeling torn between two worlds. At school she was a boisterous and popular English girl; at home she was quiet and submissive, the dutiful Muslim daughter.

'It was really hard, I used to get upset when I heard my friends making plans to go swimming or shopping at the weekend, or even to after school clubs. In the first year they used to ask me to go with them but then they stopped because they knew there wasn't any point.'

Her weekends were spent at home, indoors, except for the two hours on Saturday and Sunday when she would be sent to work in her father's shop. Those were her moments of freedom, even though while she was there her every move was monitored. 'My dad didn't want me to talk to the customers or even make eye contact. He used to sit on a swivel chair behind the counter, and I'd be on the till and if someone was like, 'Hi, how are you?' I'd pack their shopping bags as quick as possible all the time thinking to myself, 'Please don't talk to me, please, just take your stuff and go'. If my dad got annoyed that I was talking to the customers, he'd take away my little bit of freedom and I'd not have anything then, would I?'

Although marriage was never mentioned Yasmin and her sisters knew that was what their parents had in mind for them. Her eldest sister, Madeeha, was sent aged thirteen to spend a year in Pakistan. 'We were all supposed to go through that at some point, it was a good thing to have on your marriage CV.'

Garnishing that CV was a constant feature of Yasmin's girlhood: if friends came to the house for tea it was her duty to make it, to arrange the biscuits beautifully, to serve the refreshments with her hijab pulled closely round her head. If there were children present she was expected to play with them: 'Aah, look how good she is with kids.' Even her GCSE choices were made – by her father – with marriage in mind. Yasmin wanted to do dance and drama but he chose textiles: 'See, now you can sew as well.'

Marriage was all-important but, with three daughters, it was also an expensive burden. One of Yasmin's earliest memories is of piling into the family car – 'me, my sisters and my two brothers all in the back, it was so squashed' – and driving to Southall where their destination was an Asian jeweller. Hours would be spent there, admiring and then haggling over bangles, earrings, necklaces – all of them gold.

'My mum would buy loads of things and when we got home she climbed into the attic and there in the gloom she opened up a great big suitcase. Inside, gleaming up at you was all this jewellery she'd bought over the years, so she'd be ready when the time came for our dowries. The suitcase had a padlock on it and she used to put the key in this little bag and keep it in her bra.'

In the face of all this, Yasmin was the rebel in her family from an early age. She was suspended from her primary school for smoking. She reminded me of Fozia when she said, 'School was my one chance of being naughty. Seven hours in school was all I had and I was going to make the most of it.' By the time she was in year eleven she had started skiving; it was on one of her illicit jaunts into town that she met Abdul. She was fifteen. He was in his mid-twenties, he was known to the police, and he was black. 'For a Pathan a black person is the lowest of the low,' she whispered.

After her GCSEs, Yasmin persuaded her parents to let her do a business course at the local college, but Abdul lived close by and she spent almost all her time with him. Having arrived at college dressed in a full length skirt and long-sleeved top, she would go to the toilets to change into jeans and a T-shirt before skipping off. Initially they were very careful. They never walked down the street together, if she got into his car she always pushed her seat flat back, they rarely did normal things like going to the cinema. 'Really it was a bizarre relationship that just took place in his flat. If my parents hadn't found out about it, it would never have lasted.'

But they did find out. Inevitably, Yasmin and Abdul grew more blasé about the risk of being seen together, and gossip began to rustle through the community. More than one person voiced their suspicions to Yasmin's parents who began to watch their wayward daughter very carefully. She was not allowed to make or receive telephone calls, the few friends who had been allowed to come to the house were banned; the length of time it took Yasmin to walk to and from her father's shop was monitored.

One day when she was out in the street with Abdul, the police swooped and he was arrested on suspicion of peddling cannabis. Yasmin was taken to the station with him. From the first heart-stopping moment, her main concern was that her father would finally, fully, discover her relationship. 'I begged the police not to tell him. I was in the station for less than an hour and as I signed the release papers I was pleading with this Asian officer not to tell. I'd put Abdul's flat for my home address, I'd committed no crime, I'd turned sixteen so I wasn't a minor; there was no need for Dad to know.'

Yasmin didn't realise it, but PC Ahmed was his station's hate crime officer, charged with protecting vulnerable people including those who might find themselves subjected to a forced marriage. This didn't stop him from doing what he perceived to be his duty to an esteemed member of his community.

'Dad came home one afternoon. I heard him and Mum go

into the living room and they called me downstairs. The first thing Dad said to me was, "PC Ahmed came to see me in the shop this afternoon."'

Yasmin leant into the high-backed seat and closed her eyes. A shaft of sunlight fell across her face emphasising her pallor, rendering her ghostly against the green leather of the bench she was sitting on. I noticed her nostrils flare a little as she breathed in deeply, calming herself, dulling the remembered fear.

'I knew then that it was all over. I honestly thought that right there and then they would ship me off to Pakistan.'

But there was the row to get through first, voices rising louder and louder as her father reeled off her crimes: 'You have a black boyfriend.' Yasmin said he spat those words out as though the very fact of forming them had dirtied his tongue. 'You were arrested with him while walking down Glen Fern Road together. You gave the police a false address. You tried to involve PC Ahmed in your deceit. PC Ahmed – a respectable member of our community – you asked him to conceal your filthy, dishonourable ways.'

His litany went on and on, all but drowned out by her mother's weeping lamentations, 'Oh, the shame, we are ruined, how could you do this?' and Yasmin herself shouting through her sobs, trying to make her voice heard: 'No Dad, it's not true . . . I didn't . . . I haven't . . .You have to believe me. Please.'

How long did it go on for? Yasmin's last memory of it is of her mother, her greying hair dishevelled and falling from its bun, her eyes fixed on the middle distance as she rocked herself to and fro in her armchair still murmuring, 'The shame, it will kill me, the shame'. Her father stalked from the room going, he said, to arrange a further meeting with PC Ahmed. Yasmin herself slunk upstairs to her bedroom, knowing it would now become her prison. 'I didn't sleep at all that night. Every time I heard footsteps on the stairs I was like, "Oh my God, don't let anything happen to me". I was just so scared.'

News spread through the family. Yasmin only ever saw her two younger brothers at meal times, when she served them their food and cleared their plates away. They said nothing but she could feel them watching her with wide, curious eyes. Her sisters, on the other hand, made their contempt and anger clear; with their mother they stood outside Yasmin's room, whispering. 'Do you think she got close to him?' their mother kept asking, too scared to give voice to her real fear, which was: 'Did they have sex?'

No longer allowed to go to college or have any contact with the outside world, Yasmin carried out her household duties and then retired to bed as early as six-thirty. 'I started sleeping for long periods of time, just because it was another day of my life that was gone.'

I could imagine the torpor that settled on her. I felt the same before I ran away from home, when the situation I was in seemed so terrifying and intractable that it sapped all my energy and left me feeling limp and helpless. I remember yearning for someone to make decisions for me, to guide and protect me and lead me to a new, safe life. As I sat isolated in my bedroom wishing the hours away and yet dreading what the morning might bring, I longed for something to end the waiting, and of course in time it did. For me it was a moment of carelessness: my sister, Lucy, forgot to lock the door keeping me in. For Yasmin it was her father's determination to prove her perfidy. He came to her bedroom and announced that after Friday prayers PC Ahmed would be coming to the house with evidence to prove that Yasmin had a black boyfriend: there would be a meeting, all would be revealed.

'I didn't know what that evidence would be, whether it was photographs, or the slip of paper I had signed at the station but I knew that if he had something that would be the end of it for me. The consequences would be so bad, I couldn't risk waiting until Friday to find out. I knew I had to get away.'

Chance was kind to Yasmin. The following day Madeeha called up the stairs to say she was driving round to their dad's shop to drop off his lunch before going to the bank. Moments later Yasmin heard the car start up and pull away: for the first time in a week she was alone in the house.

Why did Madeeha do that? Yasmin still wonders. Had she forgotten no one else was present? Was she tired of playing gaoler? Or was it a trick – a test to see if Yasmin would try to escape. 'I didn't have time to think about it. I didn't have time to think about the fact I had no money, no documents, that I was only sixteen. I just did what my instincts told me. I rang a taxi and I tried to pack some things.'

I could picture her, no longer creeping round the house trying to be invisible and inoffensive, but rushing, helter-skelter, blindly hauling clothes out of drawers and stuffing them into black bags, cursing as the bags split ('always buy the Value bags, Yasmin, do you think we're made of money? And anyway, why does rubbish need a bag so thick?') Instinct sent her to the living room, to the massive polished cabinet. The china figurines so proudly arranged on its shelves rattled as she yanked open the drawer that held the family photographs and pulled out a handful at random, stuffing them in with her clothes.

'But then the taxi was outside and I knew it was time and the panic rose up inside me and I left with nothing; I didn't take any of the stuff I packed. I ran out to the taxi and just as I was about to climb in I had this split second when I wondered if I ought to throw a brick through the window and leave the front door open so it would look like I'd been kidnapped. I thought that might make it easier for my dad and mum to bear.'

14

I remember that point in Yasmin's story so clearly. She had been carrying those details in her head for years, but I could tell the cataclysmic emotions she felt as she ran from the house that day were still very raw and real for her. There she was in the pub with me – fastidious as she placed her slender forearms on the table, careful to avoid the stickiest beer stains – but the best part of her was absent, reliving the moment when she crossed the Rubicon, the point from which, although she hadn't thought it through at that point, there would never be any return.

For me that moment – the split second in which I decided to run, a decision for which my parents never forgave me – took place more than twenty-five years ago, and the wilderness that followed it felt like a lifetime. Listening to Yasmin that afternoon I offered up a silent prayer of gratitude that I don't have to live through those years again because I don't think I'd make it; they were just so hard. Even now it hurts me to look back and I was looking back that afternoon because the mistakes Yasmin made – no, mistakes is too harsh, the things she was driven to do – were so like mine.

Had Yasmin not run away that day her relationship with Abdul would never have lasted, she's adamant about that. It was a flirtation – with forbidden fruit as much as with each other – neither of them wanted it to continue, from the very early days there were incidents of physical abuse. But in running to him, she changed their fate. She arrived at his flat asking him to pay her taxi fare, spilling out her terror: 'They're worrying that I'm not a virgin, they're going to kill me, how will they get me married if I'm not a virgin?' By using him as a refuge from her parents she tied herself to him and for the next four years there was no escape – for either of them.

There was no romance about it. Right from the start it was awkward and uncomfortable. Because the police knew Abdul's address they stayed with a friend of his, Hussein, all three of them crammed into his one-bedroom flat. It was Hussein who told Yasmin's parents where to find her; Yasmin assumes he was handsomely rewarded. They came for her fifteen days after she fled. 'I heard a knock on the door and when I went to open it there was my sister Tasleem and my mum.'

For the first few seconds Yasmin's relatives were rendered speechless by the state they found her in. Yasmin watched her mother's eyes scan the room, taking in abandoned coffee cups, half-eaten plates of food, over-flowing ash trays, crushed beer cans and, by the sofa where he had stepped out of them when he woke up one morning, a pair of Hussein's underpants. Her gaze settled momentarily on the television ('I was watching *Top of the Pops – Top of the Pops* which my father had always forbidden') then flicked to her daughter, her hair unbrushed, her body wasted in the two weeks since she'd seen her, her eyes swollen and red from crying.

Yasmin and her mother spoke simultaneously: 'Would you

like a cup of tea?' 'How can you live like this?' Then Tasleem stepped in, her voice shrill and commanding: 'Tea? Are you mad? Look at what you have done to our mother! Look at her crying now! How can you be so selfish? Is there no place in your thoughts for your family, your family who even now despite this—' a contemptuous sweep of the hand took in the filthy flat as well as Yasmin's wretched appearance, 'have not abandoned you. We have come to take you back.'

'I'm not coming.' Telling me this, Yasmin's face broke into a smile and she shook her head, still marvelling at her own audacity. 'I could hardly believe it when those words came out of my mouth, but that's what I said.' Straight away Tasleem got out her mobile and summoned her father. Yasmin stood by the window and watched him climb out of his white work van, parked just below. The older of her brothers, Anwar, was with him as were three of his employees: big, burly men whom she knew by sight. Her father turned to speak to them, clearly issuing instructions, before leaving them on the pavement as he turned towards the flat.

'He and Anwar walked in and he just said, "Right, we're going." I love my father, very much, and usually whatever he says I say fine, but this time I didn't, I said "No". But I couldn't look at him; *Top of the Pops* was on the television and I—' Yasmin's voice was very small and her eyes were on her lap, bright spots of colour flushed her cheeks. 'I was wearing the salwar kameez I left home in, which was see-through; you were meant to wear it with a petticoat so you couldn't see your bra or anything, but I was wearing it with nothing underneath.'

At that moment Abdul walked in, carrying a box of pizza. Again there was the frozen moment, the horrified silence as the disparate parties recognised each other, the initial shock and then the rush of heat as their bodies flooded with hate. Abdul spoke first – and whatever else he might have done I have to say I admire him for this. He asked Yasmin's family to leave. He told them that their daughter would not be going with them; she would be staying where she belonged, with him.

Yasmin's father might have been deaf for all the effect this had on him. Nothing about him suggested that he heard what had been said. He walked across to Yasmin and, standing right in front of her, spoke in Pushto, his voice low and threatening. His message was simple. 'Come with me or my employees will come inside now and beat up that man.'

I don't know how she found the strength but Yasmin still refused him. We've talked about it since and she says it was desperation: 'My dad's a Pathan, Jas. He knew for sure that there was no way I could still be a virgin. In Pakistan it's death by stoning if you have any sort of contact with a man.'

But her compliance proved unnecessary. Grabbing a thick hank of Yasmin's hair, her father swung her round in front of him and began to march her out of the flat. It felt, she said, as if she were performing in some strange avant-garde ballet. She was on tiptoe, trying to minimise the tearing on her scalp, tripping when she failed to find her feet; her father – rigid as an automaton – moved behind her and behind him, her mother and sister scuttled like frightened mice. Hussein's flat was part of a student block and Yasmin remembers doors opening, curious faces emerging, a small gawping crowd congregating as she stumbled down the stairs. Before she reached the bottom, Abdul told her later, he had dialled 999 and told the police she had been kidnapped by her family.

The police were already aware of Yasmin's situation. Her parents had reported her missing and when a police officer tracked her down, she explained why she had run away and made it clear that she had no intention of returning. This should have been on record. It should have been referred to when Abdul reported that she had been kidnapped by her family. If it was, why did the police make so little effort to rescue her? 'They claim they looked for me, but they can't have looked very hard.' Yasmin broke off from her narrative to tell me this, her voice rising with her indignation. 'All they had to do was tap my father's name into the computer, find out what properties he owns and search them. I've written to them asking to explain why they didn't do that, and I've also queried PC Ahmed's behaviour in talking to my dad, but I've heard nothing back.'

Her father took her to a relative's flat where plans were made for Madeeha to escort her to Pakistan as soon as possible. She was closely guarded – 'my sister even came and watched while I was in the toilet' – but it was not until the following morning, during which the police did search the family home, that Yasmin's father sent her to the police station. His instructions, accompanied by threats, were that she was to report herself safe and well, and regretting her silly mistake.

'Madeeha took me and we sat on hard plastic chairs and waited for what felt like hours in reception, but I was really happy. I was convinced that once I'd explained my situation everything was going to be sorted out and I could get on with my life. It never occurred to me that they would let Madeeha sit in on my interview.'

But sit in she did and with her sister beside her Yasmin had no choice but to say what was expected of her. The CID officer who conducted the interview read the statement back, his flat, expressionless voice unconsciously echoing the desolation Yasmin felt as she said the words:

> I have now returned home of my own free will, because I wish to continue living with my family and I regret any distress I caused them by running away. I regret having done so, it was all a mistake.

'Have we got that right then, Miss?' The officer looked up expectantly. He failed to notice Madeeha's elbow shoot backwards in a vicious nudge, but smiled when he saw Yasmin nod.

'Good, well if I could just get you to sign here.' He was pushing the pen and paper across the desk when the door burst open and a female police officer with an unruly mass of ginger hair burst into the room.

'Right. Stop. Interview terminated, I want to speak to Yasmin on her own,' she said, tweaking the statement off the desk and running her eyes rapidly down the page.

'You should have seen my sister's face! She knew straight away what was going to happen and she tried to stop it, she tried to insist we were doing an interview but this female officer wasn't having any of it. She finished reading my statement and then she asked me, "Do you want to go home?" and I said, "No of course I don't." So she said, "Well, we'd better start this interview again" and as she was sitting down, getting her pen and paper ready, she looked up at Madeeha and said, "There won't be any need for you to stay. You heard what she said: she's not coming back."'

That was the start of Yasmin's peripatetic life. She went from the police station to stay with a school friend, but when her brothers started haunting that area she felt she and her friend were no longer safe. Knowing nothing of refuges, she could think of no one to turn to except Abdul so she went back to him and together they moved into a filthy bed-sit shared by two other men. While they were there Abdul went out a great deal; Yasmin spent most of her time in bed. To see her now – vibrant, enthusiastic, greedy for life – it's hard to imagine her in such a state of apathy and yet I understand it. Those moments of triumph when she refused to go home with her parents had flickered and died leaving her nothing but virtual imprisonment with a man she didn't love.

Within weeks Abdul was in trouble with the police again and had to leave town and Yasmin, for want of a better solution, went with him. For two months they lived with his mum in west London but then she turfed them out because, she said, men – Pakistani men – had been watching her building and she feared they were Yasmin's relations. Back in her home town, back in the same foul bed-sit, Yasmin, like so many others in her situation, took an overdose of paracetamol. The passer-by who found her collapsed in the street was kind enough to call an ambulance.

At the hospital they heard her cry for help ('I told them everything, start to finish') patted her kindly on the head ('they kept me in for a couple of days for observation') and then they sent her on her way again. 'Before I left I was visited by this social worker who said, "Who's picking you up? Is it your partner?" She seemed to think that was all right, even though she knew he'd been abusive to me. The last thing she said was, "If you need anything, call me," and I thought, why would I call you? You've offered me nothing.'

How many frightened women have felt like that? Experience has shown me that Yasmin's experience is, sadly, very common here in Britian. Look at Heshu Yones, who turned to her teachers for help three times before she died, or the tragic, tormented Banaz Mahmod. In the weeks before she was murdered by her family, Banaz went to the police four times to tell them she was frightened for her life. She told them of the death threat she received, she even named those she thought might kill her. But it didn't save her life.

Two days after Banaz made her last visit to the police, her boyfriend reported her missing. Three months later – after what was described as a 'massively challenging' search – her body was found crammed into a suitcase and buried in the garden of a deserted house in Birmingham, more than one hundred miles from south London where she lived. The bootlace that had been used to garrotte her was still around her neck. The subsequent investigation revealed that her murder had been arranged by her father and her uncle and carried out by three men, two of whom fled abroad boasting as they went that they had raped Banaz before they killed her because they wanted 'to show disrespect'.

Why? That's always the first question in these terrible, tragic cases and the answer is always the same: because her family believed she had shamed them. First she had the audacity to walk out of her arranged marriage to a man who raped and routinely beat her and then, worse, she fell in love with a man who was neither part of her family's Kurdish clan nor conspicuously religious. For her father – whose honour had already been compromised by an older daughter, Bekhal, who ran away to escape his violence, whose position as head of the family had already been usurped by his younger brother because he failed to bring that daughter back – this was too much to bear.

But how could the police allow it to happen? Why didn't they stop it, those officers who had already been alerted to the danger Banaz faced? Despite the criticism that has come from so many voices – including mine – there has to be some sympathy for their handling of this case. When I discuss it at conferences now, I put it like this: 'Imagine you are manning the front desk at a police station and a pretty young woman comes in and says – as Banaz did on her first visit to the police – 'I've been seen kissing a boy outside the tube station and now my uncle's going to kill me'. Would you find that easy to believe?'

There is also the way that Banaz herself behaved. Like Kiren and like Shabana, she appeared to seek help from the police and then reject it. The first time she went to the police to report that her uncle was threatening to kill her, she asked them not to get involved and refused their offer of a refuge place. Reports said she thought her mother would protect her. When an officer called at the family house the following day, she would not let him in. When she subsequently went to the police to report threats made against herself and her boyfriend, Rahmat Suleimani, she again refused the offer of safe housing. It was not until that final visit, in which she reported that an attempt had been made to kidnap and kill Suleimani, that she agreed to bring charges against her family. That was the day before she disappeared. She had made her decision too late.

It is in that context 'I want help, no I don't' that we could, perhaps should, look at the way the police behaved on the night Banaz's father first tried to kill her; but even then certain of their actions are inexcusable. It was New Year's Eve and Banaz's father had summoned her to her grandmother's house in Wimbledon, supposedly to discuss her divorce. When her father plied her with brandy – the first alcohol she had ever tasted – she became suspicious. Banaz fled barefoot into the street, and smashed a window her bare hands in order to get out.

Her description of this ordeal was recorded by her boyfriend Rahmat Suleimani on his mobile phone: the grainy footage shows Banaz still trembling, stammering out her story from a hospital bed in which she begged nurses to hide her from her father. But that came later. Before she got to hospital she was seen by the police, who answered the 999 call made from the restaurant in which she sought refuge. The police arrived to find Banaz bleeding and distraught and, nevertheless, refused to believe her story. She was dismissed as a melodramatic and attention-seeking drunk.

Well. It *was* New Year's Eve – high point in the calendar for melodramatic drunks. And here – in multi-cultural, twenty-first century Britain – some Muslims do drink, so a sobbing Muslim girl smelling of alcohol might not have rung alarm bells. But that does not excuse the fact that the report of the incident did not include Banaz's allegations of attempted murder. Nor the fact that these allegations were not followed up. The police also approached Banaz's father, thus alerting him to the fact that she was seeking help.

I'm not sure anything can excuse that.

15

The number of calls to Karma Nirvana rocketed when Banaz's story hit the press. Women were scared that if they went to the police they would be turned away or ignored, as they perceived she was. To me that points yet again to the crying need to educate the people in the front line: teachers, health visitors, social workers, police officers like PC Angela Cornes. Honour-based culture proliferates in Britain and yet to those not brought up trapped inside its tangled web, its mores – the behaviours it disapproves of, the loyalties it insists on, the fear it engenders, the punishments it metes out – are incomprehensible, or simply unbelievable. For instance, what westerner would understand, let alone anticipate the fact that while she was in the hospital recovering from her overdose, Yasmin had been unnerved by the presence of an Asian doctor. 'I didn't trust him, I thought he must know my dad, I thought he was bound to be part of the network.'

It was this anxiety that finally drove her to move on. Again she went with Abdul, clinging to their destructive relationship because in her guilt and confusion she felt it was all she deserved.

With no idea of where they might go, no reason to go anywhere, they put a pin in a map and it landed on Bangor. 'I knew nothing about it; I didn't even know it was in Wales until I got here.' Yasmin smiled and I did too. She had been living in Bangor for five years by the time I met her and the Welsh lilt she's acquired makes it hard to imagine that she has ever lived anywhere else.

For the first eighteen months her relationship with Abdul continued to deteriorate. They moved into a council flat, and he became so violent that the police were regularly called out by neighbours. Yasmin could never bring herself to prosecute and so it went on until, after one particularly savage beating left her covered in cuts and bruises, a friend from the college where she was doing business studies finally rescued her. Lesley arrived at the flat, helped Yasmin to pack and took her home. She never saw Abdul again.

Yasmin was twenty then and she set about putting her life together; she took bar work to finance her studies and gradually began to relish her independence. But she still felt threatened by her family; even now she still does. It took them two years to track her down in Bangor.

'About seven months after I left Abdul, the postman came to the door with a registered letter. It was from my parents and it was all emotional blackmail, things like: 'Your brother is depressed because your mother is crying all the time; your father's business is suffering because he drives around looking for you; how are you going to manage your bills, you've never known the value of money.'

Yasmin is convinced that the police in her home town had passed on her address, taking it from her letters of complaint. She no longer felt safe. She moved in with Lesley where she stayed until, having taken a second bar job, she had saved the money to pay for a deposit on a flat. She began to feel settled, to buy a bit of furniture, to decorate a little; she was happy in her new home until the morning she went to open her glass-panelled front door and found her mother and Madeeha standing on the other side of it.

Yasmin called the police, shouting above the cacophony made by her mum leaning on the doorbell and Madeeha hammering on the door. When two officers arrived, the younger of them advised Yasmin to go outside and talk to her mum. He said he hated to see an old lady so distressed. 'She was doing the whole Asian thing, wailing really loudly and tearing at her hair and saying she was going to kill herself. It took me a while to persuade him that I was the one in danger and she was the one doing the persecuting.'

'What did it feel like when you saw her?' I asked Yasmin. It was one of the few times all afternoon that I interrupted her.

'At the time I was numb, there was so much going on in my head that I couldn't cope with any of it. I couldn't even cry. Mum looked so different, she'd aged a lot and that saddened me. It was years since I'd seen her, and I'd had all the pain of missing her but when she was stood there outside my door what I mainly felt was anger that, yet again, I was going to have to uproot myself and move on.'

After this incident a meeting was held at the local police station and plans were made to keep Yasmin safe; these should have included a proper risk assessment, the installation of a panic alarm and a regular checking system. 'A lot was planned but nothing actually happened,' Yasmin said.

'So I started all over again. I found another flat, moved in, got settled and after a few months Madeeha turned up in a pub where I was working. I wasn't there at the time, but a customer told Madeeha the name of the street I was living in. He didn't mean me any harm, he didn't know my story, but luckily for me there was a barmaid there who did.'

Alerted by her friend, Yasmin moved again immediately, back to Lesley's, back to square one. 'It's like this game of cat and mouse: I move, they find me, I move, they find me.' Yasmin paused and sighed. Her pale skin was ashen and there were dark circles under her eyes; her shoulders drooped. 'I'm twenty-two now, Jasvinder and I'm still paying rent. I'm earning decent money in the refuge, I could get a mortgage, buy a house and do it up, but what then? My parents are going to turn up and I'll have to move on again. When is it going to stop? Am I going to be running for the rest of my life?'

16

The summer holidays – those long weeks when a child has no business being anywhere but home – are dangerous for girls at risk of being forced into marriage because their parents know that outsiders, particularly teachers, won't notice the ones that go missing. It is always a very busy time for Karma Nirvana and for the Forced Marriage Unit because in the weeks leading up to the end of term the anxious girls start ringing. Last year I decided to pre-empt this.

During the summer term Shazia and I targeted those Derby secondary schools we knew to have a high percentage of ethnic minority children, focusing particularly on those from which we'd had referrals. We asked if they would display the poster that had been designed by the Forced Marriage Unit. It has a striking image on it of a male and a female hand chained together, but it's not inflammatory. It just says FORCED and YOU HAVE A RIGHT TO CHOOSE and apart from that all the writing on it is informative. Without even having seen it, every school refused us. They were all very apologetic as they explained that they thought it important not to offend cultural and religious sensibilities; they said they didn't want to upset the parents. Even Heather Jackson, deputy head of Fozia's old school, said her head teacher took this line and, try as she might, she had not been able to change her mind. Most head teachers weren't even open to discussion; they barely stayed on the line long enough to hear me argue that this is not about culture or religion, it's a matter of human rights and child protection.

What I find hard to understand is how head teachers can continue to deny that forced marriage is an issue when the evidence is there before them. A few years ago a local authority in Bradford decided to monitor the attendance of south Asian children throughout their school careers. They started with the names of 1,000 boys and 1,000 girls and found that, year on year, the numbers remained consistent until the girls began to turn fifteen. In the following two years 200 of the girls went missing; they dropped off the school rolls without explanation. 'Where Have All The Girls Gone?' was written all over the report describing this project. And nobody knows the answer.

I decided I couldn't accept the schools' decision and I made an appointment with the local council to discuss it. When the day came, the meeting began badly. One of the Asian men present waited for me to sit down and then cleared his throat and said, 'Before we begin, can I say something?' All eyes turned to him expectantly and he sat back in his chair, hands folded on his stomach.

'You do realise don't you, Miss Sanghera, that you are not well liked in this community?'

His remark was so personal – so rude – that for a moment I was dumbfounded. But I was determined to ignore the impulse to fight back and, as reasonably as I could, I stood up to him.

'I haven't come here to be liked. I have come to represent

the interests of a significant proportion of the community that it is the council's duty to safeguard.'

'Yes, I know that. And what is it you are expecting us to do exactly? Arrange for teams of people to go round our schools tapping every Asian child on the shoulder and asking them if they are at risk of being forced into marriage?' He looked to left and right, seeking approval for his cleverness but although no one would meet his eye, nobody objected.

I took a deep breath. 'No, I don't expect that. Just as I don't expect you to go round tapping every teenage pupil on the shoulder to ask if they smoke, or take drugs, or drink alcohol. But – and I say this as the mother of a teenage daughter at school in this city – I do expect her teachers to educate her about the dangers of smoking or of abusing drugs or alcohol, and I expect them to display material and literature pertaining to that, and to sign post agencies that could help if she felt she had problems. To my mind forced marriage should be dealt with in the same way: it's a problem kids might have to contend with and they ought to be told where to find help if they need it.'

But my arguments didn't seem to convince anybody. Just one councillor supported me but even his pleading – 'Why are we tiptoeing round this subject? All we're talking about is putting posters on display' – seemed to fall on deaf ears. After half an hour I left feeling I'd achieved nothing.

The only route that seemed left to me was to publicise the issue in our local paper, the *Derby Evening Telegraph*. It has been supportive of our work in the past and it was again, giving us a double-page spread in which Shazia and I were photographed holding the Forced Marriage Unit's poster between us. It appeared just before the end of term and by 10 a.m. on the day that it was published Shazia had taken the first call from someone who had seen it.

John Stone is a child protection officer and he was ringing to talk to us about a sixteen-year-old girl from a college in the Birmingham region. This girl, let's call her Tarvinder Kaur, had approached the college counsellor some months before complaining that her Sikh parents were too controlling: they wouldn't let her have a mobile phone, she wasn't allowed out at weekends, she couldn't cut her hair and so on. As John Stone described them, Tarvinder's problems had been just like those of so many other Asian girls until – just the week before – her mother discovered that she had a Muslim boyfriend. I could imagine the uproar.

Tarvinder was convinced that, with the summer holidays beginning, her parents would seize the opportunity to take her to India and force her into marriage. 'I'm a bit out of my depth with this one, and I'd be really grateful for some back-up from someone who knows more about these things than I do,' John said to Shazia. 'Would you have any time today to come to college and speak to her. She's quite upset and, because it's the last day of term, I'd like to think that we can sort her out before she disappears for the holiday.'

Shazia was there as soon as she could be. She told me later she was so glad she'd gone because there was Tarvinder – looking no more than twelve years old and terribly vulnerable – in a state of confusion. She was crying and she kept repeating herself, saying over and over again. 'I must decide what to do. Once term is over I will be trapped at home, I'll be trapped, no one will help me. If my parents take me abroad no one will even know about it. No one will know where I am, no one will help me.'

I've often watched Shazia supporting distraught girls like Tarvinder: she's calm, unhurried, so full of warmth and empathy. I could imagine her sitting beside the poor girl, gently outlining all the options open to her, never rushing her decision. Apparently she was clear from the outset that she wanted to leave home – she was frightened not just for herself but for her boyfriend to whom her parents had been sending threatening messages – but she couldn't envisage an alternative. She had imagined herself alone and hungry, sleeping on park benches. 'Once I'd convinced her that wasn't going to happen, she made up her mind to leave quite quickly,' Shazia told me.

It was a situation in which everyone had to act fast. John Stone arranged for a policeman we know to escort Tarvinder to her home to collect her possessions. As luck would have it there was no one there and she was able to come and go without an ugly scene. Shazia went back to Karma Nirvana to begin the trawl for refuge provision. There are some days when the first refuge you ring has a free bed, but that doesn't happen very often. Shazia rang seventy refuges before she eventually found one that could take Tarvinder. By 8 p.m, with a bed secured, word came through that Tarvinder's mum was watching for her at the station. Clearly it was too risky for her to travel by train, but it took Shazia another hour to persuade the police to drive her up to the refuge.

'I don't want to see Mum, I don't want to talk to her, I don't want any contact. Please don't tell her where I am.' Those were the last words Tarvinder said to Shazia before she climbed into the police car. Shazia promised to respect her wishes.

The next morning the office answering machine held two or three messages from Tarvinder's mother. The first one was tentative: 'This is Kamal Kaur, Tarvinder's mother. Please could you let me know if you have information of my daughter, I am concerned about her.' The second, less so: 'Please ring back, I know she is with you.' When Shazia failed to respond, Kamal enlisted the police who rang to ask if we would mediate between mother and daughter. Then inevitably, Kamal turned up in reception and rang Karma Nirvana on the internal phone. This time I spoke to her. I said,'If your daughter asks if you have been in contact I will tell her the truth, and I will give her the information you want passed on but until she asks I will not be telling her anything about you.'

Kamal began to wail. 'But I am her mother, we are a very tight family. How will I hold my head up? What am I going to tell my sisters-in-law, we're very close.'

'Well, if you are so close I am sure they will be full of sympathy and ready to support you,' I said, but she was having none of that. She started talking about her health and how this would affect it; she grew louder and more argumentative until eventually, with a firm apology, I called a halt.

Over the next two days she rang sporadically and then, on the date we knew to be Tarvinder's birthday, a letter arrived for us to pass on to her. Like all such missives it was full of emotional blackmail. Her mother wrote that since Tarvinder left, her little sister had repeatedly searched the house for her, and her grandmother had completely stopped eating. It pointed to all the good things her parents had done for her: driving lessons, gold jewellery, trips. It reminded her that her grandfather was ill and said he was now making himself sick with worry.

Next time Kamal rang she was aggressive. 'I know all about you, Shazia. I've researched you and Jasvinder, I know exactly what you do and let me tell you, I will go – *we* will go – to any lengths to get our daughter back.'

But then she went quiet. Shazia remained in touch with Tarvinder who she felt was shell-shocked but coping well. She was still adamant that she wanted no contact with her family. We began to relax about her until, one Friday morning as I was standing on Derby station waiting for a train to London, I got a call.

It was Shazia and I could tell at once that something was seriously wrong. 'It's Tarvinder,' she said. 'Her mum's kidnapped her last night and brought her home. The police just rang us; they're bringing Tarvinder back here now.'

I looked at my watch: my train was due in three minutes. I was travelling to a committee meeting called to provide recommendations to be passed to the IPCC independent investigation into police conduct surrounding the death of poor Banaz Mahmod. It had been arranged at my instigation and I was keen to go to it, but I've always maintained that the root of my work is supporting women and I stick to that. I rang one of the investigation organisers and quickly explained my situation. If, I said, I get my thoughts on this typed up and sent to you in time for the meeting, could you make sure they get read out. He agreed and so, having made a second call to make my apologies to the IPCC commissioner Nicola Williams, I headed for Karma Nirvana where I typed up my suggestions and then called the police in Tarvinder's home town.

It seems that the previous night, coming out of the Odeon cinema with a friend, Tarvinder saw her mum standing in the foyer. She made a run for it, but out in the car park she hurtled straight into the arms of her cousin. 'There were about eight people there and all together they were too strong for me. They were slapping me and punching me and they pushed me into the car. I was screaming for help, but nobody came.'

In the early hours of the morning, Tarvinder was forced to call the police and say that she was safe and well, that running away had been a mistake, and that she had returned home of her own free will. Luckily the PC who took the call had already read the Karma Nirvana brief about Tarvinder. He understood the situation and had the presence of mind to react immediately. 'It was about four in the morning when he tracked me to the house where my grandma lives. That's where they'd taken me. I think my mum thought the police might come looking for me because she told me that if they did come to the door I was to say I was happy to be home. I didn't think that I'd be brave enough to go against her on that, but when I saw the police standing in the doorway I was brave; I told the truth.'

Tarvinder was removed from the house there and then and we had her safely back in refuge provision later that same day. We're still in touch with her and she is doing well. Her mother and her cousin were arrested, charged with kidnap and put on remand awaiting trial. Shazia spent three hours giving evidence to the police. Both she and I were frightened of reprisals from her family, but so far they have left us alone.

When the time came Kamal, her mother, and her cousin pleaded guilty to kidnap but you wouldn't guess that from the sentences they received. Both were given a one year suspended sentence. Kamal was also given a one year supervision order. To my mind these sentences are so light that they all but got away with it. The presiding judge justified them by saying he felt the kidnap was well intentioned, even though the kidnappers were guilty of poor judgement in carrying it out.

Why did he think that? A statement was read out in court in which Tarvinder said she was terrified of being forced into marriage. Why would she make that up? On the day the sentences were announced I was sharing a platform with the solicitor general, Vera Baird, and I was able to tell her how very disappointed I was. I told her I firmly believe that until the establishment faces up to the reality of these issues, we will never make progress. Refusing to acknowledge the seriousness of crimes such as kidnap just because they take place within a family all but condones the actions of people like Kamal Kaur. It sanitises what they do and allows them to cling to their skewed, self-serving view of honour.

Nicola Williams sent me the minutes of the meeting I missed on the day after Tarvinder's kidnap. It was held in consultation with community and honour-based violence support organisations, and among the people there were Hannana Siddiqui of Southall Black Sisters and Diana Nammi of the Kurdish and Iranian Women's Rights Organisation. I was glad to see the notes I'd sent in recorded in the minutes: one of my key suggestions was a re-think of the Witness Protection Programme so it could benefit young women like Kiren and Shabana who need protection but do not wish to prosecute their families. Apart from allowing these young women to be included in it, the programme needs to be adapted to suit their needs; in particular change is needed to the requirement that – once accepted into the programme – they should sever contact with everyone in their previous lives. They have already lived through months if not years of isolation and trauma and to expect them to be able to start a new life without the support of anyone familiar is unrealistic as well as unreasonable.

I found the notes on the general discussion that took place that day made for depressing reading. On one hand they spoke so clearly of the frustration that we in the voluntary sector feel at what we perceive to be police failure to properly engage in these issues; on the other they showed the fear – and occasional resentment – of the police, who feel they are being criticised for not handling these very complex problems right. I read to the end and then, for a moment or two, I sat there feeling futile. My feeling is that the two sides are often at loggerheads with one another when actually what both sides want is to engage in constructive debate. It's the only way we will move forward.

A few weeks after this IPCC meeting Shazia received an email from a young woman living in a refuge in Scotland. She had fled a forced marriage and the most appalling abuse meted out by her mother, but since she ran away she had, like Yasmin, been traced repeatedly by her family. She was writing from her seventh new address:

> *I have been to the Police Station in Glasgow. I explained everything to the officer and got told if I don't feel safe to get a bed and breakfast and go homeless again. How this is resolving my problem I have no idea. I was crying and very scared and asked him for his help. He told me I had wasted his time and told me to get out and stop thinking about things that haven't happened yet. He also said when your parents found you in your refuge they could have been stopping by just to say hello.*

As I write it is almost a month since we've had contact with this woman. I've rung, I've emailed and so has Shazia. We can't find her. I hope she's still alive.

17

As soon as I started the research for my PhD proposal, I knew that this work was what I wanted to do. Very few of the books I found in the library contained anything relevant; there was quite a lot of feminist material which touched on the subject, but I found it either strident or dry and nothing came close to examining why survivors survive. I began interviewing disowned women – there was a steady stream of them approaching Karma Nirvana – and looking for trends in their behaviour, common patterns and reactions. I became so absorbed in the research that I found myself at odd moments jotting down my thoughts and observances. I've always been in the habit of keeping diaries and now I put that habit to good use. I was enjoying myself, but I still didn't believe I had the ability to work what I discovered into anything approaching a PhD. 'I don't understand statistics or quantative analysis, I don't even know what that means. And the language – I've looked at other people's work and I just can't write like that,' I wailed to Gordon.

'But you've got the knowledge, Jasvinder. That's the important thing,' he said. 'I'm sure your proposal will prove me right.'

Presenting it was terrifying. There was an open invitation to other PhD students to come and listen and various lecturers also attended: there must have been more than thirty people in the room. Despite trying so hard to fit my research in between Karma Nirvana, my family and my speaking engagements I still felt I was under prepared; I hadn't done enough reading and I'd put the proposal together in a hurry. I knew that and so did Gordon but he went on believing in me, bless him.

I remember standing at the front of the small lecture theatre waiting to start when, quite unbidden, my mind slipped back to Bradford where I lived twenty years ago. Twenty years: it feels like a lifetime. I was married then, to Lisa's dad, and he and I were working the markets. We had stalls in Leeds and Bradford and we sold watches which we bought in box-loads for twenty-five pence each and sold for what seemed to me an outrageous mark-up. I can remember my sales patter to this day: 'Time-date-stop-watch-digital-display-fully-luminous-all-for-a-knock-down-price-of-one-pound-fifty. What about you Sir? Don't hesitate, they've been selling like hotcakes this morning and I've only three left.' On a good day we could sell one hundred.

'Sell, sell: all you have to do today is sell this idea.' I kept repeating those words to myself like a mantra as the stragglers came in and got themselves settled. I knew I could talk about my subject for as long as anyone would listen, but I dreaded the questions that would follow my presentation. I knew some of the other PhD students from the canteen and the library and as far as I could see they were all younger than me and better educated. They also had the luxury of focusing on their studies for five days each week. They could show me up so easily.

The first question threatened to do just that. It came from a young woman with straight fair hair, pale features and a crocheted waistcoat. 'How do you intend to analyse your data?' she said.

I swallowed hard. 'As discussed with my supervisor, my approach will be very much narrative.'

She gave a sharp, little nod which meant, I hoped, that she was satisfied.

'You're so close to the subject, do you really think you can be objective about it?' This came from a man with John Lennon spectacles.

'I do have a lot of experience in this area, you are right. But there is still an enormous amount I don't know and haven't yet considered. I intend to create a bit of distance between myself and the subject by having someone to interview me.' I knew I was waffling but he didn't question me any further.

Reprieve came in the form of an older man who introduced himself briefly by saying he had done a lot of research into child abuse. 'The similarities between these two fields are striking, and I think with what you suggest you could make a huge contribution to knowledge and understanding in your chosen area. I wish you luck with it.'

A few days later I was given the go-ahead. I was so delighted to have been accepted that I brushed aside the practicalities of finding time to do the work. 'I'll make it happen,' I told myself and in fact, once I embarked on my PhD, I believed I could. I was given an office, a neat little box as plain as a blank sheet of paper. I carved out slivers of time that I could spend there: early in the morning, between meetings, or occasionally, when the kids had extra activities, on the way home. I began to see the university as a retreat, an oasis of calm where telephones didn't ring and nobody wanted my advice or my opinion or for me to sit with them offering comfort. Sometimes when I arrived I would sit down, rest my cheek on the cool, smooth surface of my desk, shut my eyes and breathe in the silence. Peace. I saw the couple of hours a week that I managed to spend there as time in which I could work without interruption. It was time for me, private time when – just for a while – I could forget about all the advocating I was doing, forget about the world outside, and focus on my research. I was spending so much time speaking on public platforms that I really appreciated the opportunity to be just another anonymous student burying herself in books.

It never occurred to me, ever, that the university was a place where I'd feel threatened so when it happened – on just an ordinary day – I was totally unprepared. I was hurrying along a corridor when I heard a voice behind me. I turned and saw one of the lecturers, a woman I scarcely knew.

'Jasvinder, I've got to talk to you. Can you spare a minute?' She sounded very agitated and her face was creased with concern as she gripped my arm. I couldn't think what she wanted: was my work not up to date?

'I've got to talk to you,' she said again after she'd bustled me into her office and locked the door. She leant against it for a second, then darted over to the window and tweaked the blinds shut a little. 'We need to talk about risk, Jasvinder. Are you aware of the precautions you should take?'

I answered without thinking: 'Yes, I—'

'Because I hear that some people are not happy with what you're doing. Some people don't like it at all.'

That stopped me in my tracks. I stood there staring at her.

I know she was trying to be helpful, but I felt as though I'd been slapped.

'I hear these things when I'm out in the community. Only last week I was at a Sikh women's group.' She picked up a big red Filofax from her desk. 'It was so shocking I wrote it down,' she said, leafing through until she found the place she wanted. Reading straight from the page she carried on: 'Jasvinder must be silenced. If she appears on *Panorama* she will be killed, we will kill her. She knows our tradition of honour killings.' She stopped and looked straight at me, anxiety pooling in her eyes. 'You do know that women are capable of murdering women?'

My heart was pounding and my hands were damp with sweat but my brain wouldn't process the shock. I was clinging to normality rather than face the fear that was building inside me.

'There's nothing to stop them saying what they feel. I'm happy to meet them to have a dialogue,' I stammered, as if this might be another date in the diary, another chance to spread the word.

'Have you been taught how to look under your car?' she asked, looking very serious.

'What for?' Even as the words left my mouth I realised. A hundred television images kaleidoscoped inside my brain. The sudden explosion. Burning wreckage. Panic-stricken people. Running. Screaming. Broken, bleeding bodies. A shoe, empty and forgotten. I wanted to recoil from her terrible warnings but I also wanted comfort, someone to protect me and for one insane moment I imagined myself crawling into her arms. But I didn't. I forced myself to stand there and listen until I was sure she had nothing more to tell me, no other information that I could use as a shield against harm. Then I said, 'I must tell the police. They'll need to know who these people are.'

'I wasn't able to get their names.'

'Why not? You were there. You must know who they are. You've just told me they're threatening to kill me. . .'

'I'm sorry, Jasvinder. Tell the police to contact me and I'll try to help.' She bent over her desk and scribbled something on a Post-it note. 'Here's my mobile number.'

I took the note and whispered my thanks.

I wanted to get out of her office and far, far away, to put distance between me and those terrible warnings. The passages I've always been so proud to walk felt like suffocating tunnels. I hurried down them, fumbling in my bag for my mobile phone, fighting the temptation to turn and check behind me. Her words seemed to be spinning round me: 'aggrieved', 'precautions', 'murder', 'car', 'check', check' 'check'.

As I stumbled through the double doors I pressed my friend Trish's number on my mobile and stood there in the sunshine, shaking.

Trish says she'll never forget the fear she heard in my voice when she answered the phone: 'It was really raw emotion, Jas, almost like a wild animal.'

It's not like me to cry in a public place, but I was verging on the hysterical; I was trembling so much that at one point my mobile fell out of my hand. Standing there in the middle of her office, Trish did her best to calm me down and then, once I'd stopped crying, she agreed to meet me as soon as she finished work. That meant two hours to wait and as the minutes crawled by I couldn't relax for a second. I checked the back seat of my car before I climbed into the front; I looked over my shoulder as I walked down the pavement, I hurried past corners. By the time I met Trish I felt so tense I thought my nerves would snap.

'Why am I working in this field? I think it's time to stop,' was the first thing I said to her.

I'd never felt like that before. I believe so strongly in the work I do, Karma Nirvana is such an important part of me that giving it up would be almost like abandoning one of my own children. And Trish knows that. She thought for a bit, then she gave a big sigh, stubbed out her cigarette and said, 'You should only stop because you want to. Don't be bullied into it.'

She brought me back from the edge that afternoon. She talked me back into composure then came with me when we left the café and went to report the whole incident to the police. Going through it, making a record of exactly what was said, got me upset again. 'A Sikh women's group was it?' said the police officer. 'Can you be more specific?' And of course I couldn't. I felt my skin creep and a pulse in my temple started ticking. There are Sikh women's groups everywhere in the East Midlands: was anywhere safe?

When I left the police station I still felt scared and I'm not used to that. Discussing threats and assessing risk is part of my life now and usually, when I've reported an incident I feel reassured. The officers have this solid, sensible way of reminding me of all the safety measures that we're taking: 'You've got your blue box, you've got your panic button . . .' A soothing litany that ends with: 'All right then, Jasvinder? Don't worry, we've got you in our sights.'

But this time they got the ending wrong. This time the officer, with a frown creasing her forehead, said, 'Okay. I've got all the details. As soon as possible we'll be in touch.'

Two days later I went to a conference in London with Trish; the police had advised me not to travel alone. We arrived back in Derby at about 5 p.m. and we were heading for the station car park when I saw two detectives from our local police station walking towards me. My heart missed a beat; my mind flashed to the children, running quick as a Rolodex through their daily routines. I quickened my pace but as we got closer I could tell by their easy gait that as far as the policemen were concerned, this was business not bad news. 'If you could spare us ten minutes or so, we'd like to show you how to check for devices under your car,' said one of them as they approached.

I stopped dead; I didn't trust myself to speak. In the past couple of days I had made a conscious effort to shelve the dire words I'd heard up at the university, to put them aside so I could get on with the everyday business of life. Now they came back to me, lead weights smashing through my fragile peace of mind.

> Jasvinder must be silenced. She knows our tradition of honour killings.

I stood, rooted to the spot.

'It's nothing to worry about, Jasvinder, just a routine precaution. Do you remember we mentioned it the other day?' One of the detectives touched my arm, urged me forward as they fell into step on either side of us. Trish and I lengthened our stride to keep up with them as we marched down the line of cars to mine. My heart was pounding and I felt light-headed. There I was on a summer evening, the air still heavy from the heat of the day. Over my shoulder Derby's rush hour traffic was roaring past and I should have been part of it but instead I was standing beside my car with Trish at my shoulder watching a man show me how to check my car for bombs. I felt strangely detached, as though I was watching myself through the wrong end of a telescope. Surely this couldn't be real.

We stood in a huddle as one of the officers unpacked the device. It was a long stick with a mirror attached to one end of it. He flourished it in front of us before beginning his demonstration – like a conjuror showing off a new wand I thought, and then felt ashamed that at a time like this my mind could be so frivolous. 'Pass it under the car like this,' his arm went backwards and forwards one way, 'and then like this', he changed direction. 'If you hold it at this angle you will always be able to see . . .'

'Excuse me, but what sort of thing would she be looking for, how would she recognise the . . . um . . .' Trish faltered for a second, having momentarily lost the carefully neutral, sanitised word that was meant to protect us from the fact that we were looking for something that could blow me and my children into bits.

'The device?' interjected the stick wielder. 'We would usually expect it to look something like an ice-cream carton. We would expect to find it around here on the car's chassis.' He stopped his sweeping movement and wiggled the mirror in one particular place. 'Now, Jasvinder, it's important that you do this every morning . . .'

'Every morning?' Suddenly I dropped the telescope and was fully present in the scene. 'You expect me to do that every morning! What do I say to the children? "Don't get into the car Maria, hold on Joshua. I've just got to check the car for bombs. Don't worry darlings, it doesn't take long. We won't be late." '

Anger replaced fear and my voice was trembling with it. I felt the prickle of heat on my back as my body was flooded with white hot rage. I was angry not with the hapless policemen – I know them well and they were only doing their jobs. My rage was for the nameless, faceless people – craven cowards who wouldn't even criticise me openly – who had put us all in this ludicrous position. I could feel all the emotion of the last two days boiling inside me and I was about to give in to it, when Trish suddenly leant in towards me. I felt the warm solid bulk of her press against my shoulder and in an instant I changed my mind. I didn't want to embarrass myself there in the car park, ranting at my anonymous enemy as the weary commuters trudged past, and the policemen – tired men who probably wanted nothing more than to get home to their tea – acted as blotting paper for my anger. I took a deep breath, and thanked the policeman as he handed me the stick which I put in the boot of my car. It sits there to this day.

The following Saturday Trish came over and we sat and talked for hours about whether I, as the mother of three children, had the right to put myself at risk. How great was the danger? Did they pick up on the fear I sometimes felt? What about their feelings? Were they frightened? Was I being selfish? Irresponsible? Did I owe them my entire life? What would happen to Karma Nirvana if I deserted it? Did those poor disowned women who approach it not deserve help?

Round and round the questions went, sharp and insistent as a swarm of angry bees until well after midnight when, with the dregs of our coffee gone cold and the frantic buzzing in my mind slowing to a dull throb, I was left with just two certainties. There have been times when the children would like me not to do the work I do; I know that and it tugs at my heart and stings my conscience. But I also know that, apart from my children, that work is my reason for being alive. I'm not sure I'll ever be able to give it up.

18

The debate didn't end there. The thoughts it provoked stayed with me, forcing me to examine the work I have chosen to do and the hold it has on my life. The arguments I'd put forward to Trish and to myself echoed through my mind, distracting me when I was working late, or trying to read as I travelled by train to a weekend conference. Because as the days and weeks rolled on with me feeling that I was forever running just to keep standing in the same place, I realised it wasn't just about risk and danger, it was also about guilt, about having to put my kids in breakfast club, or saying goodnight to them by telephone twice too often in a week. Like any working mother, there were times when I felt a jagged tear between the different elements in my life.

There was no easy answer, every working mother knows that, but then within the month I came across a girl – let's call her Lamika – whose case convinced me that I had to keep going, that I couldn't give up because if I turned my back on such cruelty and injustice I would never sleep easy in my bed.

Lamika was very young, just thirteen. She and her father

had been arrested on suspicion of murdering a 21-year-old man who was known to be her boyfriend. He died of head injuries believed to have been caused by a baseball bat. Her teenage brother and her mother had been arrested over allegations that they conspired to pervert the course of justice and Lamika was being questioned about perverting the course of justice too.

Her case notes had been sent to me; the police handling the enquiry had asked me to advise on whether Lamika might now be at risk from her own family, whether I thought they might resort to honour-based violence, or even murder.

I read through all the notes, which were extensive, and my blood ran cold thinking of that girl – a child, the same age as my Maria. I would say that any Muslim girl having a boyfriend might be at risk from her family, let alone if she was only thirteen and he was twenty-one. The murder and the arrests were widely reported in the press and one newspaper quoted 'a family friend' as saying, 'You can imagine how upset the girl's mother and father were to know that their daughter was seeing a man of twenty-one. Although the relationship was in its very early stages, they wanted it to stop as soon as possible.' Theirs was a very public shame and at the very least I thought Lamika was likely to be bustled back to the homeland and married off to anyone who would take her.

Why was she being suspected of murder anyway; that's what I would like to have asked. There have been cases enough in which the younger members of an Asian family are made to take the rap for crimes committed by their elders on the assumption – probably correct – that their punishment will be less harsh.

In giving my opinion I was very clear. I said I thought Lamika was at grave risk of forced marriage or honour-based murder, and I also said that while she remained in the family home all the words that came out of her mouth would have been put into it by her parents. While they still had their hold on her, I said, it would be impossible to reach the truth. I said I thought she should be put into care, preferably with a non-Asian family and I hoped by that simple measure we might manage to protect Lamika.

When he had read my notes, the police officer who sent me the case notes said he would get her social worker to ring me so we could do a proper risk assessment, I never heard another word. Sadly that is a typical social services response, and it sometimes makes me despair of ever seeing any real change. For nights I was haunted by thoughts of that child, creeping fearfully through each day, lying sleepless in her bed at night, tormented by her past, afraid of her future and with no one to turn to for help.

On the day the incident occurred, Lamika's family made several 999 calls in which they voiced their concerns about her boyfriend, but the police failed to respond promptly, arriving at the scene only when the young man was already on the brink of death. Had they acted more quickly his life might not have been lost, nor Lamika's ruined.

So often it's the speed of response that's crucial; the minutes, seconds even, that make a difference between life and death. Detective Superintendent Tony Hutchinson from Cleveland police force appreciates this more than most. He believes, particularly in cases of honour-based violence, that timing is all and when I met him he was hatching a plan which acknowledged that.

I liked Tony immediately: he's a big, burly man with a bald

head and the kindest face you've ever seen. Having spent the last twenty-five years in Cleveland's criminal investigation department, he was now head of its murder team and he's got the reassuring presence of someone who has been around a long time but – and this is what I admire about him – he's still not afraid to admit what he doesn't know.

He knew nothing about honour-based violence and forced marriage until he went to a conference on the subject in London where, among the speakers, he heard Anna who was representing us that day. (She and I look back and laugh at that now: I was speaking elsewhere and I asked Anna to stand in for me. I told her it was just a workshop for twenty or so policemen – had I told her the truth, that it was a conference for two hundred plus people, she would never have turned up!) She did well. Tony told me that she left a big impression on him: 'All the way home on the train I was asking myself whether these issues were present in Cleveland and my mind kept turning back to the houses I'd attended where Asian females had set fire to themselves in what I'd always seen as suicide. I was sat there thinking: I joined the force twenty-nine years ago to protect the weak and vulnerable but am I doing it? Or am I lying warm in my bed at night while there are people on my patch trapped in forced marriages or worse still, living in abject fear for their lives?'

After a bit of consultation with his colleagues, he organised his own seminar to raise awareness of these issues. I was invited to attend as a speaker. 'The easy option would be for us to ignore what's going on with these women, but the easy option is not always the right option,' he told me that day. 'It strikes me that where we – and by we, I mean society at large – stand on forced marriage today is where we were on domestic violence in the nineteen-seventies: "It happens to other people, it's unfortunate, but what can you do?" It took a massive government campaign, funding and tireless work on the part of voluntary organisations to change that attitude and – in my view – that's what we need to see again.'

Tony's idea – like Karma Nirvana when it first started out – was small scale and very practical. He wanted to introduce a twenty-four-hour free phone number, manned by up to twenty volunteers, which would be dedicated to callers ringing about forced marriage or honour-based violence. 'As I see it, Jasvinder, what these girls don't have is the time to go through the whole "Fire, Police or Ambulance" procedure,' he said. 'They may only have been left unattended for a couple of moments so they've got to make their cry for help before whoever is guarding them comes back. If you would help us with the training, our volunteers would understand the issues involved and be able to signpost them to the agencies they need – agencies like the Forced Marriage Unit and your Karma Nirvana. I thought, if you wouldn't mind, I'd start by coming to observe the work that you lot do.'

He saw his phone line as a local project, and that is what he sought funding for. 'It's a starting point; maybe in time other forces will adopt or refine it. We'll have to wait and see,' he said. It could be that nobody calls it, but my view is that if just one person does it will have been a success.'

19

I had to fight hard to keep Fozia's place in the house provided by English Churches Housing because as far as the charity was concerned, she was abusing it. In the weeks she had been back in Derby she had managed to inch her way back into some sort of favour with her sister Raveeda, and she started going to stay with her. 'I just went over to visit, Jas, and then – I don't know – it got late so I ended up stopping the night. It was so nice to see my nephew.' I had to explain that she was taking accommodation intended for a homeless person and she did understand, but she was struggling: she was trying to live like an independent woman but in truth she was a child – a child who was missing her mum. She was still craving any small attention from her family and she refused to accept that the love she gets from her sister is conditional and manipulative. It seemed harsh to disillusion her, but why else would Raveeda ring Fozia from Alton Towers to say, 'We're all here, Dad's treating us. If only you'd do what he says, you could be here too.'

Her situation really struck me one day when, by chance, I

got an outsider's view of it. I met her old school friend, Kuljit, in the road outside our office: 'I'm working not far from here, in Superdrug,' she said. I hadn't seen her since our initial meeting in Heather Jackson's office, but she and Rashpal had both kept in touch for a month or two. Rashpal talked of running away from home but as far as I know she never made up her mind to it; she stopped calling and I have heard nothing since. Kuljit did run away from home. Like Fozia she went through a boomerang period of leaving and going home again but then, quite suddenly, she seemed to have a change of heart. She told me in one hurried phone call that she wouldn't be ringing any more; she had decided to follow her parents' wishes: 'I think they know what's best for me, Jas,' she said.

'So how are you, Kuljit?' I asked, noticing her pallor, her shapeless black clothes. And she told me at once that since she left school she had been biding her time, waiting for the marriage that her parents were, even then, striving to arrange. 'And is that what you want?' I said gently, hoping that in this brief moment, this chance encounter on the pavement, I could somehow give her the confidence to drop the barrier that honour imposed on her and tell me what she really felt.

She didn't hesitate, she was speaking from her heart when she said, 'I'd rather that than the alternative, Jas. I mean, look at Fozia. I see her in the street, coming to your office or going home at night. She may be okay when she's with you but what about the rest of the time? She's got no money, no proper home. She's always alone, her parents won't have anything to do with her. I don't blame them – they made sacrifices for her and how does she repay them – by running away. You know what people say, Jas? They say that Fozia is an ungrateful slag.'

Her harsh words didn't really surprise me, although I found it painful hearing them applied to Fozia. I had already interviewed several women for my PhD who – after contacting Karma Nirvana – had made the decision not to leave home and their views about those who had made the break from their parents were, without exception, very like Kuljit's. 'They should have respect for their family and not be so selfish.' 'They left home because they want to sleep around.' 'They disgust me, trying to be like white women.' And always, of course, the one that gives the clue to their bitterness: 'We've made the sacrifice, why can't they?'

Kuljit's words made me feel so protective towards Fozia that I tried harder than ever to guide her life into some sort of structure. I told her that she ought to have a timetable including courses in English, Maths and basic listening skills and then we could fit her into our rota of volunteers. But she didn't have the motivation. She kept going into education and dropping out again. It was all a question of confidence; she felt safe with me and the other people at Karma Nirvana and she was focusing on us as her reason for getting on and living. I knew it wasn't healthy, but I found it hard to persuade her to change.

I've always known she has the guts to survive: out of all of us, she is the only one who insisted on staying in the same city as her family, which is a huge insult to them, but a testament to her courage. But there have been times when she seemed so vulnerable. I've learnt to read the signals when she wants to disclose something but doesn't know how to go about it: she stands in front of your desk, twiddling the ends of her scarf, picking things up and putting them back down again, starting conversations that never really lead anywhere.

'Jas?'

'Mmm?'

'Jas, what would you do if you knew someone needed an operation and they couldn't have it on the National Health, so they had to go privately, but they didn't have any money, and they'd asked you to help them?' Her voice was faraway and dreamy and she was spinning on her heels as though this was just some idle thought that didn't really matter.

'What would I do?' My eyes flicked back to my computer screen, half my mind still on the email I was writing. 'Well, I'd start off by asking why the National Health couldn't help them.'

'Well, the National Health waiting lists are very long, and what if this person was going to die soon if they didn't . . .'

Suddenly, she had my full attention. I said, 'Fozia, why are you telling me this?'

She looked sheepish but I think she was relieved to come right out with it.

'The woman, she's my sister's friend. I met her when I was visiting my sister in Leicester, and I've been supporting her, she needs five thousand pounds.' Fozia dropped her gaze and her voice went very small: 'I've already taken out a loan and lent her some of it.'

'Fozia!' I was so shocked I didn't stop to ask what shark or charlatan had lent her the money.

'But Jas, she's got little children and she's going to die. Look, if you don't believe me, we can ask her.'

She scuttled round the edge of her desk and logged herself on to MSN. Moving across to join her, I said, 'Right, start by asking her when the operation is.'

Fozia typed in the question and moments later we got an answer back.

Very soon. As soon as I can raise another £1000.

I said, 'Ask her the name of the hospital and the consultant.' Fozia did and the answer came back with a flash of irritation.

Why are you asking me all these questions, Fozia? What's the matter, don't you believe me?

I couldn't suppress a smile, it had been so easy to flush her out, but Fozia didn't get it. The face she turned to me was stricken.

'Oh no, look what I've done. I've upset her.'

'Don't worry,' I said. 'Move up, I'll take over now.' My fingers danced across the keys.

I just wondered what your consultant is called, that's all. Nothing's the matter.

Dr Woolacott.

The speed with which she invented that name impressed me.

Which hospital is the operation being done in?

Look I don't need this, Fozia.

I could visualise the anger on her face as her fingers hammered out her answer.

I'm very sick. Why don't I just give you my bank details and you can pay the money into my account.

With every word she typed she was digging herself in, deeper and deeper. I was almost enjoying watching her.

> *But I'd like to know the name of the hospital. What if I want to come and visit you?*

> *I don't want you to visit me. This is such a terrible disease I have to face it alone, I don't want to drag anybody else in and risk hurting them.*

I turned to Fozia. 'Okay, that's enough. I'm going to tell her that it's me now.' Without listening to Fozia's protests I rattled off my accusation.

> *My name is Jasvinder Sanghera. I understand you have been talking to Fozia, a volunteer in our project, Karma Nirvana. I understand you have been putting her under pressure to lend you money, I believe under false pretences. To my mind that is theft and I will be reporting you to the police. I know you are in Leicester, we have your address.*

I went back to my desk but I know Fozia sat there, anxiously waiting for the answer that was never going to come. She rang me later that night and her voice was shaking as she questioned me. 'How could you have done that? You've got her in trouble with the police. She's going to be so angry.'

'If it's true that she's ill and needs the money for an operation she's got nothing to worry about, has she?' I said. But of course it wasn't true: she was a woman with a drug habit so developed that she was already known to the police. Even with that knowledge, Fozia refused to prosecute; she said she would rather write off the debt and move on. She put a brave face on it, but I could see she was hurting and – although Fozia has next to nothing – I don't think it was the bad debt that caused her pain.

Girls like Fozia interpret attention as affection: this was a woman who appeared to like her, a woman with small children who might take the place of the nephews and nieces Fozia is not allowed to see. These people, she must have thought, could be my new family. It was the loss of that dream that really hurt her and witnessing her sadness – or rather, not witnessing it: Fozia always withdraws into herself when things get tough and I didn't see her for several days – strengthened my conviction that I must get the Friendship Network up and running.

By that time the training of mentors was underway, but I knew we would need further funding to provide the service I envisaged and I decided to go back to the Forced Marriage Unit. We have a good working relationship now. Karma Nirvana staff helped with ideas for the Survivors Handbook which the unit gives out to those who are trying to rebuild their lives: Fozia, Shazia and Kiren are all proud of the fact that they are quoted in it. I think we've helped with their understanding of some of the issues involved; certainly the unit has come a long way since my first contact, which still makes me smile.

I rang about a year after it had been established and introduced myself. I said that I worked for Karma Nirvana, a Derby-based organisation helping south Asian women who had been the victims of honour-based violence and forced marriage. There was a bit of a pause, and then the voice at the other end said, 'You mean forced marriages happen in Derby?'

I said, 'Indeed they do, and you are speaking to someone who narrowly avoided one.'

He was astonished. I could picture him rubbing his forehead as he said, 'I knew they happened in Bradford, but not *Derby*.'

I can remember thinking: great, now I definitely know why we have to work with these people.

The unit is now contacted by 5000 people a year, and each year they repatriate up to four hundred British subjects who have been forced into or are at risk of forced marriage. In addition to prevention and rescue, the after-care of women who have fled forced marriages or been helped to leave them needs to be an important part of their plan, and it seemed to me that our aims dovetail perfectly. I rang Peter Abbott, who was heading up the unit at the time, and made an appointment to meet him in his office. Thanks to the fact that he and I often shared a conference platform in the year he held the post, I came to know him well and I liked him. In reality we are poles apart and yet we had this common interest so we always had something to talk about. I used to tease him about being that rare creature: a civil servant with a heart.

Peter makes no bones about the fact that he found himself on a very steep learning curve when he first joined the unit; in fact he told me that some of the training was traumatic and he mentioned in particular a rescue he was sent on. It was in Pakistan – which is true of sixty-five per cent of cases that the Forced Marriage Unit deals with – and the team had been called out to rescue a British girl who they believed was being held by her extended family in a remote village about two hours drive from Islamabad.

Three of them set out together: Peter, Shailin who was also from the Forced Marriage Unit and Ammara who was a local and had been brought in to do most of the talking. Peter said he felt very nervous. The landscape, the heat, the language – everything was unfamiliar and on top of that he knew they were unlikely to get a warm reception. I could just imagine him arriving in a little village that looked like something from the pages of a medieval history book. There would be kids, a ragged tribe of them running behind the moving car and then, when the car stopped and Peter got out of it, they would flatten themselves against the walls, their big brown eyes wide with curiosity and suspicion.

He said he walked into a courtyard set in the centre of what appeared to be the main house in the village, and found it full of people standing in huddles around an old, old man who was sitting cross-legged on a low woven stool. 'They were talking before we got there, we could hear this low hum of conversation, but as we walked through the archway that led into the courtyard it dried up immediately and what felt like fifty pairs of hostile eyes were trained on us.'

When Peter told me that, I felt my own skin prickle. I could see him in my mind's eye, taking a deep breath to steady himself, bracing his skinny shoulders as a trickle of sweat ran down between his shoulder blades. 'Ammara went up to the old man and introduced us. She explained we'd come to do a safe and well check on a British subject, Mariam Khan. I didn't need her to interpret his answer. From the head-shaking, finger-wagging and shrugging that was going on all around us, it was obvious that they were saying she wasn't there. It was also pretty clear they didn't want us hanging around.'

Peter had been warned that the team might have to be persistent but in fact, getting to see Mariam was easier than he expected. Once Ammara had relayed the fact that no one could leave before they had seen Mariam, a woman emerged from the crowd and – gesturing to the team to follow her – she led them into the house, up some stairs and along a narrow unlit corridor. The woman was middle-aged and her bearing was authoritative, almost arrogant, Peter thought. He guessed she might be Mariam's mother-in-law. At the end of the corridor she stopped in front of a heavy wooden door and, before she opened it, threw him a look that could best be described as challenging.

The door opened into what appeared to be a bedroom – at least it contained a bed on which a girl was sitting. Even through the gloom Peter recognised her as Mariam from photographs he'd seen. There was no other furniture in the room, no covering on the concrete floor, no light save that let in through the glassless windows in the walls on either side of her. There were, however, other people. Peter was asking Ammara to explain that policy dictated they should see this British citizen alone, when Mariam herself started shouting, in English: 'I'm fine, thank you. Very well. Please go away. I did not ask you to come here. I do not want you here.'

This confused everybody and there was a sudden huddle of people round Ammara, asking her to explain what she was saying. Mariam took advantage of their momentary inattention to point at the open windows on either side of her, then cup a hand to her ear to show that close behind them, people were listening. She also drew a finger rapidly across her throat and mouthed, 'They're going to kill me.'

'It seemed to me there was only one solution,' Peter told me. 'Ammara went back to the old man – who was obviously the elder of the village – and told him that we would have to take Mariam back to the Embassy temporarily because there appeared to be something wrong with her passport. Well, this time he didn't waste time with head-shaking, but I still didn't need a translation of what he said. It was perfectly obvious that he was yelling, "No, you can't take her! Go away."

'I was terrified. I could see men standing on the roofs surrounding the courtyard and several of them were holding rifles; I learnt later on that they had been told to shoot at Mariam if she left the premises. We had to think fast, Ammara suggested we play it very casually, so I got her to say, "I'm sorry, I know it's inconvenient, but there's no way round it, I have to take her, but why don't some of your family come too? Unfortunately there's no more room in our car but you could bring your own and follow on behind us."'

I smiled at the thought of Peter using his British good manners as a weapon, but not for long because what he said next was deeply shocking. When Mariam was brought out to the car by her relatives she climbed in – very stiffly he noticed – and then sat there, bent double. Nobody said anything until they had driven away and the crowd that watched them go was lost in a cloud of dust behind them, but then Shailin tried to reassure her. 'It's fine, you can sit up now. Don't worry, your in-laws are following but you will be safe here with me beside you.' Mariam didn't move except to turn her head towards Shailin. 'I can't sit up,' she said in a voice as frail as her poor, thin body. 'They've whipped me so often that any movement hurts me, I couldn't lean back against the seat.'

'Thank God you got her out,' I said. 'You must have felt fantastic having rescued her.'

'No, not really,' Peter said. 'At least only for a short while. We got her to the embassy, managed to get her into an interview room without her family and once Shailin had gained her trust, Mariam opened up to her about the marriage, the beatings – everything. The man she'd been forced to marry was her cousin and he and his brothers used to take her to a shed – a sort of weapon chamber full of guns and knives – to beat her. They threatened to kill her if she said a word about it to anyone outside the family. We got it all down in writing and then we started making plans to get her back to England. She was barely more than a schoolgirl but she said she had a boyfriend whom she was fairly certain would stand by her. He was the reason that her family got her married off.

'It was going to be a day or two before we could get her on a flight to London so I arranged for her to stay in a very good refuge we have in Islamabad which is funded by the British government. It was from there she called Shailin.' Peter paused; the expression on his face was pain mixed with incomprehension.

'She rang to say that she had changed her mind, she wouldn't be going back to England. Her boyfriend had contacted her to say he had cold feet, he wasn't prepared to support her after all. "You do understand, don't you," she said, and then – these were her exact words, I'll never forget them – "I'm no one without my family. I have to go back to the village. I've got no choice."'

20

After a run of attending weekend conferences I woke up to find myself faced with the first free day I'd had in what felt like a month. Lisa had just moved into her new house, and I'd arranged to meet up with her and Shazia and go down to Pak Foods at the bottom of Normanton Road. It's one of the biggest Asian shops in Derby; everybody goes there, but you never go on your own. It's not that it's in a rough area, but there are so many Asian men working there that an Asian woman shopping alone would just get stared at. That used to make me angry, I used to long to stare them out and say, 'What's your problem? What are you looking at?' But now I just think, 'So what, let's go together.'

So there we were, the three of us, with all the other mums and daughters and daughters-in-law, wandering round the displays, the multi-coloured mountains of peppers and aubergines, spices and herbs, onions, spinach and potatoes, discussing what to buy.

'What about this melon? Do you think it's ripe?'

'I'm going to get a handful of these and look – shall we share this garlic?'

'I need some chillies, how many should I get, Mother?' (This from Shazia. I can't remember when she started calling me 'Mother', but it's stuck and she has to concentrate on remembering to call me Jas at conferences.)

I would never have known how to shop, I would have no idea what spices to buy if I hadn't learnt from my mum. Then I taught Lisa, and now there's Shazia; she and I are pooling our knowledge, some spices I have introduced to her and some she's introduced to me.

My mum never came to Pak Foods – by the time it opened up she was too frail and ill to get here – but the sharp, musky smell of spices always sends me right back to our kitchen in Dale Road and her, all pink and flushed with heat, stirring a big pot of curry on the stove.

She used to buy seed pods of all the different spices, dry them out and then grind them up together to make garam masala. There were piles of pods all over the house and every room was permeated with the smell. After Mum died, Dad struggled to manage that by himself and he took to buying the seeds, ready mixed, in bags so when he got them home all he had to do was grind them. I'm sure Mum would have done that too if she'd known.

When he died I took the last bag of masala that he'd ground – it lasts for ages and the longer you've had it the better it tastes. I used it up little by little, eking it out, stirring the memory of my dad into every dish I cooked with it. It was a link to him and I wanted it to last for ever. When it finally ran out I was so upset.

I took his roti too – the metal griddle you cook chapattis on. He made it in the foundry where he worked and the fact

I've got it now is very special to me. A roti is such a fundamental part of Asian cooking; it's the first thing the girls who run away have to buy when they're setting up their own home. But food is a big issue for a lot of them. The pungent smells of cooking, the pot of curry on the stove, the big unifying meal – those are the key ingredients of an Asian family. Leave them behind and the things that take their place – microwave meals for one, tins of beans and any kind of takeaway – are all reminders of the massive gap in these girls' lives.

Some of them deal with it by becoming great cooks themselves, others – the majority – turn away from food completely. The day I met Yasmin she came to the car with me when I was leaving and saw a sack of chapatti flour in my boot. 'Oh, look at this,' she said, and there was a note of recognition in her voice as if she'd found a once-loved toy. It was for her a very poignant reminder of home. You can't buy chapatti flour in anything less than family-sized bags – the sort of thing it would take one person living alone a lifetime to use up. 'Take some, go on,' I said, reaching to break the bag open. But she had her arm out to stop me, quick as a flash. 'No, no. No way. I don't want to have to think about cooking it – I told you I don't cook.'

We had beautiful weather that day and when we'd finished at Pak Foods I decided to pick up Maria, Joshua and our dog Lyrics and drive out to Whitby, to the beach. Lisa had other things to do, but Shazia came with us and she and I sat on the sand squinting into the horizon as the sunlight danced on the sea. There weren't many people about, the air was still and it was peaceful, except for Lyrics who kept racing into the shallows and barking at the seagulls as they sat serenely on the surface, gracefully riding the lacy little waves. Joshua, still football mad, chased a ball up and down the beach and Maria was on the hunt for shells to add to her collection, reaching into shallow rock pools, peering into crevices, completely absorbed. I envied her that. I wished, like her, that I could lose myself in our surroundings. I tried to focus on the feel of the sun, warm on my back and my bare feet, cold from where I'd burrowed them into the damp, scratchy sand, but I couldn't. There was a young girl – a child really, only thirteen years old – whose story kept niggling at me, refusing to allow me peace of mind. I didn't know her; it was an officer from the Metropolitan Police who told me her story; he said it was haunting him and now, lurking in the shadows of my mind, easing itself out whenever I sit still for long enough, it haunts me.

This child – Meera – lived in west London. Each morning, like so many other Muslim girls, she put on her hijab and left the strict confines of her family for the hurly burly of a 1,000 strong comprehensive school. I bet she enjoyed it. Like Fozia, I'm sure she loved the freedom school gave her to lead a normal teenage life.

Like many normal teenagers, she found herself a boyfriend. He was at the same school, a year or two older than her, but he wasn't just someone she giggled and blushed at when their eyes met in the playground. There was enough between them for the teachers to have noticed there was something going on, and they thought that 'something' was distracting Meera from her work. When their A-grade pupil began handing in assignments that barely merited a C they assumed her mind was on the Year Ten boy they had seen her holding hands with.

Perhaps they were right. Who am I to say otherwise? I'm sure to the teachers it seemed like the obvious answer, given that Meera came from a nice, stable Asian family where the parents always seemed so concerned. Those teachers hadn't met Fozia, they hadn't heard her spit, as I did: 'What's the point of doing my homework when I'm just going to fuck off and marry some Paki!' If they had they might have seen the situation differently.

As it was, they told the headmaster about Meera's poor performance and he saw it as his duty to ring her father and share his concerns about the child. He called on Friday afternoon. 'So you can have the weekend to talk it over with her,' I expect he said. I expect he was quite jovial about it. 'Nothing too serious, nothing to worry about, just a playground romance, but it does seem to be disrupting her studies and we don't want that.'

At 3.30 p.m. that day Meera left the school and she hasn't been seen since. When she didn't come in on Monday the school secretary rang her home but she got no reply. She got no reply on Tuesday either but on Wednesday Meera's mum answered and she said that Meera had gone missing. In answer to the secretary's kind concern she said that no, they hadn't as yet reported it to the police.

Where is Meera now? What happened to her? Try as I might, when I think of her, which I often do, it is in the past tense: she *was* thirteen, she *had* a boyfriend, she *had* . . .

The jangle of my mobile phone startled me. Trish says the sound of my mobile at weekends drives her mad, she says it's never quiet and I should ignore it because everybody needs a break from work but – as I keep saying to her – this work is different. Anyway, when I checked the screen and saw it was Shabana I couldn't leave it. Meera was instantly superseded in my mind.

A good five months had passed since Shabana's DNA

samples were taken, her video statement made, but there seemed to have been no progress; she was still in her parents' house, still living in fear. There had been little incidents, moments when the situation escalated, but she was very skilled at managing her parents' rage. The stasis worried me. I'd say to her, 'What are you waiting for? Are you waiting for something big to happen?'

When I answered my mobile she was all but hysterical. She didn't bother with 'Hello' or anything like that, it was straight into: 'Will you talk to my bank manager, it's the Nationwide Building Society. Dad noticed that I'm not receiving statements any more. I told him I'm online banking but he knows it's a lie and he says he's going to take me in to see the bank manager. He says we'll go this morning. Please ring him for me Jas, please. My dad will kill me if he knows what I've been doing.'

I was on my feet before she'd finished the first sentence. My mind was racing but I felt completely helpless. Although I didn't have the full picture, the scant details I did have, coupled with Shabana's very real terror, convinced me that she was in serious and imminent danger. But I was miles away: how could I possibly help?

'Shabana, listen, be realistic. There's no way your bank manager will talk to me. He doesn't know me, he has no proof that I know you. How am I going to do it?'

'You've got to. What else can I do? I can't get hold of my designated police officers. Please, Jas, you've got to help me.'

I'd only met Shabana once at that stage, fleetingly, when she came to a talk I was giving in the city where she lived. At the end she came up and introduced herself, but then she was gone almost immediately, before we'd had any time for conversation.

Still I could visualise her now. She's got a tiny little frame which seems to fizz with energy, as if all the nervous tension she feels is running through her body like an electric charge. She reminds me of a coiled spring. I could imagine her, clutching the phone beneath this long cascade of curls she has, and covering the room with quick, frantic paces.

'Stop! Calm down,' I spoke harshly to mask my own fear and because we didn't have time for histrionics. 'You've managed to ring me; you can ring your bank manager. Go on, it's worth a try. I'm going to ring Steve Allen.'

I got hold of him immediately. I had filled him in on Shabana's situation last time we spoke because I wanted to start a dialogue on designing a proper protection system for young women in her position. Now, hearing the anxiety in my voice, he promised to look into the situation and ring me back. I didn't dare to ring Shabana and she didn't ring me, so I sat there and waited. And waited. All the beauty was gone from the day. My mood poisoned the atmosphere. The kids lost interest in what they were doing and came and sat close, pressed up against me. 'You said you wouldn't work today,' Maria said accusingly. 'She works every day,' said Joshua, bitterly. Normally I'd have picked him up on that, but I didn't have the concentration. After forty minutes I made another call to Steve Allen.

I said, 'Listen, I'm concerned. What chance does this girl have? How are we going to keep her alive?'

'Look Jas, if she really wants to get out all she has to do is dial 999.'

'We've been through this before – you know she's never going to do that, she doesn't want men in uniforms or cars with sirens and flashing lights. There is no way she will disgrace her family with that.'

I felt so frustrated, we seemed to be stuck in a stalemate and I couldn't see how to change things. I hung up feeling I'd achieved nothing. Shazia, the children and I walked slowly back to the car. On the drive home nobody said a word.

21

The rest of the weekend passed in a fog of worry and Shabana was still at the forefront of my mind when I went in to work on Monday. I felt relief wash through me when I logged on to find an email from her: proof, at least, that at seven-fifteen the previous evening she was still alive.

I scanned it quickly. She gave me the background to her panic: she had been closing accounts, putting all her money in one place, ready for the day she ran away. She told me that she had got hold of the bank manager and he had agreed to help her: in front of her father he explained that her new pass book was in the post and that, for security reasons he couldn't give out further information.

> *When the pass book does not arrive on Tuesday my father will know I am lying and that I am up to something. It will no longer be safe for me to stay here. I need your help now Jasvinder, please.*

As soon as I had finished reading her email I rang the Assistant Chief Constable for her area and said, 'Shabana's made up her mind, she wants to leave today. Can you make sure it's all sorted?' He assured me it already was: Shabana was going to be collected from her workplace by two policemen at 3 p.m. that afternoon.

'They will be in plain clothes won't they? It's vitally important that we don't attract attention to her, we don't want to anger her family further. And what about her being put on the Witness Protection Programme? I know it's been discussed, but is it going to happen?'

'She doesn't qualify Jasvinder; she's made it quite clear she has no intention of prosecuting her parents so our hands are tied. Witness protection is for people giving evidence.'

'But that's not how she sees it,' I said, determined to plead her case as strongly as possible. 'As she sees it that Soham woman – Maxine Carr – gets protected because the public want to kill her but she, Shabana, gets ignored because it's only her father who is threatening her life. She keeps asking me why she's treated differently and I don't know what to say to her.'

There was a heavy sigh at the other end of the phone and then, 'You know the Witness Protection Programme is very costly in terms of both time and money.'

'Are you putting a price on her life?' I said, piling on the pressure. To my great relief it worked; he caved in and said he would look into it.

My next priority was finding refuge provision for Shabana. I wanted to send her to Wales because I had a hunch that she and Yasmin would get on, I thought they would be good for one another. I found a place quickly but then it took me a good half an hour to explain to the manager that, for the first few days, she would have to waive the rules in order to help Shabana protect her identity. I took a deep breath and made the time to go through it slowly and carefully because I know how difficult it is for refuge managers to buck the system. 'I realise that as soon as she moves in she's supposed to apply for housing benefit,' I said. 'I understand that's how you are funded, but the thing is this. To apply for housing benefit she has to give her National Insurance number and once that shows up on the database linked to an address in Bangor it will be easy for her family to trace her. Believe me, it's not hard: all her father would need is a contact in the job centre and, as you know, Asians do have very powerful networks. You will get your money but you may have to wait.'

Eventually she agreed, even though she wasn't happy with it. I couldn't wait to tell Shabana the good news; as soon as I heard she was safely in the police car, I rang her mobile.

'You're sending me to Wales to be supported by a fucking Paki? No! No way! There is no way I am going to have anything to do with a Paki – it's just too dangerous.'

Those were her first words to me and I wasn't surprised. So many of the young women I deal with would have said the same. They've grown up with the Asian network as an all-seeing, all-knowing, all-powerful force in their lives. We all do. It starts with the auntie who tells your mum that she saw you slipping into the corner shop instead of walking straight home from primary school – and even as your arm stings from the slapping you are given you wonder how that auntie knew because she doesn't even live in your street. Four years later, it's uncle who tells on you – he heard from a man he works with – and your reported crime is talking to a boy at the bus-stop. Then a taxi-driver from an altogether different part of town mentions to your dad that a friend of his wife's saw you outside the cinema at a time when you were supposed to be studying at a friend's house.

I think it's getting worse. Imran recently took a call from a woman in London who was ringing on behalf of her daughter's classmate, a fifteen-year-old girl at private school whose parents disapproved of her going out with friends. To monitor her activity they had passed her photograph to every Asian shopkeeper and taxi-driver in the area and asked them to report back on her – not just if she was getting into trouble; they wanted a report on every single thing she did.

Grow up under that sort of surveillance and you grow up not trusting anyone because you never know how they might link in to your family. Put that inbuilt mistrust against the fact that so many of the agencies supporting these young women instinctively put Asians in the front line for dealing with them and you've got a problem. Yasmin's PC Ahmed – with his loyalties split between his uniform and his community – is just an example. There are probably hundreds of PC Ahmeds in Britain and that's something we need to change through education.

My last – and to my mind almost most important – task that day was to persuade Shabana to let the police talk to her parents. 'I know you don't want to prosecute them, I am not suggesting you prosecute them,' I said, and my voice was getting louder and louder to drown out her protests. 'I just want you to agree to two plain-clothes policemen going round to your parents' house. They would be senior officers – I know your dad doesn't take beat policemen seriously – and they wouldn't give him a caution, it would just be a warning. I want them to tell your dad that they know what's been going on in his house;

I want them to say that they know you are missing, to tell him that before you went you gave statements and DNA samples. I want them to make clear that if anything happens to you, his door is the first they will be knocking on.'

'No, Jas, I don't want that, it will just make them hate me more, it will inflame the situation.' Shabana was adamant and I understood her reasoning. You can live in terror of your family and still love them. You can hate what they want for you, but live in hope that one day they will see reason. You can – even if you don't admit it to yourself – long for reconciliation. But the day you report them to the police those hopes die for ever; it's the one way to ensure your family will never forgive you.

'Okay, I know,' I said. 'But tell me that you'll think about it.' And she agreed, reluctantly.

When I finally put the phone down and looked at my watch it was 4 p.m. Sorting out Shabana had taken most of the day and the complications were far from over. Her funding problems were going to be drawn out because I knew that getting her a new National Insurance number – which is what she needed – wasn't going to happen quickly. In all the years I've been helping young women like Shabana, I've never been successful in getting the police to change a National Insurance number or change a name by deed poll unless that young woman was in the Witness Protection Programme.

Shabana wanted to be on the programme and I was fiercely advocating that she should be, but only because she was in danger – I was sure of that – and I couldn't see a better alternative. In truth I wasn't sure that a feisty, independent girl like Shabana would be able to stand it. After all, Kiren found it too stifling, she couldn't cope with the low-key life it meant she had to lead. Within days she was saying, 'Why can't I see my friends, why can't I go out, why do people monitor everything I do?' She said the programme made her feel she was in prison. It didn't surprise me when she gave it up.

But there has to be an alternative. Shabana, Kiren and all the others like them need the highest level of protection and if it's not the Witness Protection Programme then what can it be? I've spent a great deal of time thinking about this problem and as I see it the best solution would be to drop the word witness and design a programme tailored to the particular needs of these young people – I say people because it's not just women, there are men who need protection too.

The ones we see are like a few grains of sand in an ocean. They are the few brave – or desperate – enough to run away knowing there is no proper protection; there must be hundreds more of them hidden away, unseen and unheard of, trapped by terror. Of course funding for any new programme is a problem; it always is. But I've pointed out to Steve Allen that Victim Support gets a huge amount of money from the crime budget, and yet it has no training or experience in dealing with cases like Shabana's. There are resources there which need to be pooled, and I think it should be a priority.

22

Eight years after she had left him, Shazia's husband turned up out of the blue. He rang the office, Anna picked up the phone and of course, when he gave her his name, it didn't mean a thing. She called to Shazia across the room: 'There's someone called Mohammed asking for you. Do you want to speak to him?'

I was working at the university when it happened, but I was told later that Shazia went as pale as death and started shaking visibly. By the time I arrived at the office the capable woman I'm used to working with had melted back into the timid, retiring girl that was Shazia when I first met her. It was as if the very sound of his name had wiped out all the confidence she had gained since leaving him. And I'm not surprised. This was a man who had connived with her family to override all her rights, let alone her wishes, in pursuit of his own selfish purpose which, he freely admitted, was to get himself a British passport. Her body could not but react to the memory of the miserable months she had spent with him. And her mind must have been racing:

Where is he? How did he find me? What does he want with me? What if he comes here?

Her fears were realised. Later that week, with a friend, he arrived in the reception area that Karma Nirvana shares with all the other offices in our building. The receptionist came round to tell us. 'It was yesterday; sorry I didn't have a chance to come round before now. There were two of them, both Asian and they were asking for Alan: you know, the accountant who works upstairs? But Alan wouldn't see them; he said he had no idea who they were. I thought I'd come and tell you because there was something about them that made me feel uneasy. None of my business really, but I thought you ought to know.'

Shazia went back to reception with her to view the CCTV footage and sure enough she recognised Mohammed, although she didn't know the man standing beside him. The film showed him leaving the building and getting into a black car which was parked just opposite, and that's where he sat for the rest of the day. 'He must have watched me going home,' said Shazia. 'Look – it shows the time here: he drove off at seventeen-thirty-three and I left on the dot of half past five. Ugh,' she shuddered. 'The thought of him looking at me makes me feel sick. What do you think he wants with me? How did he find me? Do you think he knows where my flat is, too? Oh Jas, do you think I'm safe to stay there?'

She reported the incident to the police, who took a statement from her and made a DVD from the CCTV footage. They also took note of a sudden surge of silent and abusive calls we had at Karma Nirvana that week. Had Mohammed made further attempts to contact Shazia they were ready to pounce. But he never did and as one week went by without further news of him, then two, then three, Shazia's fear was replaced by anger.

'What's he doing here, Jas, that's what's getting me,' she said. Her eyes were blazing and her voice, which is usually soft and gentle, was almost growling with her rage. 'I don't mean here in Derby, I mean in this country, in England. I left him three weeks after he arrived here, so he should have been sent back to Pakistan but no, he's still here, which means that two years after I left him he must have been granted his indefinite leave to stay. How did that happen? Who was his sponsor? Who forged my signature on his papers, that's what I want to know.'

Across the United Kingdom there are hundreds of women in Shazia's position. I remember meeting Surjit for the first time, and hearing a painful story that could be the template for many, many others.

Surjit was born in India and came to England aged one with her parents. She started school in England and still recalls how it gave her a place to be herself. Home life, by comparison was a schizophrenic world where all the rules were reversed. There was no speaking in English, no English friends, no western dress, no western TV – especially no *Top of the Pops*. It was like being pinned to the wall: having eyes to see and a heart to feel but being unable to use them. Surjit's dream was to be one of those women who carry a briefcase and wear black tailored suits. But she always felt different and was reminded from the age of six how dark her complexion was, how it would be difficult to find her a husband and that she must not go out in the sun for fear of making her skin even darker. She was often hit as a child, without quite understanding why – perhaps she had walked into a room where a man was sitting or had spilled some food. Nobody ever explained, they just hit her.

When she was seven, Surjit was taken to India to learn what

she calls the Indian system. For two years she was sent to Indian school and taught the ways of a good Asian girl, which included her religion. She badly missed her life at home, but on her return to school in England she was put into the year below her friends as she had missed so much and could no longer speak English. She had to learn it again from scratch, returning home each evening where she was forbidden from speaking it. At secondary school, in a leafy suburb, Surjit was one of only four Asian children in the whole school. She remembers how she was made to feel useless and stupid, having missed so much of her education through no fault of her own. She remained in the lower academic groups and was picked on by others in her year who labelled her the dunce. She was chaperoned to and from school by her father or brother. If she ever had to stay late at school she was questioned harshly by her parents. It was her brother's and male cousins' duty to watch her all the time at school and check that she was behaving. She was reminded constantly that she must have no interaction with western children. Her father would come right up to her and shout aggressively in her face, telling her how it would bring shame on the family and diminish her marriage prospects even further.

The day of Surjit's first menstrual period arrived when she was thirteen and she ran to her mother asking her what was happening. The response changed her life forever. Her mother threw a sanitary towel at her and shouted, 'Now you're a woman not a girl, behave like one and don't shame us.' From this moment on her attendance at school dropped from 100 per cent to less than 50 per cent, and no one noticed. She longed to go to college, but was told, 'You're just a girl, you know nothing. Where you're going there is no need for an education.'

The physical violence stopped at this point, but it was immediately replaced by emotional abuse. A lot of other family members moved into the house and Surjit felt more fearful under their constant observation. She was rarely left alone and never allowed to know why she had to miss so much school. Her mother had her cooking, cleaning, sewing, and taking care of family elders and children in preparation for what she called the life of the good daughter-in-law.

In fact it was the life of a slave and Surjit felt increasingly isolated. She missed school and had no idea what excuses her parents had given for her not being there. When she was allowed to go back no one asked where she had been or cared what she had been doing. This went on for three years. On one of the rare occasions that she was in school, her class was asked to write an essay on their experience of adolescence. Surjit saw an opportunity to ask for help, and wrote the truth about her life. Her teacher was appalled. She wrote across the bottom in bright red pen, 'You make adolescence sound horrifying!!!' But nobody asked her anything about the awful things she had written, nobody told to her that this 'horrifying' experience was abnormal or wrong. In fact she felt guilty as though she'd done a bad piece of work and merely retreated into herself even more.

One day when she should have been at school, she was asked to wear something respectable for a visit to relatives. She put on her best Asian suit and was driven to a house she had never seen before. She was told to sit in a room and remembered the Asian etiquette of no eye contact, no smiling, keep your head down and act shy and reserved in the presence of everyone. It was a grand house and clearly a rich and well-known family. She dared to look out of the corner of her eye at the man sitting in the middle of the room full of people, who she realised was to be her husband. Without even knowing his name or how old he was, her first thought was, 'What an ugly bastard.' She sat in silence while all round her the wedding was planned and, in her words, the deal was sealed.

On the way home her father mentioned for the first time that this was her future husband. 'What do you think?' he asked. Surjit replied believing she was being given a choice. 'He is not for me Dad.' The response this time was brutal. 'You had better get used to it,' he bellowed. 'Whether you like it or not you are marrying him in a few weeks and if you think about running away I will find you and kill you. I am prepared to go to prison.' There were other family members present and all of them agreed. There was screaming and shouting and all she remembers was the threat of death.

These words were repeated over and over again until the day of the wedding, when Surjit was turned into the traditional bride. In the space of a few weeks her weight fell from nine-and-a-half to barely seven stone. None of the family noticed or commented on this. It soon became clear that the marriage was being rushed because her prospective husband's visa was due to expire. He needed a British passport in order to stay in the country and she had been chosen to provide it. In despair, Surjit wanted to run, but there was nowhere to go, nowhere to hide, and no-one to turn to. Who, she says, would have believed a hysterical sixteen-year-old girl?

The marriage took place in a registry office and she struggled to read her vows, willing the Registrar to take her to one side and ask if this was what she wanted. But of course he didn't, and all the families' eyes were on her even if he had. In fact she was never allowed to be on her own; there was always an auntie or an uncle there, watching and waiting. Occasionally she caught her father's eye and he gave her the same cold, piercing look that had accompanied his death threats during the car journey. 'This was not an arranged marriage, I was being forced, and I hated the man I was marrying, the family, the make-up that I had never worn before and the fact that everyone was smiling and laughing. I remember the photographer saying, "Smile, this isn't a funeral," and thinking if only you knew.'

After the registry office wedding she went home and soon after this the paperwork began to secure her husband's stay. She was forced to write a letter to immigration saying that she had fallen in love with him, and had married in haste because of this. On the day the letter was written and signed there was lots of shouting and screaming. Nobody ever communicated with Surjit in a calm way. They were always aggressive and telling her what to do, with the constant threat of death if she refused. She signed the letter as her family stood over her, and it read:

> I love him and want to be with him forever. Please don't send him back.

'I was surprised that that was never questioned,' Surjit told me. 'I could have told the people in immigration the truth if only someone had asked, and they could have saved me from what came next.'

Now that she was legally married her family started to arrange the big Indian wedding, the show piece. Once again Surjit was overwhelmed by a desperate need to run away. But how? Where to?

'I married him in full Indian style, four days of surreal

celebration and I did not feel a thing, only numbness and isolation. I just complied knowing that there was no way out.'After the wedding she was put in the wedding car. 'I heard a voice in my head saying, "It's wrong, it's wrong," but it was not strong enough for me to feel anything. I wanted to be invisible so I closed my eyes.'

Later that night Surjit was forced to wear a night dress that revealed her body, and told to take off her underwear, both of which felt wrong. Her head rang with her mother's voice telling her, 'You are now your husband's property and I don't want to hear any bad reports about you coming from this family. You must do everything he wants.' She was given some milk and advised that it would help her. After drinking it, she felt drowsy and later realised that she had been drugged. 'I woke up feeling humiliated and degraded, knowing I'd been raped by a stranger and feeling I had lost my dignity, which was something I hadn't even known I had until this time.' She knew that she had to act normally, but she was in a lot of pain and bleeding badly. She curled into a ball and cried for hours until she had no choice but to get up and face her new life.

The nights of rape were repeated over and over again for the next eight-and-a-half years. 'I was treated like a piece of meat and the British Government gave him a passport to do this.' After the first night, she froze whenever he went near her and let him do what he wanted although she couldn't bear it. 'I went from never having had a boyfriend to having a husband and I hated being naked.' She went to her GP, an Asian woman, and told her she was feeling depressed. She was desperate. The doctor didn't press her for any more details but prescribed tranquilisers and sleeping pills. Sometimes they helped to numb her body so that she didn't have to feel him, but his demands on her grew. He would drink and then, with alcohol-induced confidence, would force her to do things that revolted and frightened her. Or he might come home late and demand sex before ordering her out of bed to make food. She never fought her husband because always there were the voices of her parents in her head and the fear that she might be found out and killed. Then she discovered that the GP had told her husband about her visit and another glimpse of a way out, or at the very least some support, had disappeared.

After another two years Surjit was given immigration documents by her husband's family, which they forced her to sign, to grant his indefinite leave to remain in the country. 'I wish that somebody had questioned whether it was a legitimate marriage. If only school had asked where I had disappeared to, if only the Registrar had been able to read the pain in my eyes then maybe it would have prevented the nights of being raped over and over again.'

During these years Surjit wished she was dead. Only her job provided any relief from her oppressive family life. She tried talking to her family, but they only sent her back to make the marriage work. It was preferable to them that she died rather than dishonour them in this way, and she did try to take her own life. Shortly after she'd been raped one night, she took an overdose of the tranquilisers and sleeping pills she'd been prescribed. It didn't work, but even though she was a walking zombie for days afterwards, nobody noticed or asked her what was wrong. She had many, many suicidal thoughts. It wasn't something she felt she could discuss with anyone, but she developed a relationship with suicide in her head – it was a way out.

'The day of my great escape came after my third miscarriage,'

Surjit told me. She longed for a baby – something to love and to relieve the aching isolation in which she lived. But she was painfully thin and lived on nervous energy. The years of mental and emotional trauma had left her with debilitating mental illness. She became pregnant three times, but her frail body could not cope, the babies didn't grow, the rapes continued, and each pregnancy ended in miscarriage. The first time, she was carrying twins. Nobody, not even her mother, asked questions about how she was – she had to ask permission to go to the hospital each time it happened. The second time, her mother-in-law flew over from India to tell her how useless she was. She gave her a powder to take with water to help her get pregnant, but Surjit never took it. 'I managed to pretend somehow, because I was terrified it was poison and they were trying to kill me.'

After the third miscarriage she was sitting in hospital having driven there alone, wishing that a doctor or nurse would ask why and how this could have happened yet again. Surjit longed for someone simply to offer her some love and support. She couldn't tell anyone what was happening because of her fear of death, but she felt that if only someone would ask her then she could tell the truth. But nobody did. No-one apparently thought it was odd that she'd driven herself alone to hospital three times after a miscarriage, or that she never had a single visitor or someone to take her home. She realised that she couldn't go on, and although she was very afraid, the need for freedom was finally greater. 'I knew this was the choice I had reached: my family or my freedom.'

The day before she planned to run, she went to the police. She knew that her family would report her missing and accuse her of stealing the car, so she explained her situation and told them what she was going to do. They shrugged their shoulders and took a note. To this day, Surjit has no idea whether they made any connection when she was reported missing, and whether they thought to protect her by not instigating a missing person's report.

She planned her escape meticulously with the help of a friend at work who provided an address for letters and a new bank account. Surjit got herself to London for a job interview, telling her family that she had been on a training day. Given the state she was in, it's extraordinary that she got the job. She had chosen London as being so far away from home that nobody would think of it. All this time she had been taking her personal papers bit by bit from the house and either destroying them or hiding them at work, so that when she was gone, her family would have less with which to trace her.

On the day of the escape, she told her husband she'd lost the car keys, so that he left for work without the car. She then packed everything up with the help of her friend from work. 'We were terrified that somebody would stop us,' she told me. 'But if anybody had come to the door, I would have killed myself there and then. I was quite clear about that.' She drove all the way to London, where her friend had arranged somewhere for her to stay.

Within twenty-four hours Surjit was reported missing and her family had left leaflets all over her neighbourhood in their efforts to find her. She later found out that they even paid a bounty hunter to track her down.

Escape felt like flying, and a cloud had been lifted from her, but Surjit was terrified that her father or the 'taxi-network', as she called it, would catch up with her. She knew she would be killed. She knew nothing about refuge provision and lived her life looking over her shoulder and avoiding Asian communities. As she puts it, 'I never made one brown friend.' She was out in the cold, disowned by her family and set up to fail.

23

When I began shaping my PhD work into some sort of order I made a list of the characteristics common to women who find the courage to flee their oppressive families or their forced marriages – the survivors. The first thing on the list was that all of them, every single one, claimed to have been the black sheep in her family, just as I was in mine. I was a breech baby and my mum always said to me, 'You were difficult from the start.' The next common link was that getting a boyfriend was usually the trigger for an escalation in the abusive behaviour they endured.

Both these things were true of Maya, a Sikh woman in her thirties, a single mother of two, living in Guildford. She wrote me a long, agonised email which told of such injustice and maltreatment that it stuck in my mind. Phrases from it haunted me.

The violence and abuse and sedation carried on till my father flew me to India with the doctor and my mum.

My father had continuously threatened me that if I made

the wrong statement I would lose my first husband forever and his family as they would be killed.

. . . he drank like a barrel and started beating me up black and blue.

She had suffered for years without help. She told me that down in the south of England, there is very little provision for women like her:

I refused to go to an Asian women's refuge because I knew a few ladies here who worked with domestic violence services, but they also went to the temple and gossiped.

But her email showed that she had kept her courage and her dignity, even if they were a little shaky. She offered us her services, she said she would like to help other women in the same situation as herself and it seemed she has skills that would be useful: she speaks six languages and had recently worked as an interpreter for a law enforcement agency.

I replied to her email immediately, suggesting that we meet. I was concerned for her and hoped to arrange something quickly but the days and weeks whisked by and in the end it was four months before we found a time that suited both of us. Maya was in Birmingham by then, staying with her mother who had come to live in England with Maya's younger brother while he went to university. Maya had brought her two little boys – Jeevan and Bakshi – to meet their grandmother, and when we met it was them that she was worried about.

Her life had moved on since she first wrote to me, and not for the better. The previous year, following a nervous breakdown, she had found herself unable to cope. She handed custody of the children to her ex-husband on the understanding that as soon as she was better she would take them back. 'And now the social workers won't allow it, they say the children are settled and we cannot disrupt them. My husband has taken another wife, brought her here from India; he says she is their mother now. He only does it to torment me, he knows they are my weakness.'

She told me all that almost before she had sat down in the tea shop where we arranged to meet. I put out my hand to shake hers and she clung to it as if it were a life-raft. Shazia was with me that afternoon – I was still under police instructions not to travel alone – and afterwards we agreed that the sudden passion of her outburst was at odds with her appearance. Maya is as pretty as a picture. The day we met was warm and sunny, one of those unexpected presents that early autumn sometimes delivers, and as she walked towards us she looked fresh, composed and chic. She was dressed in a red and white striped dress under a jacket with a nipped-in waist and on her feet she had black patent shoes: she looked so lady-like that I half-expected to find her carrying a pair of crisp white gloves. There is something restrained and old-fashioned about her manner too; I wasn't surprised to learn that she grew up in what she described as a very suppressed family.

I made her tell me about them at the start; I was firm about that because, as I explained, I couldn't help her regain custody of her little boys if I had no idea of her background, of how she'd come to be who she is. At first she was impatient, keen to get back to the thing that was at the forefront of her mind – and having temporarily lost custody of Lisa when she was a child I had sympathy with that. But my interview with Fatima had taught me how important it is to get the full picture, so I insisted and Maya complied although at times it was very hard for her. When I think back to that afternoon now I remember two things particularly: how brave Maya tried to be and how much she cried.

She was brought up in Africa in what outsiders imagine as the ideal extended Asian family: three generations – at least eighteen of them – all crammed into one house. (The idea that that could be anyone's ideal has always made me smile.) 'My grandmother was very strict, she wouldn't let the girls mix with the boys, we had two separate living rooms, men and women entertained separately, everything we did was monitored – even the food we ate was rationed. I remember my aunties complaining to my mother that our family had more than our fair share of food because she had a fourth child.'

From the start Maya felt she was a disappointment. Her eldest cousin – a girl – had been the first grandchild born in the house, her elder sister had been the first child born in her family but what was Maya? Not the first anything, just the third girl. Her mother suffered for that just as Maya did – especially once she had produced Maya's little sister. 'She used to hit me and shout at me, "I am ashamed of you, you should be dead, everyone harasses me because you are a girl." I think it was partly her own unhappiness. There were one or two incidents when I opened their bedroom door and saw my father hitting her.' Violence was part of the currency of Maya's family life. 'Both my parents hit me, with hands, objects, anything that came their way. It could be every day or once or twice a week, it depended on when they wanted to vent their frustrations.'

'Vent their frustrations'. As the afternoon wore on Maya

used that phrase repeatedly. I began to build a picture in my mind of this highly respectable household – 'our family is very well known for being *the* orthodox family in our town, very strict' – seething with undercurrents of anger and, with all those in-laws and cousins in an enclosed space, sexual tension. 'It was very humiliating being a teenager,' Maya said. 'Because in our house the grown-up standards were once you start having periods and producing a chest you have to cover yourself, suppress your physical attributes so the men in the house don't see them.'

Repression extended to life outside the house too. Maya was a gifted runner ('I vented all my frustrations in running.'). She competed internationally and, at a point when she was second in her age group in the country, was offered a scholarship to train abroad. 'My father wouldn't let me go because he said girls don't go alone and, although my mother could have come with me, he said she was too busy.'

Maya sought refuge at school. She continued to run – without her parents' permission – and she became involved in fund-raising and drama. 'I used to paint stage settings and backdrops with the teachers, it helped me relieve a lot of tension.' But that went wrong. She confided in a favourite teacher that she was unhappy at home and the teacher – misguidedly rather than maliciously Maya thinks – immediately told her father. 'And the next thing that happened, my father came zooming in the room, he threw a metal chair on me and hit me very hard. He was screaming, "Why do you have to shame us, why do you have to tell your teacher?"'

That was Maya's first betrayal.

Looking back on that afternoon, on the meetings and conversations I've had with her since it always strikes me what a long, hard road Maya had to walk alone. If only I had met her sooner. By the time I got to stand beside her, to support and encourage her, she was so battered by circumstance, so entrenched in her victimhood. The stories she has told me – long convoluted, stories in which physical violence, rape, deprivation and endless cruelty and callousness all pile in on one another – exhaust me. If I'm honest, I'd rather not think about them. But I have to.

'I have spoken to a lot of people about my life but it seems that there is very little understanding unless the person you are talking to has gone through something similar,' is what she wrote to me in her first email.

'I'm not being heard,' she said, talking of the social workers who won't listen to her frantic pleas to let her take her children back.

All her life Maya has been used and abused, her feelings ignored and trampled on. Now she deserves some understanding and I am going to help her get it. I decided that the first afternoon I saw her with her sad eyes and her sassy outfit.

24

When she was sixteen, things began to spiral out of Maya's control. A boy she knew ('we used to meet and talk, there was no relationship going on or anything') spiked her drink and having blacked out she came round to find him raping her. Numb with shock she told no one until two months later when she feared she was pregnant. 'I told my best friend at school, a girl I had grown up with. I told her in confidence but she went round the school telling everyone, and saying other bad things about me.' That was Maya's second betrayal – and the end of school being a haven in which she sought peace.

At home her situation was no better; in fact as she got older and more inclined to stand up to her parents, she angered them further. One day she imposed herself between her three-year-old brother and her mother who was beating him. 'I could feel his pain. All my life I had been suffering like that and now I wanted to stop it. I put him behind me.' That enraged her mother: she went to the wood shed and came back with a plank which still had some nails in it.

Shazia gasped audibly as Maya said that, she was sitting

beside me and I felt her body jerk back in horror. She told me later that she couldn't help herself: the thought of that plank with the nails in it was so barbaric. I was shocked too, but more than that I was angry, enraged by the image of this woman swinging a lethal weapon at her child. But Maya said she stood up to her, she stood there accepting the blows until something suddenly snapped and she retaliated.

'That drove her really mad. She grabbed me by the hair and hurled me to the floor. With all the noise everyone had come to see what was happening. She hit me so the nails were piercing me and then she dragged me by the hair, along the floor all the way to my bedroom. Everyone was watching. She hit me and hit me until her anger was spent and then she walked out on me. The only person to come after that was one of our house-maids, she came and she pacified me. She said to me, "I would like to pack your bags and take you away from here. If I had the power I would do that, but your father feeds my stomach."'

But there were other people, not dependent on Maya's father, who also thought that she had had enough. Some months earlier one of her running friends, Mary, had introduced Maya to her brother. 'His name was Peter and he was twenty-two. We met when he came to collect Mary after a running tournament and then, through her, we started getting acquainted and found we liked each other very much. They were Christians from Sri Lanka.'

Mary and Peter both urged her to leave the home in which she had suffered so much battery and abuse and between them they hatched a plan. On her seventeenth birthday, Maya packed her bags, wrote her parents a long letter – she advised them to forget about her – and slipped out of the house. She went to stay with a friend and Peter went too but within two days the police were on their trail and Peter lost his nerve. 'He said to me, "Maya no matter how much I care for you, I don't want to go to jail for kidnapping you. In a year you will be eighteen and I will still be here for you. I will always be here for you." He dropped me at the hospital, not far from where I lived.'

'Did you feel he had let you down as well?' I asked, as gently as I could, trying not to spoil the shine on her knight's armour.

She swallowed hard. 'At that point, yes. Later I understood, but at the time I wasn't very well versed in the law.'

Maya rang her parents and they drove to pick her up. In her absence their fury had been stoked by her best friend who – by telling them about Maya's earlier fear of pregnancy – had convinced them that their daughter had been in a sexual relationship for some time. Their anger was so loud and uncontrolled that even though she tried to defend herself, her protestations that she had been raped, that her pregnancy scare had nothing to do with Peter, were barely heard. She was driven out of Nairobi, to a town where her father had an office and there she was interrogated.

'My father said the police were coming and I was to tell them what he told me to. I said I had done nothing wrong and if the police came I would tell them the truth. That made him so angry he lunged at me and slapped me so hard I fell off the chair. He shouted at me to get up and sit on the chair and then he hit me again. I was so scared that day I wet myself.'

But she did find the courage to tell the police the truth and they confirmed her story. They told her that other women had reported the same man for rape, they asked if she would be willing to testify against him in court. 'I said yes, I would, but my father would not let me, he said it was my fault; that I had been sleeping with that man willingly, like a prostitute. I think he did not want the stain on our family's name. That's all that mattered to him. He used to say if he had to kill one of us he would do it to keep his respect.'

There followed Maya's first period of incarceration: she was locked in her room for a month. No one spoke to her. She had to ask permission to use the toilet. Food was brought to her room, 'But sometimes, when my mum was angry, she threw it all over me. I was kept like an untouchable until the time came for me to go back to school.'

As Maya said this, pausing occasionally to try and check her tears with a sodden tissue, it occurred to me that she had come to meet us from her mother's house. 'How do you get on with her these days?' I wondered.

Maya shrugged. 'She makes it seem like she has forgotten everything that happened. I see her because my children need to know their family.' There was a pause. 'My father is one person I never speak to about anything. I find it hard to think about him after everything he has done to me. I question why he has done it, what possessed him.'

She would, she said, have done anything to get out of his clutches – even marry a man she didn't love. 'There was a man from a family we knew. I said to my father, "He knows everything about me and still he is willing to marry me." Can you imagine how humiliating that was? It was like admitting I had done something wrong. But my father would not agree to it anyway, because we were from different castes – to him it was all about status, society and respect.'

Would that marriage have worked, I found myself wondering later. Would it have saved Maya the misery she has lived through? Would she have raised children, grown plump and contented, learnt to love the man with whom she would grow old? Could hers have been the arranged marriage that worked? Or was she always destined to become the broken woman who sat beside me trying so valiantly to stifle her sobs as the waitress – a teenager with a smudged swallow tattooed on her upper arm and a frankly curious stare – came to offer us more tea?

Peter was silent for months and then he reappeared in Maya's life, saying he would like to marry her. (When she told me that, for the first time all afternoon, she almost smiled.) That autumn they eloped. She married wearing jeans and her happiness lasted one glorious, golden week before she and Peter were tracked down by their families. They were summoned, by Peter's father, to a meeting between the hierarchies of their two cultures, Sri Lankan and Sikh. 'It was at a private house owned by one of the religious leaders. I was really scared and so was Peter. About twenty people were there, all seated at one long table: my relations, Peter's family, religious men, I was the only woman. I was asked if I had been forced into this marriage and I told them no. I said I loved Peter and wanted to be with him. The Sri Lankan committee were happy with that; Peter's father did not like that we'd eloped but he knew we loved each other and wanted to be together. He approved our plan to make a new life in Sri Lanka.'

This made it hard for the Sikh committee to object. They appeared to accept what was being said but, looking down the table, Maya could see her father's fists were clenched. 'I knew he was plotting something, but he sat there and watched me as I walked out of the room with Peter – I don't think he thought I'd dare to do it, I don't think he'll ever forgive me for that.'

A week later the couple were arrested at their house by armed police. Maya says she knew at once that her father was behind it. 'We sat in the police car holding hands, Peter never stopped holding my hand for one minute, he was squeezing it so tightly.' At the station they waited and waited. No one came to see them, no charges were laid but eventually an officer arrived and said, "Peter you are going to the lock-up. Maya, your father has bailed you out, you are going to his office."'

At the office, which again was filled with armed men, Maya's male relations wrangled over her fate. Her grandfather demanded to know why she had brought such shame on them. She said, 'But I thought I was allowed to live with Peter, I thought it had been agreed'. He said, 'No, none of us want that'; he slapped her and walked out. One cousin stood up for her, he tried to placate the others saying, 'We did agree to this, come on, what harm is there? Why not let her go?' But her father was adamant: 'She has humiliated me and she will pay.'

She was bundled into a car, driven by an uncle with her father beside him. In the back seat, she was wedged between her mother and a man she recognised as a doctor who had treated members of her family. 'I was told from the start that if I made a fuss they would shoot me. At one point, when I started hyperventilating they let me out to stand on the verge and have a breather, but when I started crying my uncle placed his gun on my forehead and said, "Keep quiet or I will shoot you and throw you in the bushes." When I got back into the car the doctor sedated me. They drove me across the border into Tanzania using my cousin's passport because Peter had mine.'

How can such things happen except in a James Bond film? That's what Shazia and I asked each other later. But for Maya there was no handsome double agent coming to rescue her, no one to help at all. The next fortnight passed in a blur. She was so heavily sedated that she woke up only to eat or, more often, to be sick. They stayed in a cousin's office, in one then another hotel; every two or three days they moved on, avoiding anyone who might be trying to trace them. In each new room her father removed all the writing materials and unplugged the phone. Maya's life had become surreal.

By mid-December her father had managed to 'acquire her passport from Peter's house'.

'How?' I asked her.

She shrugged. She looked drained and exhausted. Her voice was weary. 'He knows people. He has money. I don't know how.'

The way was clear for him to remove her from the country. She was wheeled through the airport at Dar Es Salaam. 'We are taking her to India for medical treatment,' explained her mother, all solicitous and concerned. 'See here, what doctor has written – she brandished a letter – 'the poor child has serious mental problem. Doctor must give her medicine to keep her calm.'

On this pretext, the doctor sat next to her on the flight to Delhi. 'I am sorry Maya but what can I do?' That's what he said to her and shame stained his face as he said it. 'I did not realise what I was getting into but now, for what I have done, I could lose my job. I am a family man. I am now reliant on your father and I dare not cross him.'

From Delhi, Maya was driven to the Punjab, to the house of her father's parents who were delighted by this unexpected visit, pleased and proud to welcome a granddaughter of marriageable age. But again, after the initial introductions, illness was used as an excuse to keep Maya locked away. She remembers a room with a cold tiled floor and big wooden shutters that were always closed. Life passed by on the other side of her locked door, whispering. Food arrived on trays. After seven or ten or perhaps fourteen days – it was hard to tell with her brain so fogged and muddled – Maya began to think she must be pregnant. Even in her misery her heart sang a little, she was carrying Peter's child.

'It can't be true,' said the doctor, but when tests confirmed it was, no time was lost. Maya's father 'acquired some tablets' and stood beside his daughter, a lowering insistent presence, as she swallowed one with every meal. Within a week she miscarried, crouched on all fours on the bed, rocking herself to and fro against the griping pains tearing at her lower belly, stifling her sobs as the blood, thick and sticky, trickled down her legs. It was night-time and in the hostile darkness she sensed her parents behind her at the doorway, silently watching.

Several days later she was on her bed, dazed and desolate, when her father again appeared. This time he was far from silent. 'What is this?' he screamed, striding across the room brandishing a letter. His open palmed slap threw her face sideways, but not before she recognised the writing as her own. 'Deceitful slut. Are you this man's whore that you write to him, begging him to come for you?'

'I am his wife,' Maya said, raising herself on her elbows ready to defend herself, but then flinching away as her father brought a curtain rod crashing down on her feet.

Sitting opposite me in the tea-shop Maya gave a deep sigh and fell silent. For two or three minutes we sat there. I was studying Maya's face and I bet Shazia was too, but she didn't seem to register. I no longer felt her yearning towards me, she seemed to have withdrawn, drifting back down the years to the moment her hope died. When, finally, she met my gaze her eyes were dull, her voice flat.

'The girl who was going to send my letters was told not to come back to work. I don't know what happened to her, but at that point I collapsed. I allowed myself to. I made peace with myself and shut down. I said to my father, "If you want to get me married you can."'

She set about making herself the accomplished Asian wife: learning to read and write Punjabi, showing off her cooking and practising her sewing skills. Her parents started taking her to the temple and making her pray. 'They wanted me to be religious and good.'

The proposals started coming. Families arrived and Maya served tea, head covered, demure in her Asian suit. 'I felt like I was in a cattle market, up for auction,' Maya said. And she was a prize catch. Shortly after Britain colonised Kenya her grandfather had been called to Britain to work on the railways; the citizenship he acquired then had been passed down his family. Knowing that she was a ticket to England made her suitors bold: her dowry must include televisions, video players, cars, a house. 'I was supposed to stay quiet and accept, but despite my resolution I couldn't bring myself to: I kept saying no.'

But then her father met a middle-man, a matchmaker, a *bachola* – all false sagacity and oily charm. 'I have just the guy for you, a very handsome guy. His family is modern in outlook, liberal too so they might be interested, although of course it's difficult, very difficult, things with your daughter being the way they are. Still, let us try. No ifs and buts – get the girl ready and I'll bring the family over. The guy? Param? No, he's already in England, no, no – not legal yet, you know how these things go.'

Maya was dressed up. Her mum got her special plates out. Her would-be in-laws arrived. 'Everybody was staring at me and I thought, this is not good. I looked at my mum and she looked the other way. The next thing I knew I had sweetmeats placed on my hand, and money and a red scarf and I realised the deal was already done. It was a *fait accompli*. I was going to be their bride.'

She travelled to England to meet the man to whom she'd been betrothed: he was working in a factory in Leeds and he spoke almost no English. Perhaps her father was not impressed because after the first meeting (all Maya said to her fiancé was 'would you like to come and eat?') he put her back in the cattle market. 'I must have seen five or so other boys. I got sick and tired of it. I said to my dad, "Come on, why don't I just marry the one you have chosen?"'

But then something happened that seemed to promise Maya a new and very different future. She was summoned to London to be interviewed by Interpol. Peter – unaware that Maya's father had annulled their marriage – had been frantic in his efforts to track her down. 'My spirits danced that day. In my head I really believed that everything would be okay again. I thought I would ask for Peter to be flown out here, we would be protected and together we would start a new life.'

How naive she was. Her father escorted her to the interview. 'Just before I went inside he said to me, "Right this moment there are many men roaming around where Peter and Mary live. Men I know. Men who enjoy rape and torture. Their deaths would not be quick." What could I do?' Maya's face twisted with anguish. 'I told the police what my father wanted me to. I could not put Peter and Mary at risk.'

Her wedding to the handsome guy with the liberal outlook took place in India. Maya was treated kindly by her in-laws who were careful of their new, prized possession. Their neighbours were impressed. 'The day after the wedding, people came to look at me. They lifted up my veil and peered at me. They didn't talk to me but they talked to my mother-in-law: "Isn't she beautiful?" "She's from outside, no?" "She has opened up your feet, you can go to UK now."' In those early days – with his British visa not yet applied for – even Param, her new husband, seemed kind.

25

The afternoon had dwindled away; the teashop was empty save for the waitress, sullen now as she leant against the counter, propped on her elbows, staring into space. It was time to go but too soon, I felt sure, to abandon Maya. She had not even arrived at the point of her story that now most concerned her: her boys. I paid the bill and the three of us walked out into the still city evening. The warmth of the day was gone, the light was fading. I checked my watch, it was already half past five.

I felt the need to move, to shake off the harsh ugliness of Maya's story. I wanted to feel cool air on my skin, to clear my head and stretch my legs. And I wanted her walking beside me, looking forwards, finding something positive in life. I touched her elbow and we turned towards New Street. For a while the three of us walked in reflective silence and then suddenly Maya said, 'My ex-husband is an alcoholic. From the start he was quite violent towards me. He would twist my wrists and slap me when he was drunk. He frightened me. I felt very alone, my parents had gone back to Kenya and when I spoke to my father on the telephone all he said was, "Are you expecting yet? Until you make a family you will never earn any respect."'

Like Surjit, Maya found that once her husband got rights of residency, his behaviour towards her grew worse. He became very controlling: forcing her to give up an accountancy course she had started, preventing her from going out alone, forbidding socialising, monitoring her calls. He called her names: 'fat bitch' was a favourite. It amused him to make her ask to go to the toilet; he would force her to wait fifteen or twenty minutes, catching her wrist and pulling her backwards if she tried to walk past him before he gave her permission to go.

He expected her to come home and cook for him on the very day that their first son, Jeevan, was born. By that time the household seemed to be disintegrating: Param had a job in a bakery, but there was rarely any money for food; he was often drunk and inclined to invite his friends into the house at 6 a.m. when they'd finished their night shift.

Two weeks after Jeevan's birth Maya was woken at 2 a.m. by the sound of brawling outside the back door. 'I went downstairs with the baby in my arms and through the window I could see two men beating Param up. I don't know where I got the courage, but I went out and grabbed him by the shoulder – he was bleeding and half-unconscious – and dragged him inside. I kicked one guy who was standing in my way, and he punched me in my face and then the other one punched his fist through the window and the smashed glass sprayed on my son and myself. I rang the police and said, "Someone is attacking us," but in the morning Param was so angry about that. He said, "Why did you call the police? Those people are my friends."' Maya sighed. 'That's how drunk he would get.'

Her marriage continued to degenerate. On a trip to India to celebrate Jeevan's birth, Param delighted in humiliating her in front of his family, insulting her and throwing his slippers at her head. He made no attempt to conceal the fact he was sleeping with one of the housemaids, and when Maya questioned him he punched her, splitting her lip. Maya's mother – visiting her new grandchild – noticed. 'She said, "He's beaten you up hasn't he?" And I said, "If he has, what do you care. You didn't want me happy in this marriage and I'm not." My father ignored my bruises and just hugged me as if to say now you are respectable, at last I can be proud.'

Back in England, before the birth of Bakshi, Param's mother came to stay and Maya found herself waiting on both her husband and his mother who – now she had the prized ticket to England – was vocal in her criticism of a daughter-in-law tired by the demands of her job (Maya was by then working in Boots), pregnancy and a toddler.

'After Bakshi was born that was the end of our relationship. I never slept with my ex-husband again. But that's when he started hinting he would leave me. He said to me, "It's so hard for me staying with you because I know you were married before." Four years after our marriage he said that! I told him, "I've tried to be the best I can for you. I've done everything for you. I've stood by you and been the ideal wife for you." But he wouldn't listen, he just kept repeating, "I'm not happy that you were married before."'

How much can one person stand? At what point does the spirit suddenly snap? That's what I found myself wondering as Maya's soft, insistent voice filled the space around me. There were times during that long, sad afternoon when I wanted to put my hands on my ears and shout, 'STOP! Please, no more!' but there could not be any respite, not until this poor tired woman had reached the end of her litany of ill-treatment and abuse.

We walked, without discussion or decision, to the station, arriving just as the street lights snapped on. We sat on the concourse sipping coffee out of polystyrene cups and Maya told us of a second trip to India during which she was treated by her in-laws as a slave. She told us of the evening there when Param, stinking drunk, dragged her into a shower room and violently raped her. She told us how he forced her to abort the pregnancy that resulted, accusing her of carrying another man's child. And she told us of the final, furious row that ended with Param screaming at her, 'I want you out of the house and take the fucking kids with you.' That was how her marriage ended.

It didn't surprise me to hear that Maya's health eventually gave out. Soon after she became a single mother, she got a job, a good job as an interpreter for a law enforcement company but – after all she had been through – the pressure was too much for her. Social services began to notice that the children weren't in school; support was given but still Maya couldn't cope. She had a nervous breakdown and was hospitalised and when Param requested an interim residency order, giving him custody of the boys, it seems it was almost with relief that Maya agreed – on the condition that once she had regained her strength Param would give them back. And now he wouldn't. Instead, he sent to Pakistan for another woman to be his wife, their mother: his last casual cruelty.

'I'm taking him to court, for the residency of my boys and now also for the rape. I might not have had the courage to report the rape if it were not for the fact that I am desperate. He would have got residence at the last directional hearing if

I had not brought the police proceedings.' Maya turned to face me as she said this and for the first time that afternoon I saw a spark of strength in her – a ghostly reminder of the girl who could have run for her coutry, the girl brave enough to defy her parents to run away with the man she loved. But then she wavered. 'There is another hearing next week, but I don't know if I will succeed. The social worker seems to be against me.'

'What do you mean?' I said.

'He says I agreed that Param should have the boys and they are happy with him. He wants to know why I have brought the rape charge so late.'

'Have you told him what you have just told me?' I asked her.

'About what?' she said. Her face was blank.

'About the abuse from your family, the kidnap, the forced marriage, the abuse from Param. Does your social worker know the background to your nervous breakdown?'

'Well, no, he has never asked me.'

'He needs to know. So do the police and your lawyer. I need to speak to them; I think we should delay the hearing, we have to make a case for why you had that breakdown. Maya,' I took her hands in mine, squeezing them tight as if I could pump hope into her. 'Look how strong and brave you are: after all you've been through you have held yourself together because you want your boys back. You have to focus on that. Everything you've done so far you've done by yourself but now I'm going to support you. You no longer have to walk alone.'

As our train home pulled into Birmingham New Street that evening, I noticed a Derby police officer, Detective Andrea Parkin sitting in one of the window seats. Instinctively, I waved, but even though the train was slowing down I don't think she saw me. Shazia and I climbed into a carriage that was empty save for a young Asian man, sitting at the far end by himself. I remember a vague stirring of recognition as I noticed him; I clocked his face and his dark leather jacket before I turned away and settled myself in my seat. Shazia and I sat side by side in silence; ugly fragments of Maya's terrible story kept playing through my mind as I tried to remember everything she had told me. If I was going to write a report for her social worker I needed to have all her details straight.

The first time the man in the leather jacket walked past us I assumed he was going to the toilet; on his way back he lurched against my seat and brushed my arm, which surprised me because the train wasn't travelling fast, there seemed no need for it. I watched him get back to his seat, stand beside it for a moment and then – as if he'd forgotten something – he turned round and started walking back down the carriage. My eyes were following him, but my brain wasn't really registering what I saw. Until I realised he was staring at me. Discomfited, I dropped my gaze. He walked past me and then, seconds later, he went back past, reached his seat and turned again. I looked up, and in the split second our eyes met I realised with a jolt that I had met him before. The expression on his face was menacing.

He was on his way back. I counted the paces between us: two, three, four . . . I nudged Shazia who was looking out of the window. Eight, nine, ten . . . I turned to Shazia but still I could sense that at fifteen he was level with us. 'I know him,' I whispered as he passed us.

'Who?'

'Him. Wait, you'll see.'

Seconds later I could feel his presence again. He paused just before he reached our seats; I think he sat down in the row behind, on the opposite side of the aisle. I willed myself to look straight ahead. I wouldn't give him the satisfaction of seeing me turn to check on him, I wouldn't let him gloat at the fear that must be written on my face.

After a couple of minutes I heard him move again, only this time he didn't walk past me. Where had he gone? Not knowing was almost more frightening than having him near me. My heart was pounding and my hands were wet with sweat.

'Who?' Shazia whispered.

'Ssssssh.' I couldn't stand it. I was about to turn, to try and find him when he walked past again, his pace slow and arrogant. 'Him,' I whispered, my eyes fixed on the seat in front of me. 'I know him.'

'Who is he?' Shazia craned her neck, trying to get a proper view of him, but I yanked her back down. 'What's he doing?' she whispered.

'Trying to intimidate me.'

'Why?'

As he started up the aisle yet again I began to dread what would happen when we got to Derby. What would I do if he followed me to my car? I could feel myself breathing harder as I started to panic. I felt trapped. I wished the carriage wasn't so empty; if only there was someone else around, a witness to this threatening behaviour. Suddenly I remembered Andrea Parkin, in the carriage up ahead.

'Shazia.' I turned right in towards her, but I was still whispering. 'When we get to Tamworth we're going to get out of the train and get back in another carriage. Don't ask me why, please, just do what I say.' I checked my watch, gathered my bag in readiness.

As it happened, he was behind us when the train pulled into Tamworth. Without looking back, I strode down the carriage, jumped out and ran down the platform, Shazia hurrying behind me, until I spotted Andrea. I banged on the glass and quickly made for the door.

I was panting as I fell into the seat opposite her, and Shazia was too. For a moment I couldn't order my thoughts enough to explain myself and we all three sat there, looking at each other.

Then: 'I need your help,' I said, quick and urgent. 'There's a man in the carriage we've just come from who has reason to dislike me. I helped his sister leave home two years ago. I met him when he came to Karma Nirvana looking for her; he was very angry and aggressive then. He's been trying to frighten me. I know he lives in Derby and I'm scared he'll follow me when we get off the train. Would you mind escorting me to the car park, just seeing me into my car?'

Of course Andrea said she would and straight away I felt much safer. Alone with Shazia in that other carriage I had felt so vulnerable and exposed. And I wasn't being fanciful. I don't know what would have happened if Andrea hadn't been there. When we got to Derby he did move towards me on the platform, but then Andrea stepped off the train and stood beside me and he swerved away.

She took my arm and Shazia walked the other side of me – as if they were physically guarding me – and they stayed like that until we reached the car. I locked myself in but still, as I put my feet on the pedals my legs were shaking. It was several minutes before I could drive away.

26

Being taken into the confidence of women like Maya is not something I will ever take for granted. I see it as a privilege that someone who has suffered so much chooses to take me into their trust, and if by listening I can help them I am glad. But I never feel I'm on a one-way street. Hearing these women's stories helps me too. Each new reminder that my experience – often magnified in horror a hundred times – is shared by so many other women vindicates my decision to leave my family and then stand up and tell the world exactly why I couldn't stay with them.

Also – and I'm at last beginning to accept this – sharing their pain allows me to forgive myself for the fact that even now, all these years on, my disownment sometimes makes me ache inside. Sometimes I have a dream about my funeral so vivid that I can see the cemetery and my coffin and the kids and the friends I hope would be there but then, in my mind's eye, there's a gap where my family should be standing. No one from my family comes to say goodbye to me, not a single one. Sometimes when I dream that I wake up to find tears rolling down my cheeks and I can hardly breathe because my heart feels so heavy. When that happens I scramble out of bed because the feeling is so intense I think it's going to crush me. But even when I'm wide awake and thinking rationally – as I'm standing in the shower with the water drumming on my head, beating the nonsense out of me – there are days when the thought that the dream might come true still hurts.

This year on what would have been Robina's birthday I heard that my family was having a get-together, but I wasn't invited. It was a Saturday and I woke up that morning feeling that everything inside of me had shrivelled. I wanted to crawl away and hide. I didn't think that I could face the world.

I'd just finished eating my breakfast when Yasmin texted me. The text read:

I'm having a low day. It's my dad's birthday.

I'm very fond of Yasmin, she's one of the women who have become special to me, but that day I couldn't find anything inside myself to give her. She wasn't to know that, she certainly didn't know why. She must have been hurt and surprised when she got my cold reply:

Actually I need some space. I'm grieving my sister.

I did apologise afterwards; that evening I sent her a text explaining the significance of the day and how I felt about it. I hope she understood; she said she did. I hope she wasn't hurt.

Earlier I took some flowers and went up to the crematorium where Mum, Dad and Robina were all cremated. Robina's ashes aren't there – I don't know where they are, my sisters took them – but I had to go somewhere I could link with her. The children came with me and we stood there for a while, very quietly, without talking.

I was thinking about how close Robina and I were, about the things we did as children. We used to play 'Knock out Ginger' when we lived in Northumberland Street and Robina was the brave one, always standing longest on the doorstep before she lost her nerve and legged it. I remember her doubled up in the safe haven of our doorway, hands on her hips, trying to catch her breath, gasping through her laughter. In Northumberland Road days, she and I and the youngest of us, Lucy, were small enough to go in the bath all together. Our oldest sister, Ginda, would line us up, three in a row and wash our hair. We were as close as sardines in a tin in those days and now look at us: all three dead to one another. And Ginda – who all but brought me up – as distant as a stranger to me and my children.

I made a choice and that's the price I paid.

27

The struggle to get schools in Derby to display the Forced Marriage Unit's posters focused my mind on how important it is to reach young people because it showed me that – even for girls who have the freedom to live a normal life – accessing help is very hard. I try never to turn down an opportunity to speak in any school that will have me, and at the end of my talk at least one, often two or three girls will want to discuss things further. It's not unusual to hear a whispered: 'You know what you were saying, Miss, well that's what it's like for me.'

Only once has a boy spoken at any school I've been to; he was at a comprehensive in west London, a big school with boys and girls from fifty-four different nationalities. I'd been asked by the head teacher there to give the same talk to two groups of students aged about fifteen. The first one was fine. We were in the library which was much more informal than the silent, austere room I remember from my school days: there were soft chairs, computers, magazines and a big semi-circle of upright chairs arranged around the place where I was supposed to sit.

I guess there were about sixty of them, and when the kids filed in there weren't any spare seats.

Once I started a few of the boys were boisterous and stupid, but most of them were quite attentive. At the end two girls came up to me – like most of their classmates they were wearing hijabs – and hugged me and thanked me and asked if I knew about Heshu Yones, the Kurdish girl whose father slit her throat. I said I did and they told me that she had lived not far away; they said they remembered all the talk, the terrible whispered details that rustled round the classrooms in the days after she was killed.

The second talk was marked for me by a heavy-jawed, broad-shouldered boy who looked much older than the rest. I noticed him when the pupils walked in and when I asked about him the teacher who was with me raised her eyes and gave a cynical little snort of laughter. 'He looks nineteen doesn't he? He probably is, but his dad insists he's fifteen, so what can we do? It happens all the time – kids miss out on education in their own countries and when they come here their parents want them to catch up. He's from Saudi.' I wouldn't have given him another thought had he not subsequently challenged me. I thought the second talk went well. This time I mentioned Heshu Yones, I wanted to stress the fact that her father murdered her simply for having a Christian boyfriend; I thought that would have a lot of impact in such a multicultural school and certainly a lot of glances were exchanged, there was whispering behind hands.

As soon as I'd finished talking the Saudi boy put his hand up and said, 'Who do you think you are, coming here and telling us how to live our lives?'

He said it with all the arrogant confidence of the man he

appeared to be and the words were hardly out of his mouth before the teacher was up on her feet, simultaneously trying to shut him up and apologise to me. But I was curious, I told her not to worry, to let him carry on and, with his arms folded across his chest and his chin thrust high, he did: 'If my sister was doing the things that you said, I would kill her.'

'Really?' I said. I looked round the semi-circle of chairs in front of me; none of the kids reacted, no one challenged him, all eyes avoided mine. 'Well, while you are living here you ought to know that in this country it's illegal to kill somebody because you see them talking to a person of the opposite sex.'

He came back at me, quick as a knife. 'I don't care which country I am in. She is my sister and it is my duty to guard her honour. If she did the things you talk about I would kill her.'

The teacher wrapped it up very quickly after that. As the kids filed out of the library, pushing and shoving, fooling about, she was full of apologies: 'He was showing off, I'm sure he didn't mean it.' But I couldn't accept that, I said, 'He did mean it. You saw him, he was very clear – and if he has any sisters I'd be very concerned for them.'

It was about 7 p.m. by the time I got back to Derby. My friend Maureen who has known the kids since they were tiny had picked Joshua up from school and was at my house with him.

'I took him to buy a comic at the corner shop on the way home,' she said, almost as soon as I walked in. She waited just long enough for Joshua to have turned his attention back to the television. 'You know how he takes ages choosing? Well, I went outside to wait and I was chatting to a group of girls I know, fourteen- and fifteen-year-olds, all of them Asian. I often see them there outside the shop, they're at the local school.'

I eased my shoes off, wondering where this was leading. Maureen was keeping her voice low, a frown creased her brow.

'When Joshua came out of the shop I introduced him to them and I told them who his mummy was. They'd been talking about that poor girl Surjit Athwal and I thought they would be interested to know that you'd spoken with her brother.'

My mind flicked to the man she meant, Jagdeesh Singh. Two days earlier we'd spoken on the same radio programme, both rejoicing in the fact that nine long years after the disappearance of his sister Surjit, her killers were being brought to justice. Throughout those years – when all that was known was that Surjit had vanished from the face of the earth while visiting India for a family wedding – Jagdeesh had doggedly pursued his 'Justice for Surjit' campaign. He was insistent that, although his sister was unhappy in her marriage, she would never have run off, abandoning her two small children, as her husband Sukhdev claimed she had.

But now the truth was coming out. Surjit had been murdered, killed in the name of honour while on her trip to India. She had brought shame on her husband by asking him for a divorce and both he and his mother Bachan had determined she would die. Bachan had allegedly called a family meeting and decreed, 'We must get rid of her', before arranging for her own brother to strangle Surjit and dump her body in a river. Once the deed was done, Sukhdev returned to England and, within months, he had divorced Surjit on the grounds of desertion and married again.

Surjit's body has never been found and the truth might not have been uncovered had Bachan not boasted of her cleverness.

On her return to England she told certain relatives what had happened and now – after years of living with this information on their consciences, of being unwilling to come forward for fear of reprisals – these relatives had passed the information on to the police. Sukdhev and Bachan had been brought to trial and the press was full of it.

To me this case was good news and I said so on the radio. It seemed to me such progress to have relatives cooperating with the police to investigate an honour killing. It also highlighted the police's responsibility to pursue justice for all British citizens who disappear abroad. I agreed with Jagdeesh Singh when he pointed out how little publicity Surjit had when compared with Lucie Blackman, the blonde British girl who disappeared and was later found murdered in Japan. I was impressed by the way he fought for justice for his sister and we both agreed we should consider what we might do together in the future.

Exciting though that news was, it all seemed a very long way from our quiet little corner shop. I couldn't think what it had to do with Maureen or Joshua. 'Were the girls at all interested? Did they want to know what Jagdeesh said?' I asked her.

'I didn't get a chance to tell them.' Maureen looked quickly over her shoulder to check that Joshua was absorbed in the television. 'As soon as I said your name their faces froze and they all stepped backwards, literally, as though they were trying to get away from us. They were exchanging funny looks and then one of them – the one I've talked to most often – said, "Sorry, but we're not allowed to mention that name in our house. We get in trouble if we do." Then she turned to the other girls and said, "Come on, we better go."

'Joshua was quite upset by it, bless him. He kept asking me,

"Why aren't they allowed to mention her name? What's she done wrong?" Honestly Jas, I didn't know what to say.'

Nor did I. Joshua didn't mention it until the next morning. It was Saturday and we were walking the dog in the fields behind our house when he told me the story, just as Maureen had. 'Why don't they like you, Mum?' he said. I told him that it was natural for people to hold different views; I tried to explain that the important thing is to believe in yourself and not worry about what other people think. I kept my voice calm and positive as I said it, and he seemed reassured, but I couldn't convince myself. In truth I was unnerved by the fact that in our little village – the haven I chose as an escape from the sharp tongues and disapproving glances I meet everywhere in Derby – there were people who hated me, people who wished me ill. I couldn't bear the thought that the children and I might be walking among them, not knowing who they were. I felt the familiar queasy fear settle on my stomach.

I'd been away most of the week and that morning I had to go into the office to pick up some files. Against my will I found myself looking over my shoulder as I unlocked the car, I couldn't help watching the people I drove past, trying to see if anyone was clocking me or my route. More than once I checked the mirror to see if anyone was following me. 'How fast can news travel?' That's what I kept asking myself. Only three days earlier I had agreed to address the jury at the beginning of a forthcoming murder trial in the West Midlands. The victim was a young Muslim man who had been shot, execution style, in the back of the head. As far as anyone knew he had no enemies, there was no one who bore a grudge – apart from his brothers-in-law who had made it very clear that they didn't like the fact their sister had chosen her husband for herself. In fact, some of his in-laws are standing trial.

I had agreed, in the role of cultural expert, to explain to the jury just how strongly Asian families can feel about young men and women who reject arranged marriages in favour of relationships they've chosen for themselves. I was going to explain the concept of honour, how easy it is to sully it and the lengths to which some families go when they feel their honour has been compromised. When the chief superintendent in charge of the case asked me to do this, I agreed with alacrity, I didn't even think twice. But that morning, driving through Derby, it occurred to me that I was putting myself in the way of a family who – although the trial had yet to prove it – seemed willing to kill people who they deemed dishonourable. Was I mad to do it? Should I say I'd changed my mind? The questions darted through my mind like fireflies. It was months since I'd felt so vulnerable and on edge.

I parked outside Karma Nirvana and reached onto the back seat of the car for a woollen hat I keep there for moments like this when I don't feel too safe. I jammed it on my head and pulled the collar of my jacket up to my ears. 'You're being stupid,' I told myself as I hurried across the car park, head down, shoulders hunched, heading for the back door of our office. Because I wasn't looking where I was going, it was the smell that stopped me in my tracks just before I reached the building. It was vile and it was unmistakeable: human shit.

I looked up to see it smeared all over the office windows, great brown streaks of it spreading out from the splat where it had hit the glass and the remnants of it, stinking fragments on the ground beside the wall. I stood rooted to the spot. My heart was pounding. My first instinct was to turn and race back to the car, to pretend I hadn't seen it, to deny it, to run away. I couldn't face any more fear, I didn't want this to be my drama, at that moment I didn't want this to be my life.

But I didn't run. Clinging to my last shred of calm and common-sense, I told myself that just inside the locked door to my office was a panic button that would summon the police within seconds. I groped in my handbag for the keys, fumbling in my haste to fit them into the lock, checking all around me as I did so. There was nothing to see, nothing but a couple of beer cans and a discarded burger, dropped and trodden on, a footprint still visible in the mud and ketchup smeared across the polystyrene box.

I pulled the door open and my eyes swept the office rapidly, checking for anything unusual, anything that had been disrupted or moved. Nothing. I hesitated for a moment on the threshold, eyes fixed on the partition that, from where I stood, hid a quarter of the room from view. 'Hello? Is anybody there?' I called, my voice sounding forced and unfamiliar in the dead silence of the empty room.

The latch clicked, solid and reassuring as I closed the door and leant against it, breathing consciously, in out in out, until my heart slowed. Once I was safe inside I made myself look at the window, at the vile mess that clouded it and suddenly, as if someone had pulled a plug out, my fear drained away. Looking at the sordid threat – or perhaps it was a protest – wondering who would clear it up, I felt a dull, tired anger. Literally and metaphorically this was shit, nothing more. It could have been thrown by somebody wanting to frighten or threaten me, it could have been thrown by drunken kids having a lark; either way I would never find out. But I wasn't going to let it get to me. The panic button forgotten, I picked up the phone on the nearest desk and dialled the police. I could hear the weariness in my voice as I made my report, noting dully that repetition was beginning to make even this process workaday. When we got to the end of it, the officer who had taken my statement made soothing remarks and – as I knew was expected of me – I politely agreed. No, not much could be done about it; yes, I would be vigilant, and of course I wouldn't worry unduly, no point in that.

I collected the files I had come for and then, with a feeling of defiance, I tugged my woollen hat off my head and shook out my hair. As I walked back across the car park it occurred to me, for the first time, that I didn't have to stay in Derby, I could live anywhere, do this work from any place I chose. Like a pop-up, an image flashed into my mind of a cottage by the sea. I couldn't help smiling at this revelation; it was as though I'd opened the door of a dank, confined room, just enough to let a shaft of sunshine slide inside and pierce the gloom. It was the spark of an idea, and I found it immensely comforting. As I reached the car, I turned back to look at the office building, at the shit which, from that distance, was nothing but a smudge, an indistinct smear. 'I could go,' I told myself. 'But I won't be driven out. I'll go when I'm ready.'

28

As soon as I could I contacted the various authorities attached to Maya's case. I spoke to the police officer to whom she had made her statement and a couple of days later he sent me the following request.

Jasvinder,

With regard to the allegation of rape by Maya Sandhar, I need an expert statement from you in relation to the cultural pressures that Maya would have been under at the time.

I would be grateful if you could include explanation of:

The culture of arranged marriages and the attitudes of her own family and her in-laws

The potential consequences for someone in her position had they chosen to disclose this matter despite these pressures.

The perceived 'shame' that such disclosures and the leaving of her husband would have brought on her family/in-laws.

Thank you very much for your help in this matter.

I look forward to hearing from you.

Jim

I wrote a careful and considered reply in which I aimed to put all Maya's suffering into the context of the culture she was raised in. I thought immediately of Surjit: two women, two marriages and yet in both cases the essentials were the same.

Both women were forcibly married to men who were considerably less well-educated than themselves which – as I pointed out in Maya's report – is in direct contradiction of the accepted practice of arranged marriages in which compatibility is supposed to be a concern.

I highlighted the fact that, as is so often the case, Param only gave full vent to his abusive behaviour once his British residency had been confirmed. I also made clear that because south Asian communities generally consider women to be lowly beings – the possessions first of their fathers, then their husbands – he would have considered his behaviour quite reasonable. As I wrote that sentence my mind flashed back to the reaction of Fozia's father when he heard that one of his daughters had been violated by her husband: that's not rape, it's a husband's right.

I stressed the isolation that Maya – and others in her position – accept as normal and explained how difficult it makes it for them to access, or even be aware of, any external sources of help. They would have been brought up to keep silent and to believe that to do otherwise would be to bring dishonour on themselves and their families. In the happiest of circumstances – which Maya's clearly was not – once married, she would have been expected to make the marriage work and not go moaning to her family; hence her silence. Almost more important, I explained – and here my mind was full of conversations I'd had with Kiren and Shabana – she would have been terrified that by disclosing the abuse to any outsider, she might sever what little contact she still had with her family. It's hard to emphasise enough just how desperate these women are to maintain any sort of link. I finished up by saying:

> The complexities of the honour-based culture she grew up in have also meant that Maya's family had a role in colluding with the accused, Mr Param Gupta and so she has not received the family support one would expect in such cases.

This continues to be true for Maya. When Param discovered that she was not only challenging his custody of the children but also intended to bring a rape case against him, he turned immediately to her parents for support. Having, without success, badgered Maya to drop the charges they then decided to do what they could – as they saw it – to salvage the situation and save their face, by marrying her off to someone else.

'They have found a man they think is suitable. Do you think I should consider it, Jasvinder?' she asked me when this happened and I had to count to ten before I told her that to do so would be madness. But I understand the topsy-turvy world that she exists in. Her father, concerned for his honour, tells her that she will be less lonely, more likely to get custody of her children if she marries again.

And she would like to believe that.

But she is cautious; she can't quite forget his past treatment of her so she challenges him about it and he says, 'What treatment? I don't know what you are talking about; I have always had your welfare at heart.'

And she would like to believe that too.

'He still has this power over me, Jasvinder. I don't know why.'

'Because he's your father, Maya. At least in name he is. You want him to behave like your father, to love you and care for you, to protect you. But if past experience is anything to go by that's not going to happen. You have to remove those expectations from him, Maya, or you will keep on getting hurt. Look at it this way: if your house was on fire you would run away from the flames not into them, wouldn't you?'

For several months I had this dialogue with Maya – or variations of it. There were times when I worried for her future, but usually, eventually, the women I see find within themselves the courage to move on. One Saturday morning Maya rang to say that she was moving up towards Birmingham to be closer to her mother who – suddenly and of her own volition – had changed her stance and offered to give evidence to the police about the violence she had seen Param inflict on her daughter.

'You know he has been charged with six counts of assault, I am waiting to hear whether or not he will plead guilty. I don't know what my mum's statement said, but I hope it will help.' Maya was quiet as ever, almost cautious. 'She says she will also give a report on my welfare to my lawyers so perhaps that will help with the custody case.'

These remarkable – wonderful – changes of heart do happen. Several months after I first met him, Imran told his story on national television; he was taking part in a debate about forced marriage on the Jeremy Kyle show. The next morning his mum rang the office – the first time she had contacted him in seven years. We all held our breath while he took the call, but what she said was, 'I saw you on the programme son and I was proud of you. What I did to you was wrong and I am asking now for your forgiveness.'

I don't know whether those two mothers had gone through years of internal struggle before finding the courage to stand up to and reject the culture that ensnared them and persuaded them to treat their own children so cruelly, or whether their acts of support were a private defiance, an isolated moment of truth that – as far as their community was concerned – they would keep to themselves. I won't waste my time in wondering: either way, they give their children such a lift.

'I can never bond with my mum, but she has in some sense realised what I've been through and I have learnt about her too,' Maya told me. 'She suffered violence from my dad as well. Did I tell you Jas, I just discovered that he has three other wives apart from her? Now I appreciate how difficult her situation must have been, I can connect with her somehow. Anyway, as you have told me so often, it is best to put the past behind you and get on with life. Once I am nearer to her I will be very glad of the practical help she can give me.'

It turned out that the help she gave was not just practical: Maya's mum has proved to be an inspiration to her timid daughter. At fifty-plus, she trained to be a Montessori teacher and now she has a teaching job she loves. 'She is an independent woman, Jasvinder. I want to be like that, I want to go to university.'

I wish Maya could have seen me when she said that, seen the grin of pleasure that spread across my face. I felt a wave of relief wash through me and with it came an idea that would help Karma Nirvana and allow us to keep an eye on Maya as she built her new life: 'We need more volunteers. While you're planning your future, would you consider it? Could you do two days a week?'

* * *

It struck me the day I first met Maya, and I have often revisited the thought since then: she spent so many years suffering alone. The research I have done for my PhD shows that the turning point for survivors – the critical moment when they decide at last to let go of their victimhood, to stand up for themselves and have faith in the future – comes when they meet someone who understands what they have been through because they have experienced something similar. For Maya and for Surjit, I was that person. But whereas Maya – with almost two decades of abuse and isolation behind her – needed a great deal of support in her recovery, I was amazed by how quickly Surjit grew from a frightened, if resourceful girl into an independent, optimistic woman. Some time after her escape she plucked up the courage to phone her mother and was told, 'You are dead in our eyes and we want nothing to do with you.' In fact her family had moved to a new city to escape the dishonour she had brought on them, and in their new life they told everyone that she had died.

Gradually, however, she found she could build up little pieces of hope and empowerment, and she decided to divorce her husband. She searched for a solicitor in her home town, to avoid being traced, and told him about the forced marriage, the rape and mental abuse, the mental illness and miscarriages she'd suffered – everything in fact. The case was so compelling that her husband was unable to contest it, and she even managed to win back her dowry of five thousand pounds.

A few years ago, Surjit met the man of her dreams, someone who has given her unconditional love and support, and a wedding she had only ever imagined with three hundred guests. She told me sadly that she set a table aside for her family, hoping that even one of them might turn up. Even then, after everything she'd been through, she still hoped that someone would. None came. 'The family who have disowned me for thirteen years no longer deserve my tears,' she says. 'My friends have become my family.'

She worked very hard to get where she is today. In spite of her unsatisfactory education, she now has two diplomas, a career in business and travels the world. She has sky dived, walked on glaciers and even been to rock festivals. She still suffers nightmares and flashbacks from the past and relies on tranquilisers and sleeping pills. There is no contact with her family, but she longs one day to have a child of her own.

29

Almost a year after I first interviewed Fatima I was called as a cultural expert to a court hearing regarding the custody of her children. She had been tried for her crime by that stage. I wasn't able to attend her trial but her solicitor told me that all three of Fatima's brothers were present in court and when Fatima took the stand she insisted she had acted alone and on her own initiative. She was found guilty of arson and lying to the police and sentenced to two years in jail.

On the train on the way to Liverpool I looked back at the report I had written after I first met her and Rafiq. It was pages long, but I turned at once to the conclusion.

> Fatima has stated that she no longer wishes to have any contact with her family . . . She understands that she is at risk from her family and that her children and her husband will be at risk too . . .
>
> I believe that by breaking the silence Fatima's risk has been heightened . . .
>
> I am not convinced that either Fatima or Rafiq will be able

to separate from her family even though they recognise that there is significant risk to them and their children.

I also said that I thought they were both in urgent need of emotional support, particularly Fatima who had been a victim of emotional cruelty all her life. She had grown up believing that her brothers' controlling behaviour was reasonable and her fear of them was such that she had allowed herself to be bullied into her crime. I suggested that on her release she would need help in freeing herself from the emotional hold they had on her if she was ever to lead a safe, independent life.

I was due to meet her before the hearing, in the cells below the court. I followed a prison officer down the steep stone steps and felt a sudden shudder of claustrophobia as the iron door to the outside world clanged shut, trapping us in a narrow beige corridor with heavy doors on either side. The temperature seemed to drop at least five degrees and I pulled my jacket close around me. The officer clinked her way round a hefty bunch of keys until she found the one she wanted, opened the door and ushered me inside.

Fatima had been in prison for about three months at that stage and I had anticipated finding a paler, more wretched-looking version of the woman I had met before. I expected her appearance to reflect the fact that she had been separated from her children and locked away but – to my astonishment – she looked really well. In any other circumstances I'd have thought she'd been on holiday. Her face had filled out and her eyes were bright. She was dressed in a track suit and I could see wasn't bony any longer. When I walked into the room her smile was so wide that it almost touched her hijab on either side.

'I'm in good health, Jasvinder,' she said, acknowledging my

surprise. 'Prison is great.' She offered me a seat on one side of the narrow table that bisected the room (as I tried to pull it out I realised with a shock that it was screwed to the floor) and sat herself down on the other side. All her nervousness had gone, it was as if I was a friend who had dropped in for a cup of tea.

It's not often I'm lost for words but they failed me this time. I didn't know what to make of her extraordinary revelation. Eventually I said uncertainly, 'Great? Really? Tell me why.'

She leant right across the table and her eyes were shining as, keeping count on her fingers, she said, 'I've been to the gym. I've been to the library – I can read what I like for the first time in my life. I've watched *EastEnders* – I've never been allowed to do that before. I don't feel I'm being watched by my family all the time. I can make friends with whoever I like. I have company. I'm not treated like a slave . . . Prison is freedom for me. Can you understand that?'

I felt my handle on this meeting slipping away from me.

'Yes, but . . . don't you miss your children?'

'Of course I do, but being in here is making me stronger. For the first time in my life I'm my own person, I'm in control. You told me yourself that's what I should aim for. I'll be a better person for them when I come out. My solicitor says with good behaviour that will probably be next summer.'

She paused and her face clouded. 'I'm sorry that I only got two years. I wish I could stay longer.'

The change in her was so remarkable that I thought she might at last see sense. I said, 'Fatima, now you are so much stronger, I'm sure you see things differently. I heard that at your trial you took all the blame for what happened yourself, but we could change that. Don't you think it's time to tell people about your brothers' role in all this?'

Her new-found confidence evaporated instantly. She shrunk back from me, fiddling with the edges of her scarf as if to use it as a shield between us. 'I couldn't do that Jasvinder.' Her voice dropped to a whisper. 'They'd kill my children if they did. And I'm worried about my children, I wanted to talk to you about that.' Having changed the subject she hurried on, leaving me in no doubt that discussion of her brothers was now closed. 'Rafiq has been to see me. He is concerned that the children's foster carers smoke . . . so many white people smoke, it is very likely. He thinks the children are not learning the Koran and that the morals in the house are very liberal.'

'But I hear that the children are happy and well, Fatima. Have you not been told that?'

'Happy and well, maybe. But that does not mean that their upbringing is correct.'

'Right.' I glanced at my watch. My allotted time was almost up and what I had to say to the court was clear in my mind, but there was one last question which had been niggling at me. I said, 'Fatima, why was it so important to your brothers that they find Jamilah? Had she dishonoured the family in their eyes?'

Fatima's head bobbed from side to side, weighing the question. 'To many people's way of thinking a woman who tries to be independent is not good, we both know that. I think my brothers wanted to make an example of Jamilah, they wanted to show their own wives that Asian women cannot get away with copying western ways.'

'And what would they have done to her if you had found her, do you know?'

Fatima shrank back again, this time not from me, but from the vision in her mind. She shook her head vigorously as if to physically remove the image that upset her. 'I would not like to say, I cannot say for sure. I don't know why people from the Pathan culture care so much about what other people think. So often it leads to bad things.'

Upstairs in the court room I listened as the children's social worker reported that they were thriving in the care of their foster parents despite their birth-parents' often-voiced reservations about the suitability of white family life. I said my piece: that I feared Fatima's children might be in danger from her family if they were returned to her or Rafiq. And then I left the court with the fate of that sad little family weighing heavy on my heart.

Next day I heard that no decision was made and I wondered how Fatima – in the gym or the library or even the private peacefulness of her cell – would take that. I wondered about Rafiq, waking alone each day to the knowledge that his family – the only thing that tied him to this country – was broken and scattered. I thought back to the days when my children were so small that I alone controlled the landscape of their days and nights and I wondered how they would have coped if they had been uprooted and re-planted in someone else's family life.

Two weeks later – with a decision still pending – I was asked if I would consider acting as a cultural adviser to the foster parents; brokering an understanding between them, Fatima and Rafiq. I said I would. I hope that such a thing is possible.

30

I was in regular touch with Shabana in the days after she left home. She settled into the refuge; she met Yasmin and they got on famously as I knew they would. She had finally taken control of her life, and each time I spoke to her she sounded stronger. Once there was distance between herself and the threatening oppression of her family she agreed that the police should visit them as I'd suggested. Two officers went to her father's house and told him that Shabana was safe and well and that they knew where she was living. Then they made it clear that they knew exactly what she had been through in the months before she left home, and they warned him that, if anything were to happen to her, he would be top of their list of suspects. Before they left they removed a licensed firearm from his house.

'That must be the gun he used to threaten me with Jas.' Shabana was elated when I told her the news. 'You were right. Getting the police to go and see him is the best thing that could have happened. I feel like the power over my life has been given back.'

She was still frightened enough to have her car crushed. 'I

feel much safer now I know my father can't trace me through the license plate.' And she went on with her struggle to get herself what she perceived to be adequate police protection. Although the police had finally agreed to consider taking her onto the Witness Protection Programme, she is feisty enough to have refused point blank to stop all contact with me or friends like Sheena who had given her such support while she was trapped at home. Her refusal led to a stalemate which made me more convinced than ever that we must find a proper solution to this problem. I resolved to make time to travel down to Bangor to see her; I also wanted to catch up with Yasmin who I knew was still concerned about her safety.

I decided to take the train the following Friday night. I asked Shazia to come with me because the three of them are close in age and I thought they would enjoy each other's company. Also, I'm sure Yasmin won't stay in Bangor for ever and she will need as many friends outside the city as she can find. On the way to work that day I stopped and bought two *thals* – circular stainless steel containers filled with individual pots of all the essential Asian spices. I wanted to give one each to Shabana and Yasmin to encourage them to cook. I wanted to remind them that even though they have run away from home there are bits of our culture they can still hold dear.

That evening, as Shazia and I walked to the station from the office we passed a young Muslim woman who I recognised despite the fact her scarf was covering half her face. I had spent some time with her the year before and she is so tall and thin that I'd recognise her anywhere. Benazir had come to Karma Nirvana in fear that she was facing a forced marriage. It was the usual story: her two older sisters had already been married off to strangers during a family 'holiday' in Pakistan; now she'd seen some air tickets, her mum was packing suitcases, it seemed her turn had come. She stands out in my mind because she was better educated than a lot of those that come to us; at nineteen she had done her A levels and was in the first year of a degree. I think it was chemistry she was studying. I spent several hours with her. I outlined all her options, promised to support her; I think we actually got to the stage of finding her a refuge place. But then she changed her mind. I remember her so well, sitting in the office with tears pouring down her face saying, 'I'm sorry Jasvinder, but I can't go to the refuge. I'm not brave like you, I can't face disownment from my family. I'd rather get married to a stranger than let them all down.'

Of course, that does happen sometimes and it always fills me with such sadness. When Benazir left our office for the last time I could have told you exactly what she would look like twelve months on, and there she was, just as I'd imagined: eyes on the pavement as she trudged along behind a pushchair, deaf to the angry wails of the infant inside.

'Benazir!' I said as she drew level with us, and I know she heard because she turned towards me: blank face, grim set mouth, hollow, dark-ringed eyes. For the smallest moment I thought she was going to stop and talk to us, but no, on she went, a respectable woman headed for the cold comfort of her family, a married woman able to hold up her head in the community to which she belonged.

Shazia and I didn't discuss Benazir afterwards: we had seen the same thing before with other women, there was nothing more to say. But I was glad to have Shazia with me, right there beside me as we queued for tickets, bought ourselves a coffee, found two seats together on the train. I know she was thinking of Benazir, just as I was. And I know too that having her there

– a blooming, happy, independent, working woman – was proof to me that everything I do is not in vain.

I felt weary that evening, setting off on a long journey at the end of a working week but in fact the hours passed quickly. I spend so much time travelling now that I have learnt to make the most of the time I'm trapped in my seat. I use it to catch up with my case load and that evening I wanted to speak to Kiren, who had sent me a text message earlier in the day saying 'my life is shit'.

I felt such sympathy for her. For many months after she left home she battled to contain the anger she felt towards her family and occasionally she vented her feelings on the people closest to her, lashing out at those who wanted to help. Emotion sometimes clouded her judgement and brought a chaotic quality to her life: she moved to Derby, started college, dropped out, moved to Nottingham, found a job, left it, came back to Derby. But she never gave up. Kiren has guts and I admire that. She was struggling to find her feet but she was working: in a call centre during the week and then a couple of shifts in a chip shop at weekends. The jobs weren't worthy of her and she knew that, but she also knows she needs an income and, until she has got herself some qualifications, she has to take what comes. She was trying: she had signed on at college again, this time she was doing evening classes.

Kiren has the potential to do great things with her life but it's so hard for these girls without any sort of guidance from their families. I wish I had more time to spend with her. If I could only give her what I gave to Shazia I know she'd be all right. But I first met Shazia years ago, when twenty-four hours in the day seemed to be enough.

I rang Kiren and when she didn't answer I sent a text saying:

Will u come 2 KN. Ages since we talked. We need a 1-2-1

It was after 7 p.m. by the time we got to Bangor but Yasmin was there to meet us. She had just passed her driving test and bought herself a car. 'Now I'm really free; nothing can stop me now,' she said, as she ushered us into it. She looked so proud, but as she drove us to collect Shabana from her refuge, her smile faded and she said, 'I think my family might be on to me again, Jas.'

She stopped at a red light and turned towards me, her face anxious.

'My friend Lesley – the one who let me stay with her, remember? Lesley got an anonymous call on her mobile yesterday. It was a man asking her to tell him where Nabeela was. Nabeela's me, Jas. That's my old name. Nobody I know now calls me that. When Lesley asked him who he was, he wouldn't say; he just hung up.'

'You're sure it wasn't a wrong number?'

'No, he began by asking her if she was Lesley.'

'Have you told the police?'

'Yes. They said "Keep calm, there's no point in getting yourself all worked up."' She sighed. 'I suppose they're right, but I can't stop wondering who it was, or how he made the connection between her and me. Still . . .' She gave her head a little shake as though to clear it. 'There's definitely nothing we can do about it now, so let's talk about the good news. I applied to join Operation Black Vote, like you said.'

That definitely was good news. Ten years ago I took part in this shadowing scheme which is designed to encourage black and ethnic minority people into public life; I shadowed Jim Cunningham, the Labour MP for Coventry South. The scheme has grown since then to include magistrates and councillors as well as MPs and I knew Yasmin would learn a lot from it; I certainly did.

By the time I finished congratulating her, we had arrived at the refuge. In the months since I caught that one brief glimpse of Shabana, I had held a picture in my mind of a tense little figure with hunched shoulders and a bowed head. The Shabana I've known on the telephone and through emails has always been scared, sometimes scared and angry and – feeling a bit apprehensive if I'm honest – that's what I was expecting.

The woman who came skipping out to meet us now could not have been different. She was as tiny as I remembered, but far from looking cowed and miserable she had a grin that split her face. She was dressed up to the nines with her shoes matching her bag, matching her dress. She was the height of fashion.

'All right, Mother?' she said, as I climbed out of the car to greet her and I knew then that I would have to rethink Shabana completely. This woman was so vivid, so alive. As we stood there looking at one another, both of us studying faces that belonged to voices we already knew so well, I realised the tangible thing that made her look most different. 'What happened to your hair?' I asked, reaching out to touch the ends of the elfin crop that had replaced her mane of curls. She shrugged. 'I've got alopecia, it was all falling out anyway. The doctor said it's stress-related,' she said, then slid into the back seat beside Shazia.

Yasmin drove us through the city streets to a Turkish restaurant which she said was a favourite of hers. 'She brought me here the first time we met,' said Shabana. 'The food is very good, but let me warn you: don't eat too much of your starter or you will never be able to finish everything.'

She was fizzing that evening. For two years all her energy had been spent on controlling her fear and placating her parents while she planned her escape; now it was as though someone had popped the cork on a bottle of champagne. She was on top of her feelings, in control and clearly relishing her freedom, although she was frank about the downside of her new life. 'I'm learning what it's like to be poor. I've got my savings but I'm still worried that if I use a cash machine to access them, my dad will track me down. I'm spending as little as possible and I'm learning how to improvise. Look,' she touched a dramatic diamante brooch pinned to one of her lapels. 'I got this in Oxfam for seventy-five pence and this,' she lifted a big straw bag from the seat beside her 'was one pound fifty. I may be poor but I still know how to shop!'

She could joke about it because she hoped her new-found poverty would be short lived. Despite her continued fears about safety, Shabana – I was fast learning – is too dynamic to put her life on hold. Within weeks of arriving in Bangor she had applied for a job with a travel agent in York. She had already been interviewed and was so confident of getting it that she was going to flat-hunt in the city the following week.

'It's great isn't it?' said Yasmin, raising a glass to toast Shabana. 'But I'm not letting her get away that easily; she has to spend Christmas with me before she goes.' Yasmin is far too generous to let her personal sadness show, but a tiny catch in her voice made me realise how much she had come to rely on this new friendship, how much she would miss it.

Ignoring the warning Shabana gave us, we ate so much that evening that we had to go outside and walk it off before we could finish the food on our plates. The four of us laughed and talked and talked and laughed until we cried. We were high on intimacy if you like; I don't know when I last felt so close to other people. Memories of that evening still warm my heart.

We spent the night, the four of us, in Yasmin's flat which is all dark leather sofas and artfully arranged pebbles and style, and in the morning I made a big breakfast for us all – scrambled eggs and toast and mushrooms. While I cooked the other three gossiped and giggled and lolled about in front of Saturday morning television, and it really felt like we were family. I felt a warm rush of pleasure as each of them said, 'Thanks, Mother,' as she took her plate.

I'd never considered it before and I don't know that it's been a conscious choice, but since I ran away from home all those years ago, the friends I've made, the women I've confided in, have tended to be white. Perhaps I felt safer steering well clear of anyone who might be in the Asian network; perhaps I felt that among white people who couldn't possibly understand all the rules and strictures of the close-knit community I grew up in, I was less likely to be judged. Either way, the result was that all my friendships tended to be marked by big gaps in our experience. I think that's why I found that visit to Bangor special. The atmosphere between us was something that I'd not experienced before. We all felt the link between us, there was no need to explain things: we'd all suffered at the hands of our families and we'd survived.

31

When Kiren finally responded to my text message she said she didn't want to come into the Karma Nirvana office, so we agreed to meet in a pub instead. She came straight from her shift at the call centre and when she arrived she had that bug-eyed pallor that comes from spending too long shut up inside. As soon as she walked in I knew something had happened because she looked tense, almost defensive, she found it hard to look me in the eye. I bought us both half a lager and once we were sitting down, she made conversation for a moment or two. It was nothing but inconsequential pleasantries and I knew she was just avoiding a silence while she plucked up the courage to tell me what was really on her mind.

I didn't have to wait long.

'I'm going home, Jas, back home. I've been thinking about it for a long time and now I'm sure. I've made up my mind.'

'You what?' I couldn't believe it. If the pub hadn't been as quiet as a grave at that moment I would have thought I'd misheard her, but I knew I hadn't. Surprise, disappointment, concern – concern more than anything – all jostled for space in my mind as I said: 'But Kiren, why? You've come so far, you're nearly there. I know not everything is perfect at the moment, your work's not great, you wish you had more money, but believe me that will come. Don't give up now.'

'I've really thought about it, Jas and it's what I want. I'm missing my family. It's not just the financial security – although that's hard enough. It's the guidance, the sense of belonging; I'm tired of being all alone. I just feel like I'm nobody. And I miss the seaside, I really do. This part of the world's not me, I've got no roots here. I took the train back down the other day and spent an afternoon just walking round the streets near where I used to live, where I went shopping with my mum and, you know what, Jas, it felt so right it was . . . it was like being back in my own bedroom. It's where I'm supposed to be.'

'But are you not concerned for your safety? What's your mum going to make of it? I thought she'd disowned you.'

'I'm not going to my mum's. She's in Pakistan anyway. I've been talking to one of my uncles, the one who lived nearest us, and he's said I can stop with him.'

'Kiren.' I was feeling upset but I tried to keep my voice calm and even. 'Have you really thought this through? You've been away for . . .' I did a rapid calculation. 'It must be eighteen months and in all that time you've been living like a westerner: you've been clubbing, you've had boyfriends, you've worn the sort of clothes you like. Have you thought what it's going to be like, going back to being the dutiful Muslim daughter?'

'My uncle says it's not going to be like that,' she said. 'He says I can lead the life I want – you know, I don't have to get married, I can go to college, things like that – but whatever I do my family will be there to give me guidance, like they should be. That's what he says. Trust me, Jas, it's going to be okay.'

'Trust you? Of course I do. But do you really think you can trust him? Wasn't it your uncle who tricked you and then shopped you to your parents the first time you ran away?'

'That was a different uncle,' she said and she was beginning to sound impatient with me. 'I'm nearly twenty, Jas. I know what I'm doing.'

There was no point in arguing any further. We discussed the practicalities, how much notice she had to give for her job, her flat, that sort of thing. It wasn't until she bent to kiss me goodbye that I twigged the fact that her pallor wasn't due to the length of her shift in the call centre. She wasn't wearing make-up; for the first time in all the months I'd known her, her face was bare.

I watched her walk away and she had a spring in her step which seemed to suggest just how relieved she felt to have got that conversation over. I stayed in my seat and rang Brent Hyatt. He and Kiren had remained in touch since he first rescued her and I wanted to discuss my worries with him; I wanted to ask if we could set up some system for checking she was safe. He said he shared my concern and we talked for a while and then, when he rang off, I stayed there, sitting by myself in the pub. For at least forty minutes I sat staring at my empty glass, wondering if this could have been avoided, what else I should have done to help.

The next morning I told Gordon Riches about Kiren. 'It shows me just how right you were to make me do this research: I need to find out what survival strategies people do use successfully and then I can pass them on to women like Kiren who try so hard but, in the end, can't resist the pull of home.'

It was a way of easing him into what I really wanted to say which was that I couldn't keep up with the pace he had set for me. I was dreading this discussion because I was afraid he'd tell me that if I couldn't cope, it was best to forget the PhD. I didn't want that. I've never been a quitter and anyway, I love the work. Finding the time to do it was the problem. I don't know how many times in the past six months I had woken in the middle of the night with my bedside light still on and the book I was reading open on my chest. I'll swear my biceps had grown bigger from continually lugging round a briefcase full of photocopied pages that I hoped to snatch a moment to read. When I sat down to watch *Coronation Street* with the children I kept my gaze fixed on the television because I didn't want to glimpse the coffee table laden with interview tapes that sat there waiting to be transcribed.

The trouble was that with so much going on at Karma Nirvana, that had to be my priority. The PhD felt like my own private pleasure and I wanted to go on with it but I was struggling. Gordon, bless him, understood. He made me work out – realistically – how much time I could give to my studies and then he said, 'Face it Jasvinder, it's not enough. You mustn't let this hang like a dead weight round your neck. Why don't you put it on hold.' I left his office feeling that a burden had been lifted off my shoulders; for the first time in months I was confident that I could get my life back under control.

I left his room that morning and went on to Karma Nirvana where I found the office full and busy. Shazia was on the phone to a young woman called Laila who first contacted us only recently, a woman whose life has been a living hell since her older brother started sexually abusing her when she was ten. At the time, in pain, ashamed and – without fully understanding why – aware that what was happening was profoundly wrong, she told her mother who instantly turned on her. She accused her cowering daughter of provoking her brother by being sexually active; she slapped her face, screamed at her, called her a slag, a slapper, a bitch. She then swore Laila to secrecy, saying that if one word of the abuse reached her father, he would kill the brother and then no one from the extended family would ever speak to them again. She said it would be the worse for Laila if the entire family was to be ostracised on her account.

Not long after she reached her teens, Laila's trauma was compounded when her family betrothed her to a man in Pakistan. Her parents persuaded her to agree to this marriage by beating her, often with a baseball bat. They then removed her from school and confined her to the house, locking her in when the rest of the family went out to work. This miserable existence had continued for several years. She had no confidante, no source of comfort. Until she saw a news item on Karma Nirvana she had no idea of where she might find help. Since her first call two weeks ago she had spoken to Shazia almost daily; she was slowly mustering her courage to leave the prison she called home.

At least there are escape routes for women like Laila. When she is ready, there will be a refuge place for her and there will be specialist help. There's not enough of it, and there are still far too many frightened, isolated women who don't know how to access it, but a start has been made and we are building on it. Now – both Imran and I are agreed on this – it's time to do the same for men.

For over a year Imran has been our male project worker and he's grown so much in confidence during that time. I look at him, striding into work in his crisp suit and his shirt and tie and I think, if your mum could see you now she'd be so proud. He has a new authority about him. I heard him talking to Fozia the other day, telling her how he wants to go round the mosques and talk to the imams about forced marriage. 'I always go to Friday classes at the mosque now. I never used to because of what I've been through, but now – with where I am today – I've started going. I read the Koran every day as well, and you know what it says? It says you are not supposed to use force with your wife and kids. Well, why don't the imam *sabhs* ever say that? There's millions of Muslims who would listen to them if they did.'

As far as we know Imran is the only person working specifically for male victims in this country. Within months of starting with us he had a caseload of twenty-five and his dedication is such that as the demands of his job grew so did the shadows under his eyes. The long hours he was working were beginning to take their toll. When he told me that he had had a series of calls at one o'clock the previous morning I knew the time had come to tell him about the importance of looking after himself as well as the men he was supporting.

'But he was in such trouble, Jas, someone had to help,' he said, his eyes sharp with the fury that we all feel when presented with terrible cases of on-going, calculated abuse.

I sat down and he told me this poor man's story. 'You won't believe what he's been through. His wife brought him over from Pakistan four months ago and since then he hasn't been allowed out except to go to work – and even then his wife pockets his wages so he is totally dependent on her. She keeps a knife under their bed and says it's to use on him if he makes any trouble. Her family say they hate British culture so he's not allowed to have a phone, or make friends or even go to English classes. He is totally isolated; I'm telling you Jas he's that cowed, she's destroyed him as a man.

'A couple of weeks ago he got desperate and confided in his supervisor at work, but his wife found out and it made her so angry – disloyalty she called it – that she got her brothers to beat him up. One brother pinned him to the wall by his neck while she kicked him in the testicles and tried to burn him with a hot iron. That's torture in my book. And then last night he called because she said she was going to get a gang to come and kill him. He was absolutely terrified Jas. I had to help. I called the police and they went round and got him out.'

It was contact with men like him that convinced Imran and me of the need for a proper male refuge. To date whenever Imran has needed to provide accommodation for a male victim he's had to take what he can find, and it's often unsuitable. 'These are gentle, delicate men who have been traumatised anyway; they hate being put in hostels that are meant for ex-convicts,' Imran said. 'And it's not just single men. When couples who have run away together contact us we're not really helping either of them if we can't help them both.'

It's a problem we must address urgently because Imran is starting to have referrals from across the country. Only last week a man from Bradford arrived in our office having fled from his parents who were trying to force him into marriage. He had his meagre possessions – all he had to start his new life with – crammed into two black plastic bags and he was urgently in need of a safe place to stay.

He was brought to us by Philip Balmforth, an ex-police

inspector who is employed by Bradford police to be responsible for the welfare of vulnerable people within the city's Asian community. Philip works flat out. His popularity is partly due to the fact that in the first case he ever dealt with he inadvertently settled a dispute between a pair of sisters and the parents from whom they'd run away. The sisters were brought to his attention as missing persons and his first instinct was to ring round women's refuges. He started with those in Bradford and worked outwards until he found the young women in Sheffield. Once he had established they were fleeing from forced marriages, he made the call to their parents saying they were safe and well but they would not be coming back.

Within half an hour those same parents, plus a posse from their extended family, were in Philip's office. Their daughters, they said, had taken with them passbooks giving them access to £35,000 of family money: could Philip please get those pass books back. Amid the clamour and cacophony, Philip managed to establish that the money was in two accounts; one in each of the two sisters' names. 'If the accounts are in their names, then as far as I'm concerned it's their money and they can do what they like with it; end of story,' Philip said. At this the shouting grew louder and more insistent until the sisters' father managed to make himself heard. 'It is family money, put into their accounts temporarily to show the Home Office that they have the ability to support the husbands they will bring over from Pakistan. Once the Home Office is satisfied, the money will go back into the family account, ready to be used elsewhere.'

He clearly saw nothing wrong with this arrangement and was most indignant when Philip insisted that legally the money belonged to his daughters and nothing could be done to get it back. Reluctantly, still muttering their dissatisfaction, the family allowed itself to be ushered out of Philip's office and that would have been that had the sisters themselves not rung Philip the very next day. They asked to see him in Sheffield and when he arrived there they explained that they could not live with having taken what they too perceived to be family money. They gave him their passbooks and asked Philip to return them to their father.

'After that I became known as the man who finds your daughters and gets your money back,' Philip said, smiling at the memory of this extraordinary saga. Each year since then he reckons he has seen or heard of about one hundred and fifty cases of forced marriage in Bradford alone. I don't know how many young women he has bundled into his car and driven to safety, but his reputation is such that they have come to expect a good service: he made me laugh recently with the story of one young woman he was transporting to a refuge; she piled all her possessions into his car and then was furious because he couldn't fit her oil-spattered industrial sewing machine in as well.

Philip and I have shared a platform at so many conferences – and afterwards shared our problems too. We face many of the same obstacles: for instance, although Philip has won the trust of many individual teachers in Bradford, the fact that they ask him into schools to advise pupils who are facing forced marriage is kept very quiet. There is one head teacher who begs him never to sign the visitors' book lest the governors find out he has visited; she knows they would see his intervention as 'offending cultural sensibilities'.

But he continues to get results. I wish every police force had a Philip because time and again his casework shows exactly what can and should be done – even for brides who have been taken abroad to marry. At the end of last year he was instrumental in bringing a young woman back from Denmark, rescuing her from a forced marriage that had been sprung on her only hours before it happened. The young woman's plight was brought to Philip's attention by her sister, who rang to ask for Philip's help. She wanted him to stop her father and brother travelling to Denmark to punish the young bride for refusing to consummate her marriage.

'Out of the blue this woman appeared on our doorstep and said, "I'm going to be your mother-in-law" and that was the first my sister knew about the marriage. She's still in shock – the ceremony happened next day and as soon as it was over she was bundled back to Denmark with her in-laws. My dad's in a rage because it's not been consummated; he's determined she should make the marriage work and I'm scared of what he'll do to her. You've got to help,' the sister said.

Philip immediately rang the Forced Marriage Unit, and staff there contacted the High Commission in Denmark who apparently floundered about, not knowing what to do. It was several hours before some bright spark suggested making the young woman – who was just seventeen – a ward of court. That done, the police were able to remove her from her in-laws' house and take her to a hotel, from where the Forced Marriage Unit arranged safe transfer back to Britain. 'But she couldn't stay away from Bradford,' said Philip with a sigh. 'She came back to be near her sister and then, within a couple of months, she rang her dad who said, "I'm sorry, I should have told you before about that marriage. Let's forget about it. Let me take you to Pakistan and we'll find you a husband there."'

Philip says he sees no sign of change in the attitudes and traditions of the community he serves – nor even any hope of it. But he keeps going, just as I do, and knowing that we are fighting the same battle is a source of strength and comfort. I just wish that every police force in Britain had an asset like him.

32

Tony Hutchinson's dream of a helpline was becoming a reality. It was to be called Choice-Line. During the planning of it, I caused some controversy by advising that all twenty of the female police officers who had been selected for training should be white. We later heard that one Asian officer would like to have been involved and she protested vigorously, clearly feeling she had been excluded from something that should have been hers by right. But I was adamant. I got them all together and said, 'It is vital that those who answer the phone are able to establish a relationship of trust very quickly. The callers will be stressed enough without worrying that they are speaking to someone who might know their family. I don't have to tell you what the network is like.' They seemed to accept that.

Anna Hardy and I both went up to Cleveland to take part in the training programme which ranged from how to log calls properly, to active listening, to which agencies to refer women on to. Our role was to share the experiences of Karma Nirvana victims. The launch then took place at a seminar for more than three hundred people. It was a great day, the atmosphere was buzzing and the speakers included the Solicitor General, Vera Baird, Nazir Afzal, Hannah Buckley, the policy advisor to the Forced Marriage Unit, me and, of course, Tony Hutchinson who summed it all up when he said, 'By working together we can make a difference. We can bring about change. Our message is simple: there is help and there is hope. Forced marriage is wrong.'

That launch was on a Friday and the first call came through on Saturday morning. In the first three weeks the operators took over one hundred calls involving twenty-two different cases – and this is in a part of the country where the minority population is less than three per cent. Thirteen of the women who rang the number requested police assistance and at least two of those were successfully escorted from their family homes and relocated to another part of the country. In one instance, the police linked in with the woman's employers and they were able to transfer her job to the town she was moved to. In his understated, modest way Tony was obviously pleased: 'That's thirteen people who couldn't have rung and wouldn't have rung if they hadn't had the number.'

To my mind one of the most encouraging things is that as I write this, almost a month after the line was launched, posters advertising Choice-Line are still up in several of the city's mosques. On one of them someone had scrawled: 'Ten Years Too Late!'

I felt sure that my planned friendship network would have just the same sort of instant take-up and I was longing to get it started, but I knew we had to get it absolutely right. I was clear in my mind what I wanted: my initial vision was for a national number to be answered by a team of people, preferably survivors, with specialist skills. Women – and men – who call the number would not only be given support, they would also be able to get advice on practical issues and be signposted or referred to all the other organisations that can help.

I also wanted to establish local and regional support groups as well as a website and an online newsletter for postings such as: 'Lila has passed her driving test'; 'Sameera's birthday is this week'; 'Anamika has completed her access course'. People could post on it all the things that, normally, you would rush to tell your mum, all the bits of information that, gathered together over weeks and months and years, make up the web of common understanding that puts the soul into a family. But this would be a family of friends, both survivors and others who support our work.

I organised a consultation day with representatives of the Forced Marriage Unit and a number of senior police officers joining Karma Nirvana staff and our guests the survivors themselves. These included women like Yasmin whom we already knew and about twenty people from our database, most of whom Shazia or I had spoken to on the telephone but none of whom we had met.

Yasmin, Shabana and Maya all agreed to make the effort to come up to Derby for the day and I was so grateful that I invited them all to arrive the evening before and stay with me. I asked Shazia over for the evening too; I thought it would be a good opportunity to pool our thoughts before the consultation. What's more, it was my birthday so I decided to celebrate: I said I'd cook a feast.

As soon as I announced this Yasmin texted me asking if she could choose the menu and when I agreed both she and Shabana bombarded me with suggestions. By text we discussed all the home-cooked food they had loved and now missed and it took us some time to settle on chapattis filled with spicy potatoes, lentil dahl, saag bahji and karelas which Maya, who is so good at languages, translated as bitter gourds. The preparation of it gave me real pleasure: each onion chopped, each spice added seemed to me to be going towards giving these young women simple, tangible comfort. Good food was one facet of their lost homes that I could – at least for that one night – replace.

I was determined to make it an occasion: I bought flowers, candles and wine and we sat round my table and ate until we were replete. That evening – all five of us sharing food and friendship, trusting and supporting one another – seemed to me to symbolise everything that I hoped the Survivors' Network would achieve. It ended just as our evening had in Bangor, with us all on a high, and that feeling stayed with me. The next morning, as I stood on the stage with Hannah Buckley and Tony Hutchinson waiting for the event to begin, I was convinced it would go well.

In my introduction I gave a potted version of my story as I always do, I explained how I ran away and how I had to learn to live with the fact that for the last twenty-seven years I've been disowned by my family. I described how, for months after I left home, I was paralysed by feelings of guilt and loneliness and that it was only the death of my beloved sister Robina that gave me the courage to turn my life around. 'I've said all this before many times,' I said. 'I've criss-crossed the country ten times over telling people what I went through, because I believe that if women like us suffer in silence we will go on suffering for ever. I believe that it is only by standing up and telling the world about forced marriage, honour-based violence and disownment that we can bring about change. But let me tell you,' I said, and I dropped my voice low, drawing the listeners in to me. 'I find it lonely standing up here on this stage. It's very lonely, and if any of the survivors in this room today would like to share their story too it would mean a lot to me.'

Instantly one woman put her hand up and said, 'I've been disowned for thirty years.'

The woman beside her put her hand up too: 'I've been disowned for seven years and I still miss having a jalibi and a cup of tea with my mum.'

And that was it. A forest of hands shot up, people could hardly wait their turn:

'I've been disowned for nine years and I still can't stop myself driving past my dad's house, just to see if he's in.'

'I've been disowned for thirty-two years and in all that time I've found no one to talk to in Punjabi . . . I really miss speaking in my mother tongue.'

'I miss not having anyone to celebrate Eid with.'

'I feel sad for my kids: their family history starts and stops with me.'

Looking around the room, I saw one young couple who were sitting together holding hands. They were listening attentively but they didn't join in until suddenly he put his hand up: 'Can I say something?'

Everyone around him nodded. I said, 'Please, do.'

He looked at the young woman beside him as if drawing strength from her. 'Our parents wouldn't let us get married because we're from different castes. I never understood that; where in the Sikh religion does it say you have to marry someone from the same caste? We felt isolated and alone, we looked to so many places for support but it was in vain, until we found Karma Nirvana. I spoke to Imran and I knew that at last I had found someone who understands our situation. He gave us confidence and the courage to live our own lives.' He turned again and smiled at the woman beside him, then he said, and this time there was a note of triumph in his voice, 'We got married last week. Our families were not there, but we are learning to live without them and with the support of Karma Nirvana I know we can.'

Everyone clapped. The room was buzzing; the atmosphere was electric. It was one of those moments when a disparate group of individuals becomes a team with a common aim and purpose and a surge of energy so powerful and surprising that anything seems possible. We could have gone on sharing our experiences all afternoon but I had to call a halt because there was work to do.

We split the survivors into groups and asked them to discuss elements of the project, from its name to its logo to the range of people it should cater for. The longest, liveliest debate turned out to be about the name. At Karma Nirvana we had been favouring Survivors' Network but that didn't appeal. All sorts of things were bandied about until I said, 'What about Honour?'

The room fell silent.

'I mean, honour is what it's all about, isn't it? It's why we're all here.'

'But isn't honour what drove us from our families?' said one voice.

'The wrong sort of honour,' said another.

'I feel honourable,' said a third.

I said, 'We are honourable, but that's not how our families see it. To them our honour is their shame.'

And someone else called out, 'Yes, that's right. Let's make honour really honourable. Let's reclaim the word.'

That's how it came to be called the Honour Network. And for me one of the most exciting parts of that incredible afternoon was when we started to talk about the logo. Steve Allen had arranged for a designer to be there and when he invited people to give their ideas there was no shortage of suggestions: lilies, doves, all sorts of pretty images were mooted and rejected until finally discussion turned to a line of people with linked arms.

'Will they be models?' somebody asked.

'No! I think it should be real people. I'm not ashamed to show my face, I'll be on it,' said one woman, leaping to her feet and standing, tall and proud.

'So will I,' said another woman.

And then from all round the room the voices came, 'So will I!' 'So will I!'

'So will I!'

33

I was invited into Joshua's school to give an assembly on the work we do at Karma Nirvana. Having dropped him at his classroom door I went to wait in the hall while the individual teachers took the register. I dawdled on the way, admiring a wall full of self-portraits done by year four pupils, studying a project on recycling that had been stuck up along one passage wall. As I reached the hall it occurred to me that I feel very comfortable in this building. Parents' evenings still bring a tiny, nervous tightening in my stomach as I queue to talk to Joshua's teacher, but mostly this hall speaks to me of good times: the summer fair, Christmas concerts or the school play. I have always enjoyed visiting, having a glimpse of this other, independent world that Joshua is absorbed into each day.

Mum never saw the school I went to. Ginda took me on my very first day and after that I just tagged along, hurrying down the pavement after my big sisters. Mum never visited, not once. At the time I never questioned it; in my angry teens I took it for indifference but now – now I think perhaps she was afraid. She didn't speak enough English to talk to the teachers or read the stories proudly pinned up on the walls. Our school was alien to her and – like so much of the culture she found herself stranded in – incomprehensible. Education was the gift that she and my dad gave all of us when they left their village in the Punjab and came to live here, but she didn't presume to have a piece of it for herself. That was her tragedy and, as I see it nowadays, it was also mine.

The assembly done, I said a hurried goodbye to the head teacher and went to catch a train to Wales where I was due to speak at a conference. Yasmin was attending it, representing the organisation that she works for, and on the way to the station I stopped to buy her a card because it was her birthday and I know from my own experience and from watching all the young women that come to Karma Nirvana that it's at celebration times – birthdays, Ramadan, Eid – that the loneliness is hardest to bear. I sat in the train and wrote to her:

> Dear Yasmin,
>
> Look: I am getting to know you so well that I even bought a black and white card to match your black and white flat!
>
> You are probably missing your family more than ever at this time but I want you to know that I am thinking of you.
>
> With my love and blessings,
>
> Mother.

That afternoon I was once again sharing a platform with Nazir Afzal; he and I look at the problem of honour crime from opposite perspectives: I try to keep people alive and he – as director of the Crown Prosecution Service – strives to achieve justice for those who have been killed in the name of honour.

He organised the first CPS conference on honour crime in 2004, since when he hasn't been able to let the subject go. He says it takes up all his spare time.

I enjoy listening to him; he's a passionate and exciting speaker but – even to me – his presentation is very shocking. From the platform you can watch the audience, even those who have been dozy and inattentive, sit up and take heed. That afternoon he cited a BBC survey in which one in ten young Asians had said they could justify the murder of someone who had supposedly dishonoured their family. He listed women who had been murdered in the name of so-called honour for reasons as trivial as wanting to learn to drive and as unjust as having been raped.

He talked about the case of a young woman called Sajida Bibi who was murdered in Birmingham on her wedding day, and you could hear the outrage burning in his voice. Hers was not an arranged marriage but her immediate family felt they could live with the choice she had made. Not everyone agreed with them. On the day the marriage was due to take place two men claiming kinship came up from the south of England and stabbed her to death, then fled to Pakistan. 'I've studied the family tree,' said Nazir. 'Their relationship was so distant that they simply don't appear on it, but still they felt they had a right to grievance.'

Nazir always uses the same saying to express the hypocrisy of honour: 'A man is like a piece of gold: if you drop it in the mud you can wipe it clean. A woman is like a piece of silk: if you drop it in the mud it is stained for ever.' I think that's the perfect summation. I admire Nazir because he is never afraid to say the unacceptable. For instance, he claims that the greatest fear for a Muslim woman living in Britain is not Islamaphobia or being mistaken for a terrorist, it's the threat from her own family. He says that in his opinion if you want to re-educate people about honour crimes you have to target six-, eight- or ten-year olds: 'Anybody over the age of eighteen has already made up their mind, for them it's too late.'

But he emphasises the positive too: the fact that moves are being made to tackle the problem of honour crime on a national level. That afternoon he claimed that across the country a 'stock take' is being done to discover the extent of these crimes; that a national working party is being set up, with representatives from the Foreign Office, the Home Office and the Forced Marriage Unit, who will all be working to produce policies and products that we – organisations like Karma Nirvana – can implement. A small part of me felt cynical as I listened: in the past so much has been promised but so little achieved, and yet . . .

Normally before it's my turn to speak I try to disappear for two minutes to compose myself. I use the time to think about what I'm doing on this platform, I remind myself that I am there not for myself but for all those who cannot speak, that I am representing thousands of women in this country and – in time, I hope – across the world. In the seconds before I actually start to talk, my heart still races, not because I'm nervous of the audience – if it was the Prime Minister I was talking to or even the Queen herself I'd feel no different – I'm anxious because I want to do these issues justice. But as soon as the words start flowing, my heart and mind are wiped clean of everything except the message that I'm trying to convey.

The only time I've come close to feeling overwhelmed on stage was at the Woman of the Year lunch. As I stood in front of the audience that day accepting my award and saying my thanks, my mind was filled with the image of my mum. 'You said I'd amount to nothing and yet here I am,' I was thinking. 'Who'd have thought it? Certainly not me.'

I try to talk whenever and wherever I can and now, slowly but surely, I'm building up a team to help me spread the word: Shazia, Anna, Imran, Fozia – though she's still behind her veil. Maybe even Maya will join us next year. There was one day recently when Shazia, Anna and I spoke in three separate places to 800 people: our voice is being heard.

It's the interest, the outrage and the compassion of the audiences we speak to that keeps us going. So many people have been in complete ignorance of these issues; you see disbelief on their faces and then, quite often, shame – shame for all those years of not noticing, not understanding, not doing anything to help. There was one woman there that afternoon in Wales and she stood up and said, 'The problem as you two' she meant me and Nazir 'outline it, seems to be so enormous, so entrenched in the society that you describe that I don't see how anything can change it.'

'But it is changing,' we said, as one. Then Nazir went first, he said, 'When Heshu Yones was murdered, her father was given life with a minimum tariff of just eight years before he could be considered for release. The judge said he had sympathy with the distress he must have felt when he found out that his Muslim daughter had a Christian boyfriend.

'That was in two thousand and three. This year – not five years later – when Sukhdev Athwal and his seventy-year-old mother Bachan received life sentences for arranging the murder of Sukhdev's wife Surjit because she wanted a divorce, her minimum tariff was twenty years and his was twenty-seven. For them, being family was an aggravating not a mitigating circumstance. From an eight-year sentence to a twenty-seven-year sentence: to me that's change.'

He turned to me, and I took over. 'I've recently given evidence to a Home Affairs Select Committee which is investigating domestic violence, forced marriage and honour-based violence, and several of my staff have done the same: at last the government is listening to us. The enquiry includes an online consultation to which as many people as possible are being encouraged to contribute, so the stories of thousands of victims could be heard.'

Suddenly I found myself on my feet, carried away with conviction in what I was saying. 'It's a big step between consultation and action, but a start has been made, top politicians are becoming involved. Only last week David Cameron spoke out against forced marriage. At the request of his staff I arranged for him to meet survivors from a refuge in Bradford; he came to the city and consulted with us and on the strength of what he learnt he said he believed – what we all know – that the four hundred forced marriages reported to the Home Office each year are just the tip of the iceberg. He is in favour of raising the age at which a wedding can take place with someone from overseas to twenty-one and – and to my mind this is very positive – he says if the Conservatives come to power they will look again at criminalising forced marriage. At last politicians are beginning to understand these issues and take them seriously. To me that's change.'

There was a short burst of applause but I spoke over it. 'And the survivors themselves are beginning to take action. More and more are coming forward and in their sheer numbers they are finding strength and solidarity. I'm currently helping three British women who want to see the deportation of husbands they were forced to marry and forced to sponsor into this country. All three want to see justice done and they are brave enough to fight for it. They are the first but, once they've won, I'm sure that we'll see more.'

It was a full programme that day: after the speeches and the questions there were workshops. I had no time to talk to Yasmin, but I caught sight of her a couple of times and as I anticipated, she seemed sad. At the end of the day she came straight over to me and she said, 'Would you take me to a phone box, Jas. Now. I want to ring my family.'

I said, 'Why? What do you mean?'

'I miss them so much. It's my birthday and I haven't heard from them.'

'You haven't heard from them because you're hiding from them.'

'But that's just it,' she said. 'Maybe they are missing me and there's nothing they can do about it because they don't know where I am.'

This was in the foyer of the hotel where the conference was. People were milling past us, walking in groups, in ones and twos; we had to keep shifting a little to let them past. Yasmin was trying to hold herself together and not cry. I set my bags down on the floor by my feet and put my hands on her shoulders. I had to reach up to do it.

'Trust me,' I said. 'I understand exactly what you are going through and I know what it feels like. But you are asking me to advocate for you to have a very high level of police protection from your family. If you are then going to go and ring your family, the police will say, "What's the point? She's contacting them herself." And think about it, Yasmin. Even if you do ring them, what's going to change? You're still going to be hiding from them because you think they're going to kill you. You're still going to be peering out of the window, checking the street outside your flat before you dare to open your front door.'

She didn't trust herself to speak at that point, but she nodded. I leant forward and gave her a hug. 'Come on, come with me and we'll go and have something to eat.'

We went to have supper in a nearby restaurant and as the evening went on the warmth of our companionship seemed to ease Yasmin's longing for her family. She didn't mention them again. Instead she told me her plans: 'I want to go to college, I don't know where yet, maybe I'll move away from Bangor. But the thing is, Jas, I don't want to be a refuge worker all my life. I've told my supervisor that and she's just like you: she says if you want to get on you've got to get yourself some qualifications. And something else, Jas. You know I told you I'd applied to Operation Black Vote? Well, I've been short-listed. What do you think?'

'Fantastic. I think you'll find it really interesting; I know you'll be good at it because you've got all the right attributes and . . .' I stopped because something occurred to me. 'Hang on Yasmin, I've just realised, you can't do this.'

'Why not?' she said. She looked really taken aback.

'Well, the whole point of Operation Black Vote is that you have a public profile; they'll want you to speak on platforms, to be seen and heard. You can't do that if you're in hiding.'

There was a long pause. I could see Yasmin working this out in her head; I could see disappointment, anger, resignation, each one in turn clouded her face. Eventually she said, very quietly, 'No, I guess not.'

We both sat silent for a minute, thinking our own thoughts

and then I reached across the table and gently touched her hand. 'You know, we all have to make the decision eventually.'

'What decision is that?'

'The decision to stand up to your family. To face them. To refuse to allow them to control you any more. Think about it, Yasmin.' I sat back and looked her dead in the eye: 'You can't keep on running for the rest of your life.'

EPILOGUE

All the women whose stories are told here are part of the patchwork of my life. Knowing them has touched my heart and shaped the work I do. Some are now as close as family, some I keep in touch with by phone or email, others have drifted away, but still I wait – like an anxious mother – hoping for news.

Shazia – my third daughter – continues to go from strength to strength and the glowing, composed woman she has become is a million miles from the miserable young girl I first saw hiding behind her peaked cap. She regularly addresses large audiences across the country and I have every confidence in her as my representative. I am moved by the strength and empathy with which she supports those who turn to us for help, and grateful for the energy and enthusiasm she brings to exposing the cruelty and injustice that these women – and so many others like them in this country and across the world – still endure.

Since Imran joined us I have become increasingly aware that men are not immune from forced marriage, honour-based violence and coercion at the hands of their families. In the year after he became Karma Nirvana's male project worker we assisted over eighty-five men. The government has just begun to recognise this problem and we were recently granted the funding to undertake a feasibility study for a refuge for Asian men. Karma Nirvana has also recruited a second, part-time male worker.

Fozia is still volunteering with us, and as her confidence has grown she has started going into schools with the Karma Nirvana team and sharing her experiences. I hope the satisfaction this gives her helps to bolster her against the continuing disappointments in her life. She has yet to find proper housing, so is still living in a refuge which she has never enjoyed. Her yearning to be reunited with her family has not lessened, and my constant fear is that she will get tired of her lonely struggle, go home and give in to the forced marriage she has suffered so much to avoid.

Kiren also continues to worry me. Not long after she moved back to stay with her uncle she rang to say that it had been a terrible mistake: the clean slate, the fresh start, the freedom – these had all been empty promises designed to lure her back into the family net. Once her family had her home they made her second-hand, second-class status very plain. She quickly realised her mistake and within weeks she ran away again. I haven't heard from her since then but the grapevine tells me that, once more, she is trying to rebuild her life at university. I wish her success.

Shabana, on the other hand, is flying, literally. She loves her new job and it takes her all over the world. We speak regularly and her voice – once so taut and tense – now bubbles with enthusiasm for life. But she is still looking over her shoulder. She never got the level of protection that she asked for and I know that at the back of her mind lurks a sharp sense of her own mortality. Like me, she will never take her personal safety for granted.

Shebana and Yasmin remain firm friends although changes in Yasmin's circumstances – changes I would never have predicted – mean that their lives are now poles apart. Last Ramadan, Yasmin found herself drawn to the Muslim women staying in her refuge. She envied them their sense of purpose and their calm and she decided to fast with them. Comforted by this ritual – which she had not practised since she left home – she started attending Islamic classes and, in time, wearing a hijab. For a while she kept up with her old friends, clubbing, drinking and dancing the nights away, but increasingly – so she told me – she yearned to be completely immersed in the peace and protection Islam offered. She spent more and more time talking to her Islamic teacher whom she came to see as her *wali* or Islamic guardian. He listened and advised, and Yasmin began to believe she could not be a true Muslim if she were not married. 'That was the element of my life that was missing, but what could I do?' she said, 'In the western world I would go out looking for a boyfriend, I'd go on dates, but I couldn't do that.'

Instead, she asked her *wali* to arrange a marriage for her, which he did. He introduced her to a white British Muslim convert, and chaperoned her at their first few meetings. They were married within months; I couldn't go to the wedding but Shabana read out a speech that I sent. Yasmin says her husband's family are lovely and very understanding. She says she is very happy having found her faith. She still does not feel ready to be reconciled with her own family, but she no longer rules the possibility out. She says she remains determined to pursue her complaint against PC Ahmed of Torquay police.

I was surprised when she told me about the marriage, of course I was; the Yasmin I've known is a party animal, but equally I understood. When she ran away all those years ago, she lost her place in the world, her identity, and now she feels she's found it. She says that wearing the hijab makes her feel more empowered and independent. Her faith gives her a community to belong to, her husband gives her acceptability; she has found a family to replace the one she's yearned for all these years. I hope she has found lasting happiness too.

Maya's life has also changed dramatically. To her bitter disappointment, the Crown Prosecution Service persuaded her to drop the charges of assault she had brought against her husband on the grounds that some of the people (notably social workers) he would call to give evidence against her might dent her case. But, in the face of this, she has regained custody of her two precious boys, a joyous event marred only by their father's staunch refusal to have anything more to do with them. Soon afterwards she put her house on the market and moved north to stay with her mother, an arrangement that has come under great strain since her father moved in too. Both parents continue to bully her, but she is anxious not to rock the boat, dependent as she is on her mother's help with the boys. As soon as she can she intends to buy a house of her own. Meanwhile she has plans to go to university to study business or law and she is volunteering at Karma Nirvana one day a week. I value the work she does in the office and at conferences where she has started speaking, albeit anonymously. I think she draws strength from the support she finds among us, but she is still very fragile. There are times when I still see her as a beautiful bird trailing a broken wing.

Poor Fatima's situation has not changed, she is still in prison and her children are still being fostered by the same family. Tarvinder is working to rebuild her life. Like so many of the girls we see, she is very young to be so alone, but I know that in Shazia she has the best support available.

I couldn't finish this book without making reference to the hundreds of people whose stories aren't specifically mentioned. Since establishing Karma Nirvana I've met some of the bravest people – women and girls who've endured extraordinary levels of suffering. I've talked to many women who wanted to share their stories, but found in the end that putting their experience into words on the page was too much. This is a measure of how serious the situation is, of the damage they carry with them and the effect that taking action has on their external and internal lives. They are fragile and vulnerable, and often full of ambivalence about leaving their families, speaking out, and what the long-term consequences of that might be. I think immediately of someone who successfully prosecuted those who committed crimes against her. She was vindicated on all counts by the courts. But even then, and with her anonymity protected, she felt that the danger would be too great if she told her story in this book, and it was sadly withdrawn at a late stage.

This fact tells a different story in itself, and there are many others like it. I just hope that in time her victory in the courts will give her the courage to rebuild her life and will encourage other battered and abused women to follow her example.

There are plans for Tony Hutchinson's Choice-Line to expand to incorporate the North Durham and Northumbria police districts, and then across the North East region. Not long after the line was opened, the Cambridge police force launched an almost identical service and there is talk of expanding this to neighbouring districts too. As Tony himself said: 'the success of that line is actually the tragedy of that line'. It has certainly proved the need is there, as has the Honour Network. In the first four months of operation, the Honour Network Helpline received one thousand and sixty-nine calls from men and women needing our support. An analysis of one hundred of these calls showed that eighty per cent of them were victims of forced marriage, in seventy-one per cent of cases the perpetrators were immediate family, and fifty per cent of callers were under the age of twenty-two. My vision for the future of the honour network is a number of bases across the United Kingdom and we are currently developing this idea in Newcastle. I have also decided that Newcastle will be the first city to have a satellite Karma Nirvana office and I have started working towards this too. My vision continues to grow as the need for Karma Nirvana's work becomes more and more obvious – my comfort is that I am no longer working alone.

ACKNOWLEDGEMENTS

My sincere thanks to all the women who made this book possible by selflessly giving their stories – it has been a privilege for me to hear and to help share your stories. My sincere thanks go to you – may you own that you are honourable women.

So much love and thanks to my children who understand Mum's cause in a way that enables us to have strength and a foundation that is unbreakable. Thanks go to my close friends who in the absence of family are often a lifeline in offering unconditional love, support, and at times lots of patience that keeps me going.

A big thank you to my agent Mark Lucas for his continued guidance and assistance, but most of all for believing that I had a story to share. Thanks to Gordon Riches – a special person who has been significant to my journey by enabling me to recognise that I was not only capable, but could make a difference. Your patience, trust and commitment in keeping up with me has at times been remarkable, thank you for never giving up on me even when I felt like giving in.

I will forever be grateful to my publishers whose belief in

the story made it happen. I thank you for your honesty and commitment, with special thanks to Rupert Lancaster who has at all times supported my journey even when he was the only man at the Woman of the Year Award!

A special thanks to Detective Inspector Brent Hyatt, Philip Balmforth, and retired Superintendent Tony Hutchinson, all of whom continue to restore faith in policing this area by going over and above the normal call of duty. I know, along with many others, that you continue to be responsible for saving lives, and raising your heads above the parapet to make sure these issues are heard.

And, finally, thank you to all the Karma Nirvana team – especially Trish, Anna and Shazia – your commitment is outstanding and I thank you for your friendship. Your support and belief in the project has often been the lifeline to many out there, and my wish is that through you and many others the project goes from strength to strength.

CONTACT

Karma Nirvana can be contacted for support, advice or to give a donation at:

Karma Nirvana
Unit 6
Rosehill Business Centre
Normanton Road
Derby
DE23 6RH
Tel: 01332 604098
Website www.karmanirvana.org.uk

Useful telephone numbers:

The Cleveland Choice-Line: 0800 5999 365
The Honour Network Helpline: 0800 5999 247
The Forced Marriage Unit: 0207 008 0151

'We can all get stronger together'